The Independent Film Experience

Special thanks to Audrey Geyer,
Sid, Sophie & Spenser, Todd Pontsler,
Tim Ritter, and Fred Olen Ray.

The Independent Film Experience

Interviews with Directors and Producers

KEVIN J. LINDENMUTH

Foreword by FRED OLEN RAY

McFarland & Company, Inc., Publishers
Jefferson, North Carolina, and London

ALSO BY KEVIN J. LINDENMUTH

Making Movies on Your Own:
Practical Talk from Independent Filmmakers
(McFarland, 1998)

Library of Congress Cataloguing-in-Publication Data

Lindenmuth, Kevin J., 1965–
The independent film experience : interviews with directors and
producers / Kevin J. Lindenmuth ; foreword by Fred Olen Ray.
p.   cm.
Includes index.
ISBN 0-7864-1075-2 (softcover : 50# alkaline paper)
1. Independent filmmakers—Interviews.
2. Motion pictures—Production and direction.   I. Title.
PN1998.2.L55   2002
791.43'023—dc21   2001056254

British Library cataloguing data are available

Manufactured in the United States of America

Cover photograph: Courtesy of Kinetic Image.

McFarland & Company, Inc., Publishers
Box 611, Jefferson, North Carolina 28640
www.mcfarlandpub.com

Table of Contents

Part III: Additional Commentaries

Foreword

BY FRED OLEN RAY

Independent filmmaking more often than not means doing without. Many times I have recounted the story of pioneer black filmmaker Oscar Micheaux, who, holding a cue card to jog the memory of one of his budding actresses, heard her spout, "No, emphatically. No!"

She had just read the screen direction as well as the line, and it went into the film that way. He couldn't afford a retake.

Herschell Gordon Lewis, while making *Lucky Pierre*, knew that his 35mm feature had to be at least 7,200 feet long and bought only 8,000 feet of film—just enough to cut off the slates and splice the remaining film together. Nothing could be wasted.

Since most of the film was shot silent, he gave his directions as the cameras rolled. He told one young starlet-in-training to stretch as if she were just waking up. She thought he said "scratch" and she started scratching her sides like a chimpanzee.

It went in the film that way. He couldn't afford a retake.

The bottom line is that sometimes you just have to do your best with what you've got—sometimes you just have to do without.

There was a time way back in 1977 when I was trying to shoot my first color 16mm feature, *The Alien Dead*, out in the swamp country of Oviedo, Florida, and after driving all the way out there we discovered that the producer had forgotten to bring the tape stock for the Nagra sound recorder. It was a 60-minute trip back to Orlando, so off he went.

Becoming frustrated by the delay, I decided to try something experimental. I went into a guy's car and pulled out his eight-track tape of Elvis hits and busted open the cassette, spooled Elvis onto an empty reel and started shooting, using the eight-track tape (which was a quarter inch in width) as my recording stock. It worked.

Today things aren't so primitive, of course, and eight-tracks have been replaced by compact disks. It's no longer necessary to drag around carloads of equipment to record an image with sound.

Digital video is at the fingertips of anyone with a desire to create. More and more consumer-grade cameras are rendering professional quality video, and computers now make it possible to edit, title

Director-producer Fred Olen Ray.

and mix complex sound works—all from your desktop.

With this sea of technology accessible to the average Joe there seem to be only a few things left to address, such as how to make good films that people will enjoy watching—even when they don't have to.

It is time to start thinking of the quality of what is being recorded. It is time to work out the use of over-the-shoulder shots, hand inserts, close-ups, to match the lens to the distance for reverses.

Explore lighting. Just because you have an image in your viewfinder doesn't mean you've lit it properly, or creatively.

Work on writing better scripts. Recognize that editing is as important as scripting and shooting.

I've always said that if the independent video makers spent as much time on what was *on the tape* as they did on creating the video box it comes in, they might really end up with something worthwhile.

Think *inside* the box—literally. The box may look great, but when what's inside looks like hell, who cares? Take your time. Be your best.

And read this book from cover to cover.

Preface

This book deals with the trials and tribulations of making and participating in an independent movie at the beginning of the 21st century. Although the technology of creating a movie has changed, *how* to make a film has remained much the same for the past 90 years, particularly within the realm of low budget production. The low budget independent filmmaker is forced to do things the old-fashioned way and use ingenuity in making a film. But it is easier to finish an independent feature with that new technology, particularly since videotape has become a valid and recognized way to shoot a movie. And with 1999's *Blair Witch Project*, a Hi-8mm video movie that gained worldwide attention and made millions of dollars, low budget films may now gain easier access to a broader, more receptive audience.

In fact, the success of *Blair Witch* will probably inspire hundreds of prospective filmmakers to think, "Hell, I can do that!"

And with technology on their side, they may be right.

In 1999, I sold the Internet rights to my *Alien Agenda* trilogy for a three year period to an entertainment company. In fact, a B-roll television package that they made, which included an interview with me and clips of the *Alien Agenda* movies, aired on some Warner Bros. channels.

What interested me in this Internet venue was that this was an entirely new way to show the movies to an audience, potentially the largest audience you could have. And as far as I knew very few people were exploring this option—perhaps because they didn't know it was possible.

Here's how it worked: If someone was interested in viewing a movie, he or she could go to the site where it was playing, type in a credit card number for payment—the same cost as for a movie rental—and be able to watch the movie on computer or television. This particular site offered a free one-minute preview of one of the movies to encourage viewer interest.

The website gets most of its money from advertising, so its creators aren't depending solely upon people watching the videos for income. This should allow the website owner time to figure out the types of movies most web surfers are interested in seeing—what works and what doesn't. The movies are offered primarily to get people to go to the website so they'll see the sponsors' advertisements. I think with more people, particularly young people, spending so much time with computers, this may be the future of direct-to-video movies.

Director-producer-writer Kevin Lindenmuth of Brimstone Productions.

But remember one very important thing: Regardless of how much the technology changes, how to make a film remains the same.

Although it is easier than it was five years earlier, independent filmmaking is still a very difficult and risky business. There is no guarantee you will make your investment back, no guarantee your work will get distribution. No one will care more about your film than you. But if you're persistent and able to pull it off, you'll have a finished movie—the whole point of embarking on this adventure to begin with.

The 1990s established a growing movement of independent filmmaking, particularly with the advent of decent, low-cost video equipment. Low cost DVD duplication, even cheaper video duplication and simple ways to design and print video sleeve boxes from your home computer have made independent moviemaking easier than ever. But it's only recently that avenues of distribution for the little guy have opened. The Internet is one of these new avenues, and I think soon cable and satellite television will be better used by filmmakers. The sheer numbers of new films, it's to be hoped, will make the masses—and distributors—open their eyes. Ultimately, the times will catch up with our creative urges.

What follows in these pages is a mixed bag of thoughts and advice from producers and directors, all of whom are involved in independent, low cost filmmaking. What they have in common is their passion for what they do. They vary widely in age, experience, choice of subject matter, and the format and budgets of their movies. This diversity provides a balanced view of the filmmaking experience.

The individuals kind enough to participate were Joe Bagnardi, Pat Bishow, Michael Bockner, Mark Borchardt, John Bowker, Mark Burchett, Elisar Cabrera, Dennis Devine, Tommy Faircloth, Mike Fox, Bruce G. Hallenbeck, Andrew Harrison, Evan Jacobs, Marcus Koch, Jeff Leroy, Santo Marotta, Alexandre Michaud, Ted V. Mikels, Brian O'Hara, Andrew Parkinson, Brett Piper, Mark Pirro, Mike Prosser, Joe Sherlock, Ronnie Sortor, Mark Sparks, Dave Sterling, Mike Strain, Jr., and Paul Talbot.

Kevin Lindenmuth
August 2000

Kevin J. Lindenmuth on the set of *Addicted to Murder*.

The *Alien Agenda* Series

The idea for the *Alien Agenda* series formed during the writing and research of my first how-to book, *Making Movies on Your Own: Practical Talk from Independent Filmmakers* (McFarland, 1998), during which time I got to know some of the filmmakers quite well. Based on their films and what they had to say I knew what they were capable of. Also, many of them were frustrated that their resources and distribution were limited. During this time I also wanted to work on a new project, specifically the alien flick I'd always wanted to make. So I came up with a fairly elaborate premise and started asking people if they were interested in scripting and directing stories. Among those I contacted were Tim Ritter (*Truth or Dare*), Ron Ford (*Alien Force, Witchcraft XI*), Michael Legge (*Braindrainer*), Gabe Campisi (*The Stranger*),

Tim Thomson (*No Resistance*) and Tom Vollmann (*Dead Meat*). All people who I knew could meet a deadline and do quality work.

I came up with the basic premise of two different species battling each other for the control of the earth. The first species, the Greys are from the far future, descended from the ocean's sharks. After a catastrophic nuclear war the seas dried up, causing mutations that lead to their existence. In their future world came the Morphs, squid-like aliens that can assume the form of most creatures—but they can't tolerate the radiation of the Greys' world. Equipped with time travel technology, they go back into earth's past, when the environment was perfect for their species. The Greys, fearing the Morphs will change the timeline and therefore their existence, go back in time and try ensure that mankind is not somehow prevented from launching the nuclear war already recorded in Grey history. This is the outline I sent the filmmakers:

SYNOPSIS OF THE SERIES

This series focuses on an alien invasion by two different types of aliens and how humanity is caught in the middle. These aliens are the "Greys" and the "Morphs."

The Greys are the creatures who abduct people and do the implants, experiments, and cross-breedings. They aren't overly concerned with the prospect of humanity destroying itself—in fact, they are depending on it. Their manipulations are causing humans to act irrationally, provoking wars, etc. They want people to be afraid.

The Morphs are able to assume human form. They are colonizing the earth and because they can change their genetic structure they can interbreed with humans. The only problem is, their offspring are aliens, so that with each generation there are more of them on the planet. They are also enemies of the Greys—humans, again, are inconsequential, but they want humanity and the earth to survive, in order for their slow but eventual takeover. They control the media—they've already showed us being invaded a thousand times on television. So this is nothing new to a jaded humanity.

All the directors should keep this back-story in mind so that they integrate.

I sent this outline idea to those filmmakers I thought would want to be involved in the project, and I had interest almost immediately. I then wrote a detailed outline that was around five pages in length, outlining everything that I wanted to happen throughout the three movies.

The other directors came up with ideas for their own segments based on the premise, and I edited the scripts to make sure they were consistent with the other parts. Basically, the *Alien Agenda* movies were disguised anthologies that had a connecting story.

The first installment, *Out of the Darkness*, was the easiest because it involved me and one other person. I had worked with Mick McCleery on nearly every one of my previous projects, and there had been very little ego bashing between us. *Out of the Darkness* is a little weird in that it incorporates three very disparate stories, but, then, I wanted that strange wraparound. The story is about the survivor of an alien invasion, a hermit-like individual who lives alone, foraging for weapons and supplies. Through a sort of "mind/time travel device" he is able to go back to the time of the invasion and observe individuals—whose own stories are folded into the primary tale. McCleery's segment, about a man whose doppelganger commits murders and frames him for the crimes, was actually made two years earlier, requiring only a slight re-edit to fit the premise. This segment, along with Gabe Campisi's *The Law* (used in *AA: Endangered Species*) were always in the back of my mind for this project and helped determine the premise to begin with. My segment was about a homeless young girl in New York City befriended by a very strange—and very alien individual.

The digital effects, including the title intro scene where the credits play in all three movies, was done by Tim Thomson of Lunatic Fringe Productions, who did some amazing things. Other effects, such as creating the illusion of three incarnations of the same character, were done by me, with props I borrowed from other filmmakers.

The actors involved were Mick McCleery, as "the survivor"; Sasha Graham, whom I first used in *Addicted to Murder*, and cult film director Scooter McCrae, known for *Shatter Dead* and *16 Tongues*. Ever since I had seen Scooter act in a movie called *Original Sins*, I wanted him to portray a character in one of my movies. I would later use him in *Addicted to Murder 2* and *Rage of the Werewolf*.

Alien Agenda: Endangered Species starts off with the character of Megan Cross (played by actress Debbie Rochon), a tabloid-TV reporter who becomes victim to aliens and eventually joins a secret organization that battles them. There are also the characters of Fritz, another operative who mysteriously reappears after a five year absence, and Cope Ransom, a lone mercenary who must brave the wilds of radioactive Florida of the future and fight a mutant alligator residing there, created by filmmaker Marcus Koch. I involved Tim Ritter, Gabe Campisi and Ron Ford. Again, I came up with the connecting story, which I shot and directed, and Ritter, following the guidelines, shot his segment down in the tropics of Florida with cult actor Joel D. Wynkoop in the lead. It was sort of an *Escape from New York*–type short. Gabe Campisi's segment, *The Law*, already existed but meshed quite nicely with the wraparound segment. I even had a character in my segment talk on the phone with one of his characters— and the footage was years apart. Ron Ford, who also has a cameo, took care of the "Alien Interview Segments" that opens the movie with his stable of actor friends. As with *Out of the Darkness*, once all the footage was acquired I edited it together in New York.

The last feature, *Alien Agenda: Under the Skin*, which was done almost a year after the first one, involved filmmaker Tom Vollmann, who directed the "Unsavory Characters" segment. Originally he had wanted to do this as a 16mm feature, but funding fell through—so he sent the script

my way and I re-wrote it to fit into the *Alien Agenda* scenario. This feature concentrated more on the Morph aliens and explained what was going on with the "battle over the planet." Tom shot his segment in Chicago, I shot mine in Manhattan, and all the footage was edited in New York City. Mike Legge, probably best known for *Loons* and *Working Stiffs*, did the "Alien Abduction Interviews" from his core group of actors. Actors featured were Arthur Lundquist (*Pledge Night, The Regenerated Man*) and Leslie Body (*Contact Blow*) in mine and Nick Kostopoulos (*Dead Meat*) and Sam White (*Just for the Hell of It*) in Tom's.

After each movie was complete a box was created and the film was released. It gained a limited distribution through Blockbuster Video as well as going through many of the smaller chains. It also gained a foreign home video distribution.

This experience convinced me that part of the survival of the independent filmmaker involved collaborating and bartering services of other filmmakers.

Addicted to Murder: Tainted Blood

After doing the science fiction *Alien Agenda* movies I really had the itch to do another horror movie. In that time I had written several scripts—two with long time collaborator Ron Ford (director of *Alien Force, Mark of Dracula, Riddled with Bullets*) and one with New York filmmaker Jeffrey Arsenault (director of *Night Owl*)— scripts which would take a large budget to do justice to. In fact, I had even paid Ron Ford to write the script for the *Addicted to Murder* sequel based on my story and outline. Something that needed twice the budget of the original movie. But, with my funds tied up distributing and promoting

Top: Nick Kostopoulos prepares for a brain munching scene in *Alien Agenda: Under the Skin*. Photograph by Tom Vollmann, Cool Movies. *Bottom:* Nick Kostopoulos sucks out Conrad Brook's brains in *Alien Agenda: Under the Skin*.

the *Alien Agenda* movies, I decided to do something I could shoot within a month using local locations. Fortunately I lived in Manhattan, which is like living on a big movie set. And since I think that *Addicted to Murder* is one of my strongest movies—and because I wasn't quite finished with the characters—I decided that this would still be my next project. I would simply use the Ron Ford script as a future installment, as it basically ended the whole vampire concept.

So, over a period of several months, I wrote *Addicted to Murder: Tainted Blood*, coming up with a prequel-of-sorts that showed the vampire subculture in New York City. The script was very much determined by my budget, which actors were available from the original movie and also my locations. I would shoot and light the movie with a sound man as the only other crew, ensuring that things would go much quicker.

McCleery's life had changed considerably in the intervening three years: He had gotten married, and his wife would soon give birth to his second child. Laura McLauchlin had since moved to Los Angeles and was basically unavailable (working on the last two Clint Eastwood movies among other things) and Sasha Graham, I think, was getting a little burned out on this whole B-Movie scene after being in nearly a dozen features in the past three years. But she had a soft spot for the Angie character and would reprise her role. The majority of the screen time, though, was given to a new crop of actors who portray the new vam-

Box art for *Addicted to Murder 2: Tainted Blood*. Photograph by Bill Brady.

pires. There are some great performances here, particularly from Cloud Michaels, Sarah Lippmann, Ted Grayson and Joe Moretti. Bigger and better things are on their horizons.

The majority of it takes place before the first movie, how the Angie character deals with the wanna-be vampires and her vampire brethren, sort of like *New York Stories* but with vampires instead of humans. I think it builds on the first movie,

Actress Sasha Graham in *Addicted to Murder 2: Tainted Blood*. **Photograph by Bill Brady.**

since Tim Ritter and he are partners of Twisted Illusions, Inc., it was easy enough to call up Wynkoop and ask him to shoot a pseudo-interview with the character he was supposed to play. It was a lot cheaper than flying to Florida! He also shot a flashback sequence with R.M. Hoopes, who usually scores music for Tim's films. I also wanted a cameo with cult director Ted V. Mikels, who I've been in regular contact with the past few years, having done interviews with him for *Screem, Defekt*, and *Cult Movies*. I thought he'd be ideal for the TV vampire hunter and he was in fact great. With Ted living in Las Vegas, I resorted to a now-familiar tactic, calling up my friend Gabe Campisi and asking if he could videotape the interview segment, and he was up for it.

After the script was finished I had a casting call after placing an ad in *Backstage* magazine and spent the next two months doing the pre-production and scheduling. Most locations were friends' apartments, places people worked and some outdoor city location.

Shooting was very straightforward, and we kept on punctual schedule, primarily because it was the first time I had an uninterrupted two weeks to shoot the

adding a lot of background material that makes you nod your head and say, "Oh." The tone is very different—this is a very cynical and sarcastic movie and it moves a bit faster. I think of it as an entirely different movie featuring some of the same characters. I hope it's a follow-up done right, because I find most sequels very disappointing. A large part of the challenge was to try and make a film better than the first one.

Also, I wanted to involve some other filmmakers on this project, though not to the extent of *Alien Agenda*, and realized that the best way to do this was through cameos. I wanted to use Joel D. Wynkoop in a brief cameo and,

Sasha Graham (left) and Sarah K. Lippmann in *Addicted to Murder 2: Tainted Blood*.

Creaturealm Anthologies

Sarah K. Lippmann enjoys the holiday spirit—and some blood—in *Addicted to Murder 2: Tainted Blood*.

Creaturealm, like the *Alien Agenda* series, comprises the work of individual directors Tim Thomson (*No Resistance*), Mike Legge (*Potential Sins, Night Basement*), Ron Ford (*Riddled with Bullets, Witchcraft XI*) and me. At the time, my idea was to create more of a straightforward anthology feature, with no connecting story or host. I contacted several of the people I had worked with on *Alien Agenda* and they were interested in coming up with their own mini-movies.

Tim Thomson's "Possession Is Nine-Tenths of the Law" involved a woman on trial for killing her husband—and it looks like the devil made her do it. "Dryer Straits," Mike Legge's story of an old

Cloud Michaels in *Addicted to Murder 2: Tainted Blood*.

movie. I'm always a bit wiped out after a shoot, but it went extremely smoothly; in fact, many of the actors already knew each other from working together on films and plays, which made it all the easier. Plus, there were few live effects. Lots of blood but very little makeup effects, which is extremely time consuming.

The movie was completed within six months from when we started shooting and released to the home video market shortly after. The genre magazines and fanzines called it "better than the original."

woman's dryer creating a lint monster, provided a contrast in tone to Thomson's story, and we thought they'd go well together. These two stories were released on the video *Creaturealm: Demons Wake*.

The second anthology feature, *Creaturealm: From the Dead*, features a story by Ron Ford entitled "Hollywood Mortuary," about an unemployed horror makeup artist in the 1940s who resurrects, from the dead, the equivalents of Boris Karloff and Bela Lugosi. Things don't work out as planned, as the two go on a killing spree in Hollywood. My story, "Eyes of the Ripper," cast Sasha Graham (*Addicted to Murder*) as a woman who has recurring nightmares of previous lives—until the horrible truth is revealed by a mysterious stranger.

Although I was happy with the results of these two anthology features, and like that particular format, they sold the poorest of all the movies I've ever released. It wasn't a matter of quality—Tim Thomson's "Possession" is better than any *Tales from the Darkside* episode!—but what other people may have been interested in seeing at the time, particularly the video distributors I sold to, who seemed to have no interest in the anthology movie. One thing I learned is that the home video market is very fickle. Although the videos weren't selling right then, there was the chance they would in a year or so.

The next time I embarked on an anthology it would have to be another "disguised one."

Addicted to Murder 3: Blood Lust

After the second *Addicted to Murder* was completed I went immediately into coordinating the *Creaturealm* series *Creaturealm* movies. And after releasing the first two of the anthology movies, I realized I should work on another full-feature instead because it was so much more marketable.

During this time Tom Vollmann, who contributed to *Alien Agenda: Under the Skin*, was doing a vampire segment for the third *Creaturealm* movie called "Killing Time." But because the distribution was so disappointing on the first two movies we switched gears and decided to incorporate this story into the *Addicted to Murder* universe. Hence, a disguised anthology. His story involved a vampire who was using a maximum security prison as a sanctuary—because it was well guarded, dark and had a captive food supply. This vampire could come and go as he pleased but no one could come in after him. A new prisoner is put in the cell with him and learns his secret.

While Tom was busy shooting his segment on the streets of Chicago I shot my half of the movie in New York City. This time I had the story take place after the first *Addicted to Murder* movie and also incorporated characters from the prequel. The Joel Winter character is an active vampire hunter hunting down the remaining vampires in New York City. Two of these are the Tricia and Karen vampires from *Addicted to Murder 2: Tainted Blood*, whom the character had never met. Through a series of interviews and flashbacks we get a sense of the characters and also how much the "serial vampire killer" had transformed into a different type of creature. Bruce G. Hallenbeck, director of *Vampyre* and *Fangs*, portrayed the television host character, and Brett Piper, who is probably best known for *They Bite* and *Nymphoid Barbarian in Dinosaur Hell*, let me borrow a demon head created for a movie that never got off the ground. All the other effects were done by me.

The footage for both segments was shot around the same time. Tom then mailed his tapes to me and I started editing, which took around six months. This movie was released a year after Part 2.

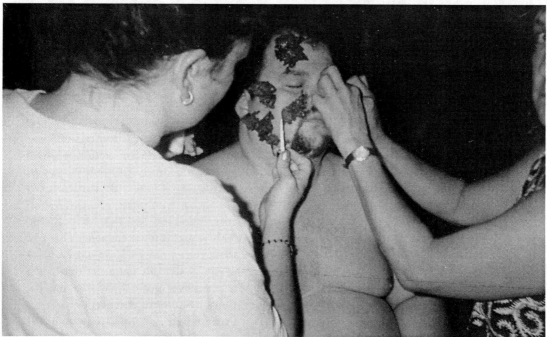

Top, left to right: **Margaret O'Brien, Randal Malone and Anita Page in Ron Ford's** *Hollywood Mortuary.* *Bottom:* **Director/actor Ron Ford getting made up as Janos Blasko in** *Hollywood Mortuary* **segment of** *Creaturealm: From the Dead.*

Adrianne Belle and stunt double from *Creaturealm: From the Dead*. Photograph courtesy Ron Ford.

Video box art for *Addicted to Murder 3: Bloodlust*.

Rage of the Werewolf

Rage of the Werewolf started in October of 1998, when Santo Marotta (Marotta Productions) asked me to collaborate on a werewolf movie. We tossed a few ideas around—Santo wanted the classic tormented-soul type werewolf, and I wanted to do with werewolves what I did with vampires in the *Addicted to Murder* series: make them a little different from the usual lycanthrope. The script, which incorporated both aspects, was written the following two months by both me and Santo, and the film went into production in January of 1999, shooting completed two months later, at the end of March.

Rage of the Werewolf is a bit different from the rest of the Brimstone Productions in that it is more of an action-adventure movie, sort of a cross between *Escape from New York* and *Planet of the Apes*, but with werewolves instead of apes. The movie takes place a few years in the future, when a meteorite collides into the moon, pushing its orbit closer to the earth and making thousands of people werewolves. New York City is designated a "werewolf habitat," and no one with the lycanthrope gene can leave the city limits. The story is primarily about two brothers, Jake and Lazlo, who were werewolves even before the moon changing orbit. Because of this, they retain their minds when they morph— and can transform any time they wish, not just with the full moon.

The character of Jake, the protagonist, was written specifically for Santo. I had previously used Santo in *Addicted to Murder* 2 and 3, and in *Rage* he was perfect for the role. In my opinion, Jake is Santo and vice versa! For casting I gath-

Video box cover for *Rage of the Werewolf*. Brimstone Productions, 1998.

Addicted 3, and I think it's the most evil part Joe has ever portrayed. There are cameos by Ron Ford (director of *Witchcraft XI*), Nathan Thompson (*Contact Blow*) and Kendra Munger.

The many special effects were done by several people. Mike Strain, Jr., of Fantasy Creations in Missouri, built the two full-body werewolf costumes, Jay Alvino and Joe Biondi did all the on-set makeup effects such as the mutants and Lazlo's demise, and Tim Thomson and Nathan Thompson both did the digital computer effects. Nathan, a filmmaker himself, was kind enough to let us invade his spacious house in Brooklyn for two long weekends, where we shot about 25 percent of the movie. The location adds a great deal of production value to the movie. The Big Apple provided the rest of the locations.

A bounty hunter in front of werewolf-head trophies in *Rage of the Werewolf*.

ered some of the usual suspects. Tom Nondorf, who was brilliant as the "crazy vampire guy" in *ATM 2* was cast as Ralph, the faithful sidekick and foil to Jake's dark brooding nature. Sasha Graham was the suspicious damsel in distress, and Debbie Rochon was cast in the key part of Kessa, a mysterious vampire woman who holds the fate of the main characters in her blood. Believe it or not, it's the first time Debbie has portrayed a vampire. For the part of Lazlo, Jake's evil brother, both Santo and I wanted someone who could be a little over the top, almost comic-bookish, like *Doctor Doom*—and actor/director Joe Zaso came to mind. I previously worked with Joe on *Alien Agenda*, *Creaturealm* and

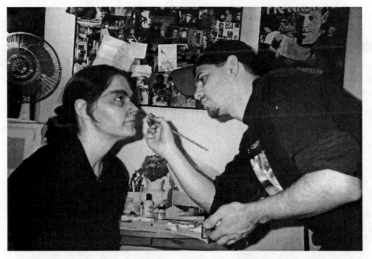

Shooting in Coney Island at 6 A.M. was an experience!

I think people will be surprised by this movie. *Rage* is much, much different from the *Addicted to Murder* movies, which are moody and non-linear in structure. In fact, one of the reviewers at *Alternative Cinema* wrote that he couldn't understand any of my movies because of this style—well, he should have no trouble following this story. Much more of a "popcorn" movie.

Top: Makeup artist Jay Alvino transforms Sasha Graham into a lycanthrope for *Rage of the Werewolf. Bottom:* Pre-production artwork for *Rage of the Werewolf* by producer Santo Marotta, showing the evil werewolf-bat creature.

Introduction

This section features a mixed bag of film directors and producers, each of whom shares his experiences in the industry. Some of them have been working in the business for decades, while others have only just embarked on their first feature. What they all have in common is a love for what they do. They are all filmmakers whose work I like, and they have valuable information for those who want to be filmmakers themselves.

When people ask me what I do for a living and I respond, "I make movies," the predominant response is "Gee, that sounds like fun." This drives me a little nuts because I don't think anyone but a fellow filmmaker knows all the pain and heartache one can experience in this profession. There is no other business like independent filmmaking. Granted, I do enjoy my work, especially when I find myself immersed in a production, but I usually pay for it by getting sick for a few weeks afterwards. When I was a teenager I used to read how some director or makeup-effects artist fell ill during a production, and I was always a little puzzled by this. Nearly a dozen films later, I can no longer claim such healthy bewilderment.

So when people say it's fun, it makes me wonder how easy their nine to five jobs are. But I'd never trade those 10 to 15 hour days. I'm a filmmaker.

Joe Bagnardi

PRODUCER-DIRECTOR

Filmography: Shadow Tracker (1998); "Manbeast" segment of *Blood of the Werewolf* (2001)

Biography: I grew up always trying to entertain in some type of story form or another. It started with acting out action figures as a live play in front of brothers, sisters, birthday parties, et cetera. My parents were divorced so I spent Sundays with my father and brother at the movies.

These movies affected me the most. Everything about them—the story, the camerawork, the music, the posters—all of it had an affect. This was a world I could escape to, no matter what was going on in my life. And I wanted to create this world for others to escape to. I wrote two-page stories, then audio cassettes like the old radio shows. In 1967 I finally received my first projector and I collected the old *Castle Films*, which were cut down to four- and twelve-minute versions. I entertained family members and friends. They'd laugh as I would repeatedly show Roy Rogers punch someone out.

But I wanted to make my own movies. In the Christmas of 1969 I got my first Super 8mm film camera. I shot a film almost immediately. It was called *Christmas Time*. The following year I did my first narrative film, entitled *Maniac's Morgue*. The James Bond films inspired me. The look, the music, the sex, the action, the posters. All of it. I created a spy series, the Jason Scott movies, starting with *To Kill a Spy*. The series went to thirty short films.

Of course, there were other inspirations. Old films, new films, horror, science fiction, action, adventure, war—everything! Over the next twenty years, through high school, college, marriage, divorce, moving, life and death, I managed to make a total of 250 short films. No genre was left untouched. These were all silent films with soundtrack music added. Then, in 1992, I sent a series called *Horror Hospital* to a Texas filmmaker. He liked the way they were shot. He sent me a script. I wrote down what I thought the camera angles should be and mailed it back to him. The next thing I knew he sent me a

Opposite: **Video Box art for Joe Bagnardi's *Shadow Tracker*. Courtesy E.I. Independent Cinema.**

SHADOW TRACKER:
VAMPIRE HUNTER

SHADOW TRACKER:
VAMPIRE HUNTER

SHADOW TRACKER:
*VAMPIRE
HUNTER*

SHADOW TRACKER
Horror / Cat # 7018
120 mins / color / 1999

plane ticket and a chance to be "assistant to the director" on a film called *Verdun Manor*. The Super 16mm film took us two-and-a-half weeks to shoot, with many 16 hour days. It was a fun experience that further whetted my appetite for filmmaking.

In 1993 I received a call from Bruce G. Hallenbeck, director of *Vampyre* and the vampire documentary *Fangs*. He asked me to help him out on his feature *Black Easter*, which starred actress Debbie Rochon. Again, a wonderful experience. That year I was also cameraman on a Gary Secors production, which featured a Witch hanging.

But I wanted to shoot my own feature, so I held auditions in 1993 for my film *Shadow Tracker*. Featuring a character named Nomad, it was originally supposed to be a post-nuclear war film called *Nuclear Rage*, based on my short film series called *Wasteland*. I felt, though, that it would be limited by costumes and location. So, I took the look of Nomad, changed it a bit, and made him into Shadow Tracker, a vampire hunter.

The crew and I started the film in September of 1993, shooting on high tech video for three days. Something was missing, though. I was not used to the monitors, cables and batteries. The video looked like a soap opera. I needed more freedom to get my various camera angles, to get that film look. The Holidays came and the project died.

In 1995 I bought a Super 8mm film camera from *Splatter* books author John McCarty and held another audition for actors. The actors were cast and we had a reading. All went well and by Memorial Day 1995, *Shadow Tracker* had come back to life, like the vampires he hunts. With help from my fellow producers—Mary Kay Hilko and Ed Dimmer—and my actors—Ron Rausch, Bruce G. Hallenbeck, Voni Powell, Amy Naple and Tom Ecobelli—things moved ahead in steady fash-

ion: after 49 days of shooting over the next two years, photography was finished; the film was transferred to videotape (for editing purposes) by Brodsky and Treadway up near Boston and then edited locally, on weekends; the all-original score was provided by David Bourgeois; the title song and love theme lyrics were written and sung by Janice Krystallis.

The movie premiered at the 1997 Chiller Convention, in Secaucus, New Jersey. Then the re-mastered stereo edition premiered at Off-Broadway Theatre and Grill in Saratoga, New York, to a sold out crowd. It was accepted at the New York International Film and Video Festival and the Philadelphia International Film Festival.

Influences/Aspirations: I've wanted to create stories and entertain for people as long as I can remember. I've had, in fact, more ideas than film to work with. That's why I did 250 short films. My influences have been the James Bond Films, Universal Monsters, Errol Flynn, John Wayne and just about every genre of film out there. Sean Connery is my favorite actor. Some of my favorite films and television are the original TV *Star Trek*, *Dark Shadows*, *The Magnificent Seven*, *True Grit*, *The Dirty Dozen*, *The Longest Day* and *Zulu*. Many inspirations from the 50s, 60s and 70s.

Film School: If given a chance I'd probably go. I learned filmmaking like a guy who learns piano by ear: I watched a ton of film and shot a lot of film. I think learning the history of film is a plus. Film school is probably great for learning equipment and technology. The only problem I've seen in some film school graduates is in their attitude, which is "I went to film school, you didn't—therefore you don't know how to shoot films the proper way." My suggestion for learning film? Read about it and then do it. Experiment, try different things, different angles, different ideas. Read Jerry Lewis' *The Total Film-maker*, in which he tells you to do films your way.

If you have the opportunity to go to film school, take it. Just don't allow yourself to buy into prescriptive filmmaking. Keep your mind open.

Script: You have to be flexible with your script on a low budget film, willing to change it as needed, yet adhering to those elements basic to its identity. During auditions, when different actors are reading the same lines, you realize they each give it a different interpretation—simply the way an actor says a line can change the context of the scene. Sometimes this is for the better. For me, a bendable script is better than a stiff one. Better for the director and the actors. In our film *Shadow Tracker* we changed the script because of actors' schedules. I think by being flexible your script will evolve. Maybe not in the way you first envisioned, but in a different way you may like.

Equipment/Format: I use Super 8mm sound film equipment in my productions. I love the way film looks. I was shooting on film before the video age, so it's been difficult for me to make the transition to video. I know that some people shoot on video and then put it through a "film look"; I just thought I'd start out with film. But it is getting expensive.

Cost/Budget/Funding: The cost of *Shadow Tracker* was around $9,000. Most of that was on the film cost itself—processing, the film-to-tape transfer, music and duplication. We had three investors on the film, none of whom were strangers. Basically it was myself and two friends.

I hope someone will recognize the film as a good product for the budget and will invest in a future project. I think that

if you can prove you can make a film on limited funds you are more likely to get investors on a bigger project.

How do you cast your actors? First, we put an advertisement in the local weekly entertainment newspaper for interested people to send resumes for our action-horror film. After 12 weeks I went through the resumes and headshots, narrowing the choices. We then called the actors and had them do a cold reading, which we videotaped. I then studied the tapes and selected the actors I wanted. Some of the other actors I used in the movie were friends I grew up with who had acted in my short films. They and the new actors complemented each other.

We needed two detectives but couldn't decide if it would be big cop/small cop or good cop/bad cop or black cop/Asian cop. After meeting actress Mary Kay Hilko, we went with the guy cop/girl cop scenario. The male lead played the older "don't like working with girls" cop to her "don't like working with jerks" cop. It seems to work.

Music: During production I met a girl named Janice Krystallis. She told me that she sang and wrote lyrics and invited me to see her do Karaoke. She reminded me of Shirley Bassey, the singer of the theme song to the James Bond film *Goldfinger*. I even asked her to do *Goldfinger* and she did. She was great. That made me decide I had to have a James Bond–type tune for my film. She told me she had written a love song called "Don't Walk Away" with David Bourgeois, who would write and perform the music that was used in the film. After seeing his set up and hearing a few improvised samples I felt that he was perfect for this film. I would describe the scene and he wrote the score. Amazing! Janice let me hear "Don't Walk Away" and I fell in love with it. It became the movie's love theme and the song that played over

Left to right: Bruce G. Hallenbeck as Jonathan Stokes, director Joe Bagnardi and Ron Rausch as the Shadow Tracker.

the end credits. Now we needed to think about the theme song.

We had already shot the slower dance scene for the title sequence and decided to go with a more upbeat theme than *Don't Walk Away*. I let David listen to the themes of *The Liquidator* (Shirley Bassey), *Game of Death* (John Barry) and *Goldeneye*, the last of which was sung by Tina Turner. All were Bond or Bond-like. The next day he called me and played over the phone what he'd come up with. It was great! I couldn't believe how Bond-like it was. Now we needed some lyrics, about *Shadow Tracker* himself. Dave and I talked to Janice, and in a short time she had the words. She sung them to me in her car with Dave's music blasting. It was exactly what we needed.

Dave and Janice then recorded it. He suggested some changes and went over them with her a number of times.

We finally had our song, which I'm proud of.

How long did it take to make your first film? One day would be the answer, if you counted my short films. In twenty years I made 250 shorts. They ranged from horror to sci-fi to comedy to Westerns to musicals. After working on *Verdun Manor* again, as assistant to the director, I worked on Bruce G. Hallenbeck's *Black Easter* in Upstate New York. My own first feature was *Shadow Tracker*.

Special Effects: Ron Rausch does our effects and makeup. We've also done stop-motion dinosaurs, blanks for guns, bullet holes, vampire teeth, hands cut off, heads cut off. Our visual and sound effects are done by Colin Lovelock.

Production Tips for the Novice Film-maker:

Left to right: Ron Rausch, Mary Kay Hilko and Joe Bagnardi on the set of *Shadow Tracker*.

1. Watch and study film angles.
2. Read about filmmaking
3. Experiment with camera angles.
4. Look at comic books; they are like movie storyboards.
5. Start with short films or videos, for practice.
6. Read books on filmmaking, then throw them out and do your own thing.
7. Hold the camera steady.
8. Don't overshoot a scene. No fifty takes.
9. Rehearse scenes before you shoot.
10. Try to plan as much ahead of time as you can.

How important is publicity for your films? Publicity is very important. It's up to the filmmaker to get his film out there. Don't wait for a distributor to come knocking at your door—they never do. Try sending screening copies out to magazines and newspapers, create promotional flyers, go to conventions, have a website—do it all. Also try the festivals. Push, push, push. As with the drive-in movies of old, advertise!

Distribution: First, you can distribute through mail order, through advertisements in genre magazines, but be prepared to work at it! Seek out distributors. They do the leg work, you still get some of the money and most important, your product gets out there. But you should try to retain your film rights, in case you want to sell them elsewhere. Don't sign an exclusive agreement with a distributor because you may regret it. Right now *Shadow Tracker* is being distributed by E.I. Cinema, which is based in New Jersey.

Future Projects: If *Shadow Tracker* is a success, I'll invest the money I make into another project. I've been the cameraman on Bruce G. Hallenbeck's movie, *London After Midnight*. I also did a short with Mary Kay Hilko, a ghost story called *Sweet Sorrow*. I may shoot two more short stories and make it into a trilogy called *The Edge of Reality*. On the other hand, I may do *Shadow Tracker II* or maybe a James Bond–type film.

Last Words: Don't let anyone discourage you from filmmaking. No matter who or what they are to you. If you want to make a movie, make a movie! Shoot it on whatever format you can get a hold of. But don't just talk about it or think about it. Do it. Believe in your dreams, and don't let anyone get in your way. So after you finish this book, get the lights out of the closet, grab a camera and yell "Action!"

Pat Bishow

DIRECTOR

Filmography: Three from the Dead House (feature Super 8mm film, 1983); *The Dead of Night Town* (feature 16mm, 1985); *The Soultangler* (feature 16mm, 1987); *Hypnolovewheel "Wow" Video* (16mm music video, 1991); *The Adventures of El Frenetico & Go Girl: The Wax Terror* (½ hour Hi 8mm video, 1994); *Whitewood Crossing* (Trailer, 16mm, 1996); *The Return of El Frenetico & Go Girl: Crimes of Fashion* (½ hour DVC Pro, 1997); *The Return of El Frenetico & Go Girl: Shades of Crime* (½ hour DVC Pro, 1998)

Biography: I grew up in Charleston, South Carolina, in the late 60s and early 70s, when I fell in love with *Planet of the Apes* and made Super 8mm films. In high school (the late 70s and early 80s), I fell in love with punk rock (Clash, Ramones, Elvis Costello). Rock was everything. I loved 50s (Holly, Berry), early 60s (Beau Brummels, Seeds, Beatles), the Motown and Atlanta sounds (Smokey, Booker T) and, again, the punk stuff. I wanted to be a musician for a long time, but I soon found out that rock stars can't age; once they do, they're out. But directors get *bet-*

ter with age, so I thought I should put my sites on that. I went to the School of Visual Arts in New York City for film and didn't last a semester. It was way too expensive, and I couldn't possibly afford it. So I dropped out.

Hard times hit in the early 80s. I was in a rock band called The Mosquitos. The lead singer sold a song to the Monkees ("That Was Then, This Is Now") and broke up the group, but I had grown tired of rock anyway. I waited around with odd jobs and still made Super 8mm films until I made *Three from the Dead House* (1983). This was my first endeavor into feature-length films. It was shot in Super 8mm and starred Louise Millmann's adult-education acting class. The ball started rolling. I went from that to making *The Dead of Night Town* (1985). Now I was in 16mm and I had someone doing special effects. We never finished that film, but I was able to sell what I did shoot to another film, so I made money!

Next up was *Soultangler* (1987). Again, 16mm and friends for actors (my brother-in-law played the Soultangler himself). This was done at the time home video first broke out, and they needed product. I was able to sell *Soultangler* for a huge profit. I thought I was now set. Troma hired me as the assistant director on *Kabuki Man*. They were so bad to work for that I quit.

In a few months, the bottom dropped out of the horror video market and I was back to square one. Dealing with that and girlfriend problems put me into a deep depression. I didn't want anything to do with film for a while. I made my living selling antique toys.

In the early 90s I made a few rock videos for friends (*Hynolovewheel*). Then Owen Cooper stepped in. He had a job working for Dow Jones Television. He had access to equipment. He offered to produce a half-hour installment (if I could come up with one)—and that's how *The Adventures of El Frenetico & Go Girl* was born.

Influences/Aspirations: I *love* films! All kinds—cheap horror, artsy foreign, old classics, comedies, dramas, et cetera. I've always loved movies. When I was in fifth grade I found out what a director did (before that I wanted to be an actor) and chose Franklin Schaffner (*Planet of the Apes, Papillon*) as my favorite director. In junior high school I learned about Hitchcock, Welles, and Whale. Later came Scorcese, Woody Allen and George Romero. And still later came Sam Raimi, Spike Lee and William Wyler (the one I would pick if I had to pick a favorite). I also look forward to Rich Linkletter and Todd Solondz movies, too.

I would love to direct features. That's what I aspire to. They wouldn't have to be expensive. I would just like to make films for a living. I have no desire to make a big epic. I would love to make small-budget movies (opposed to no-budget movies, which I make now).

Film School: I quit film school in less than a semester. It just wasn't for me. I think it's good in a way because it can hook you up with a lot of people that you otherwise wouldn't have met. I don't know if you really learn anything there, but it does get you bad jobs on big movies.

Cost/Budget/Funding: Budget is the toughest thing to a no-budget filmmaker. *No-budget* means, at least to me, that everything is coming out of your pocket. So the food becomes the most expensive thing. You have to get your locations, equipment, cast and crew for free. The money you're spending is on stock, labs, transportation, food and the little things, which tend to add up. So you have to keep the costs down. You'll have to pay for things that you didn't know you would— last-minute stuff like a blown lamp (bulb) or a broken microphone.

One of the things I hate most about no-budget is the sound. It's a tough thing. Big budget (and low budget) movies often have "sound design." Someone is controlling everything you're hearing. In our films, we're often stuck with whatever we happened to catch. Another frustrating thing is "pick-up." We get the set for today and that's it. If you don't get it then, you don't get it ever! That can be really tough if you're trying to cut a scene and find out that you need a quick shot to put it together.

How did you get your actors? 95 percent of the actors are my friends. I try to use friends that want to be actors because I know they'll be there are at 5 A.M. and work until 11 P.M. I'm very nervous about bringing in new people. The guy that played the Fop (Clark Donnelly) was new. But he became a friend fast (which is what usually happens). I guess the advantage of strangers is that it gives you the liberty of yelling at them, but at least friends won't walk out on you.

Frances Lee (left) as Go Girl in *The Adventures of El Frenetico & Go Girl*, **directed by Pat Bishow.**

How did you get your film's music? How important is music to your movies? I was lucky. I was a musician when I was younger and a lot of my friends are musicians. So I just asked them to do it. We all shared the same aesthetic. And they all did an amazing job. Basically, I give them a rough cut of the film, and then they make music based on what they're seeing. Usually I come back to them near the end

El Frenetico (Charlie Pelligrino) *and Go Girl* (Frances Lee).

of the final cut, explaining that I need something fast or slow to highlight a scene. They do it.

How long did it take you to make your first feature? I consider *Soultangler* my first feature. We shot in five consecutive days. We took over my mom's house for a week, built the set in the basement, rolled up a camper and filmed. We did pickups six months later and sold the film at a festival.

What is your experience with special effects at this level? I've done some cheap horror films for which close to half the budget went to effects. They're fun but also expensive and unpredictable. One time we decapitated a character and made a full replica of his head. The head was to tip over and blood was to pour out of the neck. When we did the shot, blood went *everywhere*. It flew all over the camera lens so you couldn't see anything. On the fol-lowing day we shot outside in the summer (about 90 degrees) and we used real meat. When we cut it open, boy, did it smell!

Another time, we were blowing up a model house and we couldn't decide how much explosive to put into it. My sound man wanted more and I wanted less. I was afraid that too much would blow out the main frame. Needless to say, he was right. It worked great. You never know what will happen. And you don't have the money to do it twice.

Any production tips for the novice filmmaker? Yes, use a good microphone! Don't use the camera microphone. Rent it, if you have to. Too many no-budget films have bad sound. Also, less is more. If you can't afford to make *Star Wars*, don't! Keep your budget in mind. Use what you have. A friend owns a boat, someone can get you into a cool building, your father owns a junkyard or some other location—use it! If it's not in the script write it in.

Michael Bockner

PRODUCER-DIRECTOR

Filmography: Reconnaissance (1975); *Generation to Generation* (1980); *Psycho Girls* (1985); *Graveyard Shift* (1986); *Johnny Shortwave* (1995); *The Night Is Mine* (in development)

Michael Bockner has been working professionally in the film industry since 1972. At 15 he secured his first film job as editing assistant on a 35mm feature, *The Merry Wives of Tobias Rouke*. He spent the next few years making short dramatic and experimental films in 16mm, which he wrote, directed, edited and produced.

One of these films, *Reconnaissance* (1975), a 20-minute drama about a Canadian soldier lost in Europe during World War II, was his entrance piece for the film program at York University in Toronto. In his four-year course at York, Bockner made several films, among them, *The Ships Come In*, a documentary about Toronto waterfront stevedores which was sold to the CBC Television Network; and *The Pedestrian*, a 30-minute drama about an inhuman, computerized society of the future, based on the science-fiction works of Ray Bradbury.

Upon completion of the York film program in 1979, Bockner traveled with a small crew to Eastern Europe to film *Generation to Generation*, a one-hour television documentary about the re-emergence of post-war Jewish communities. He co-produced and co-wrote the film while also functioning as second-unit director and sound recordist. The film was shot entirely on location in Czechoslovakia, Hungary and Poland.

Back in Toronto, Bockner made a foray into the film distribution business but later moved to Los Angeles, where he worked for Dimension Pictures in distribution and foreign sales under the late Lawrence Woolner, one of independent Hollywood's original B-movie producers.

Returning to Canada in 1982, Bockner started the feature production arm of Lightshow Communications, which brought him together with former university colleagues, including Peter Boboras. At Lightshow, Bockner produced *Psycho Girls* (1985), a cult horror film which, though banned in Canada, was acquired by the Cannon Group for theatrical distribution and MGM/UA for video re-

Director Michael Bockner.

lease. Next, under the Lightshow banner, Bockner produced *Graveyard Shift* (1986), a stylish vampire noir film which performed extremely well in the video market worldwide.

Leaving Lightshow Communications, he formed Michael Bockner Productions Inc. and, with Peter Boboras, developed several feature film projects. Bockner directed and co-produced *Johnny Shortwave* (1995), a controversial drama about a renegade radio broadcaster who attempts to foment a political uprising. The film was photographed in 35mm black and white and was written by Bockner and Boboras. *Johnny Shortwave* has played at several international film festivals since its European premiere at Mannheim-Heidelberg. It received its North American premiere at the prestigious Film Forum in New York City in July 1996. It has had subsequent theatri-

cal release in the U.S. and Canada, where it has also been broadcast on television.

Bockner will soon direct his second feature film, *This Night Is Mine*, now in development and scheduled for production in 2000. It's an ensemble character piece, set against the backdrop of contemporary theater.

Michael Bockner has also contributed articles to film publications and has worked variously as an actor, script doctor, script reader for Telefilm Canada and film editing consultant. He lives and works in Toronto.

Biography: I grew up in Toronto. I think my interest in filmmaking began in junior high school. My father was a prominent film distributor in Canada and my mother loved movies so films were always around me as an influence. I started making my first films in regular 8mm when I was eleven and then moved into Super 8. I went to New York when I was fifteen to buy a 16mm Bolex reflex camera and started making them in 16mm, one or two of which got me into the film program at York University, which had a good reputation. When I was fifteen I got my first professional job as an editing assistant on a low budget 35mm movie called *The Merry Wives of Tobias Rouke*. It wasn't a very good film but it had the distinction of being a hundred thousand dollar full-blown feature in 1972 and it was fun. It taught me a lot, about movies and life.

Influences and Aspirations: I remember in junior high coming across a book called *The Film Director as Superstar*, by Joseph Gelmis, which is really an excellent collection of interviews with film directors. That inspired me quite a bit. One of the pivotal moments in my life was seeing Stanley Kubrick's *2001: A Space Odyssey* in 1968. I saw it at the Glendale Cinerama

Director Michael Bockner (middle).

Theater in Toronto about a week after it opened. My father got us tickets to it because it was a reserved seating engagement. And I believe, during the next two years of its run there, I saw it about a dozen times. And I'm not the only one—it was a seminal film for a lot of my friends, who are also filmmakers now. It really inspired us, got us to want to be filmmakers. The reason I mention this is that *The Film Director as Superstar* had an interview with Kubrick. He definitely is one of my important influences, as much for the quality of his work as for his work methodology and independence. He was perhaps the most successful independent filmmaker working on a large scale. Another influence is John Cassavetes because I love his films, and I knew him; he was a personal influence in my life.

How did you know Cassavetes? My father distributed his films in Canada and

so I knew him over a 15-year period and used to hang out on his film sets when I was in Los Angeles. He was a warm and gregarious kind of guy, but quick tempered and mercurial. He was very nice to me, though, and to other young filmmakers who sought his wisdom, Martin Scorsese among them. Cassavetes looked at one of my early films and gave me critical commentary, support; he appraised it. It was a much needed shot in the arm, and still resonates to this day.

Who are your other influences? Truffaut, Godard. I will always watch *400 Blows* and *Shoot the Piano Player* whenever they're on television, even though I've seen them many times each. Because great films have a kind of a magic about them so that there's nothing else like them; they create their own world which comes to life every time they're unspooled. Orson Welles is also a big inspiration, for sure. Not a lot of modern directors. And there's a European influence in my work as well.

What is your take on film school? It's not absolutely necessary, though it can certainly be of benefit. If you really want to be a filmmaker you'll find a way to do it. Working on your own and inevitably discovering techniques and technology on your own has as much validity as learning something in a more formalized setting. However, in this extremely competitive world in which we work, where film schools and aspiring filmmakers proliferate and an abundance of films never get seen or distributed, it's like any other degree in that it helps separate you from the crowd. It helps to get you a job. Perhaps film school is necessary to qualify you to take a position in the film industry but not necessary for you to become a filmmaker. But film school graduates separate themselves from the crowd.

How did your recent film, **Johnny Shortwave,** *come about?* My business partner and I were anxious to make another film. So we decided on a kind of genre film, a cat and mouse game. That was the first idea. It developed into something completely different. It was strongly influenced by the politics of the country: Canada was going through some major political upheaval at the time, in the midst of an election campaign. We had an incumbent government that was running on a free-trade platform which Peter (Boboras) and I, being political people, believed was potentially dangerous to many of the industries in our country including our own. And we said, Let's incorporate this into our story. What if the guy we're chasing is a political dissident, a renegade, and the government has to send an agent to track him down because he's trying to foment an uprising. So we put words into his mouth, turned him into a radio propagandist, pro-

jected this into the future and found ourselves in the realm of science fiction. It was heavily influenced by the political trends we found ourselves in. We decided to use black and white because it seemed to evoke an earlier period, the deprivation of the Depression-era cinema and an underclass which we were trying to show. It also gave us instant production value, instant design, because black and white looks dramatic. It's a medium of preference for me but commercial death today. I've talked to kids today who won't even look at black and white films! It was artistically the right thing to do and commercially the wrong thing to do. But we stuck to our guns and proceeded artistically and are very happy that we did. We were offered a good production deal to shoot the film in color but we turned it down. It simply wouldn't have been the same movie. The film took a long time to make, and it was an organic process, stopping and starting a few times because we ran out of money and had to raise more. And I ended up editing the film myself. It is a very personal film. It's autobiographical to a certain extent because *Johnny Shortwave* is as much a political propagandist as he is an artist, sort of a metaphor for the struggling artist in all of us who can't find expression in the commercial marketplace. The film has something of a following. It's been well received at festivals around the world, particularly around Spain and Portugal, and the Germans like it. But North Americans, especially Americans, don't take to it, and it hasn't done well there. The cards are stacked against it—too European in its atmosphere and sentiments, it's not really a genre film. It's a tough thing to pigeonhole it, [a fact] which I think gives it some originality—but, then again, try to market something that's original.

It seems like most of the people who graduate from film school work on other

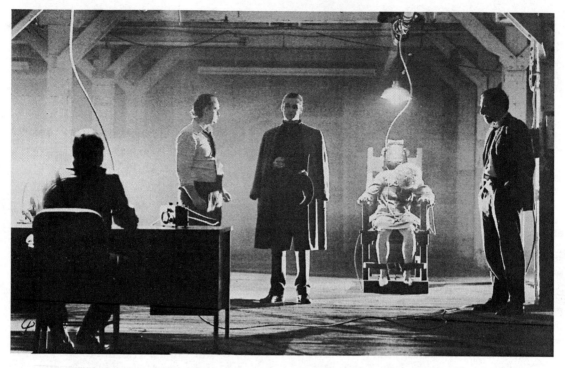

The photographer (John Tench) confers with interrogators (Doug O'Keefe, Robert Cotie, Andy Dan) after they electrocute Lotte, the polling lady (Rebecca Maynard-Nile) in *Johnny Shortwave*. Copyright 1995 MBP Inc./Mythmakers Ltd.

people's films, instead of making their own. But also those of us who are independent filmmakers also find ourselves working on other people's films. At least film school does teach you some basic technologies and, certainly, if it's a good film school, it's up on the latest technology that's changing the business and is tied into the industry. Unfortunately the one I went to did not have strong industry ties at that time, not like UCLA and USC and now the Film Centre in Toronto, with visiting lecturers and job placement programs. It's important for schools today to have a certain success rate.

How important is your script to your films? Important but not fixed. You have an evolving relationship with your script, as with your film, throughout production. I have this script right now that I think is finished, meaning that it's ready to show

other people. But I know it's not really finished. It will never be finished; it will change constantly—as new ideas come upon me, in different phases of production, as different things assert their influence on the project. I don't consider a script to be finished until you're done editing the movie, because you're always rewriting scenes and dialogue. But I wouldn't want to start a film with just an outline, although I know some people do. I would feel confident making a film from a detailed treatment which described the story in third-person narrative form and had dialogue references because I think much of the dialogue could be created as you go. But, generally speaking, I wouldn't start a movie without a full blown screenplay. And I tend to be a dialogue person—but not in the Billy Wilder sense, where every wicked word is etched in stone. I don't have to do the script verbatim.

Syd Field, who is, or was, the screenwriting guru, with his 120 page paradigm for the perfect script, was always [saying] that *Chinatown* was the classic two hour script—120 pages, 30 page first act, 60 page second act, 30 page third act, et cetera—which turned the whole process of screenwriting into a dull, structural approach to filmmaking. It also turned Hollywood's attention to his method. Now, I came across a copy of *Chinatown* and it's a 152 page script, not 120—so it shoots that theory to hell—which means that the director, Polanski, whose name was on the draft I read, was attracted to the script when it was "overlong." Field's formula has really taken hold of Hollywood. Also, from what I've read, Robert Towne, screenwriter of *Chinatown*, has great difficulty in cutting his long drafts down to the 120-page format.

Cassavetes' films, as an alternative example, are structured, but not in any way we're used to. You go along with a scene almost to the point where you can't bear it anymore. That's how long his scenes last. That interests me because there are no comfortable segues or time limits. That was part of his originality.

When you're shooting a script are you 100 percent faithful to it? If an actor is having trouble dealing with some dialogue, then we can change it to something that is more suitable to him, that he can get his mouth around. But, of course, the script is just something to interpret, anyway. Sometimes if you're the director of a script you've written, you tend to write visually. If you're conceiving a scene quite specifically as you're writing it you may stick to it. Other times it's quite loose. I stick to the structure for the shooting but structure will often change in the editing.

What equipment do you use and why? I'm a film guy. I was taught on film and my last feature I cut on a 35mm Moviola. And I noticed that *Saving Private Ryan* specified in it's end credits that it was edited on the Moviola. We're living in a digital environment today, cutting on Avid and Montage systems and whatever else is out there, yet we should not forget that the greatest films of world cinema were cut on this Moviola, so it is hardly an obsolete tool. I haven't worked on digital systems yet. For trailers, yes, but not for a feature. Some friends of mine are looking into shooting on DVD and transferring to film for release. Thomas Vinterberg's *The Celebration* was shot on video first, then bumped over to film. And film festivals are accepting films in these formats. So it's becoming a legitimate way of working. But it's not my way of working because to me nothing looks better than original 35mm motion picture film projected. I also like to hold film in my hands and hold it up to the light, the tactile aspects of filmmaking being very important to me. I don't think we have to embrace new technology to the exclusion of all else just because it exists, although that's the thrust of the business. Like any artist, you choose your tools. Some people work in watercolor, some prefer oils, and I think it's just as legitimate to cut a movie on film, on a Moviola or a Kem, as it is cutting on an Avid. The product might be slightly different, because the tools we use affect the outcome of the work, but not fundamentally. It's still the same medium, after all. The way I work on the Moviola is like a sculpting process to me, more holistic.

For cameras, I use an Arriflex BL35. Good registration. Good and solid camera.

I got rid of my 16mm Bolex years ago, for some horribly ill-conceived reason; there are some days I still want to go out and shoot some 16mm film. I like portable equipment. I'll shoot on anything, depending on the project. I prefer the look of 35mm film, overall.

Cost/Budget/Funding: I find that if you don't finance your own venture at the outset you'll never get it off the ground. One has to be his own development financier at this level of filmmaking. I fund that phase of the film myself, usually. Then, there's the actual budget. That has come from my company and private sources, an unusual method of finance for Canadian films. In Canada it's slightly different than in the United States. Canada functions as a European country in terms of film finance: we have the government agency system here. The degree to which one is successful as a producer is directly proportional to his ability to extract money from the government agencies. I've never used a government agency. It's always been myself and my partners, private funds, investor funds, loans and also presales. That's how we've done it, and I will continue to do that. The only time I'd get involved in government financing is if I had a co-producer in a European country. And then, they'll be the one accessing the government funds.

Are there restrictions to get these funds? Yes, you have to shoot a certain portion of the film in the country providing the money, or a certain amount of money has to be spent in that country [on, for instance] equipment or actors, or doing some post production there. And it can be quite tricky, if it's funded by more than one country, to satisfy the demands of all. That's part of the deal making.

How did you cast your actors? We would always contact the agencies in the city, and they would send us a pile of photographs and resumes. We might stipulate that we don't want the "usual" actors, that we want them to send us fresh faces. Or we might request certain actors. But for the last film we just got a lot of photos sent, went through them, made a short list, interviewed a lot—about five hundred actors—and chose them that way. With the next film I'd like to carefully select the actors I want from a much larger base.

We used some of the same actors in the first two movies and then in the last one I had a whole new group. You develop loyalties, you know what people are capable of doing and you get to know them well and cast them better.

Have you ever had an actor in mind when you were writing a script? I have. It doesn't mean you're going to get that actor, necessarily. It can help you nail a character, help you better write a character. Certainly, that's the way that Hollywood works. They write "Jim Carey" pictures and "Will Smith" pictures, or whoever today's stars happen to be. That's the star system, not the same way of visualizing a character.

How do you get your film's music? I have a guy I've worked with twice, Joel Rosenbaum, a very good composer. I'd want to work with him again. He's classically trained, likes to write for acoustic instruments, in the manner that John Williams composes music for the screen. I'm not really a big fan of electronic music. I tend to resist electronic scores. On the other hand, the material I'm filming might suggest different types of music. I don't do needle drop, meaning "choosing prerecorded music." This is how Hollywood works today. So many of today's films are just wall to wall pop music tracks. I think the best score one can get is either composed for the scenes that have been cut, or the film has been shot with certain pieces of music in mind. There's an old technique which was used on silent film sets. They'd have players playing atmosphere music to get the actors in mood for and during the scenes. And I know some modern directors have used this technique in some

MOS (without sound) scenes. I know Kubrick and Spielberg have done this, and apparently it worked quite well. It shows the effect that music can have at the image creation level. Ideally, I think the music should be composed for the film at the fine-cut stage.

How long did it take you to make your first feature? It was called *Psycho Girls*, a tongue-in-cheek horror film. It took five to six months to complete. It was fast, very fast. We had a company of three partners, and one of us was cinematographer-editor, another was the director, the other was producer-co-writer (that was me), and my later co-producer, Peter Boboras, was our sound recordist and sound editor. We did everything. It was shot in 13 days. When you're working on such a low budget you move very quickly. And we were young, so we had the energy and attitude that I don't have now. I would like to make a film that way again but I'm much more methodical now.

What is your experience with special effects? The gunshot effects in *Johnny Shortwave* were typical applied makeup. The gunshots were pre-made on his face and I think there was blood in his mouth that he spit out. But it wasn't anything elaborate. Quite standard but effective. In *Psycho Girls* and *Graveyard Shift*, all the effects were makeup and appliances. They looked appropriately gruesome. We had a lot of mortician's wax to mottle the skin and create wounds, and a lot of blood.

The rest of it is how you cut the film. With Sam Peckinpah, all his effects were makeup effects as well. Incredible ballets of violence, remember?

Advice to the prospective filmmaker: Get a camera—that's number one—whether it's a video camera or digital video or Super 8mm. Spend a couple of days learn-ing how to use it. I don't advise making a film unless you have something important you want to say or show, and by that I mean important to *you*. No point in making films unless you have something that's burning to get out that you want to communicate to people. It has to be something you really believe in. Otherwise, what's the point? The point may be to make money. But to aspiring filmmakers that's usually not the point. They have a need to express themselves and play at this medium. So, write a good story that's important to you, think visually and go ahead and do it. Refine your technique, maybe, by going to film school. Watch a lot of movies, surround yourself with people who can teach you, which might mean attaching yourself to someone as an apprentice or getting work in the industry as a production assistant. I guess film school is the most prescribed method of getting into the business, but even to get into film school you have to have some films behind you. Find a way to make them. Borrow money from your family.

How important is publicity for your films? Very important because it's very hard today for a movie to find its audience. It was easier 15 years ago. There weren't as many films, not as much competition and many more small screens willing to show small films. And a film could afford to run for a little time back then to find its audience through word of mouth. But that's rare today. The small screens and repertory houses have been replaced by video shelves, and the other screens are dominated by the major film companies. The only venue left for smaller independent films are film festivals—sometimes the *only* venue a film has, the only place a film will ever be released. I've seen festival films that have never been released, wonderful films, that you never get to see any other way. Publicity is

the type of film that appeals to me and people like me. And secondly, what the public wants to see is what they are offered. They have to have a choice. Often the public will be more receptive to your film than the distributor will be. "What the public wants to see" is really code for what the public already knows. "Give the public what they want" is what we always hear, an edict of North American Capitalism, and what that really means is "Give them a very slim variation on what they've already experienced so there's a consistency and no risk," and that's not what I'm interested in. Especially today, when films are mass marketed like fast food.

A good director, in Hollywood's view, is someone who gets the job done on time and on budget. They say of him, "He knows exactly what he wants." That's funny to me because I know that it's many a day that I'm standing on a set and I don't know what the hell I want. I know what I'm trying to accomplish but not necessarily the method yet. I have to get the job done and figure out what I want along the way. It's a process of discovery. If you take that element out of it and claim to know exactly what you want from day one, you're missing a great part of the creative process.

How is independent filmmaking different in the U.S. than in Canada? In Canada, film funding is the province of the film-funding agencies. There's no private financiers anymore. We also don't have venture-capital financing from the banks. Our banks are extremely conservative when it comes to film. So the film agencies fill the gap—Telefilm Canada, Manitoba Film Board, et cetera. Every province has its own agency. If you don't get funding from the government agencies, you're what they call an "outside" filmmaker, as if you're a mainstream filmmaker if you're working with the agencies!

Emmanuel Mark as *Johnny Shortwave.*

The film distributors here are all tied in with Telefilm, as well. To do what I'm doing, which is produce films totally independently and privately, is almost heresy here. It's the exception, and people are always surprised. I just do what you're supposed to do, what independent producers are supposed to do, raise the money independently. I think it's much more that way in the United States, more of an individual, freewheeling cowboy attitude there. Plus, you have ten times the population. At any given time only 1 percent of Canadian screens show Canadian films. I blame the Canadian government and blame the major distributors. The American majors own our screens. It's detrimental to the indigenous industry when we can't get screen time in our own country.

What are you working on now? I work on one project at a time which consumes and obsesses me. I have a script now that I'm trying to package. A few actors are interested, so I can attach them to the project and try to get a distribution commitment from a Canadian company. And once that's set, I'll do the same thing with some European companies—put the budget and financing together in that way. It's a character piece called *This Night Is Mine*. It has some really wonderful roles.

Last Words: It's a hostile, jealous business, this film business of ours. It's ruthless. It gets harder, I find, than easier. Just when you think you understand how to do something, it changes. Things are changing so rapidly, nothing is permanent any longer. I feel much more isolated and independent now than I have in the past. There's a learning process I have to go through now about how the market has changed. The players change all the time. It's tough. One of the things that keeps me going is to think of Jack Kerouac writing *On the Road,* of how he had to go through 27 publishers before he got one. That book has been [in] print, in 50 languages, for the last 42 years. So, we should keep that in mind.

Mark Borchardt

DIRECTOR

Filmography: Coven (1998); *American Movie* (subject of documentary, 1999)

Biography: I was born in Milwaukee, Wisconsin, and continue to live in the area. I started making movies at age fourteen with a used Super 8mm camera for forty dollars that couldn't even focus. I made my first epic, *The More the Scarier,* on one fifty foot roll of film, utilizing the local cemetery as a main location. I shot about a half dozen of these films before going into the military.

I joined the army at seventeen for a three year stint. Had I been wise I would have saved my [military] money for filmmaking when I got out. Also, I should have worked on writing scripts on my off time. That is all hindsight, of course; but the fact remains that time is valuable and money doesn't come easy, for the most part.

After I got out of the service I continued to make Super 8mm films. I also enrolled in the film department at [University of Wisconsin at] Milwaukee. I briefly wrote film reviews for a few of the local free-press papers in town. I joined the Wisconsin Screenwriter's Forum, one of the largest screenwriting groups in the country, and that enabled me to get my hands on other writers' scripts. I was exposed to the style and content of other people's work. I volunteered to be the national contest coordinator for two consecutive years, and soon after that I was elected chairman of the board of the organization.

I still felt I was treading water, filmwise, and I knew that I needed some sort of breakthrough. I decided to write a film to be shot on 16mm entitled *Coven.* Soon after production began I found myself back in film school because the cost of renting equipment out in the "real world" proved to be quite prohibitive.

I was taking a "works in progress" class taught by filmmaker Chris Smith. His first feature, *American Job,* played in the American Spectrum section of the Sundance Film Festival in 1996. He was impressed with the amount of footage I had already shot for *Coven* so he asked if he could shoot a documentary of my cinematic efforts. Three years later he completed his effort and it was accepted into

Shooting the road attack from the camera car for *Coven*.

competition in the documentary section of the 1999 Sundance Festival. In conjunction with Smith's film, *Coven* played at the Egyptian Theatre during the festival.

What are your influences and aspirations and what got you into making movies? I am fascinated by life. I am fascinated by the way people express themselves and behave. I always paid close attention to the nuances of language, the old stories and the manner in which they were told. Just as a still photographer pays close attention to the visual world he or she lives in, I was also aware of all the physical (cars, apartments, landscapes, et cetera) presences around me. With a movie camera I knew that I could capture all of that that was important to me.

Major films that have influenced me were *Taxi Driver*, *Night of the Living Dead* and *Dawn of the Dead*. The *Dead* films really got to me with their atmospheric gray skies and barren landscapes. Also, the more realistic way in which the characters spoke and the environment they existed in, as opposed to their Hollywood counterparts.

Hollywood films never turned me on and up to this point I have no desire to pursue that form of filmmaking. I wish to proceed into higher budget movies but only to get what I need up on the screen. I'm what you could call a personal filmmaker and will continue to write and bring to the screen the way I experience life and the way it affects me.

What is your take on film school? Film school is what you make of it. A lot of the students spend most of their time staring up at the ceiling or down at their shoes. They usually end up making the upside-down tree films. Film school is not necessary, and a lot of people bypass it, but it does have its advantages. You meet a lot of people with similar ambitions and they

Studying a cue card, *Coven*. Mike Shank is on the left.

can be a valuable asset to your production. They also provide moral support and a sense of cinematic community. As some of [your classmates] enter the outside world of filmmaking, they will also be valuable professional connections.

Most equipment rooms in school are run by volunteers. Don't be a fool. Volunteer. Get in there. You'll then have access to the equipment you'll need. You will also circumvent the dreaded waiting lines and, most important, [you'll have] first dibs on the equipment. Once you have left the school system you'll realize how valuable the free access to the equipment was. On the outside you will have to pay for everything you can't beg for or borrow. Also, you'll need access to a credit card to rent equipment to cover possible damage or loss.

Don't just go through the motions while you are in film school. Become technically adept at the mechanical workings

of the equipment. Crews will respect you for this knowledge and not just consider you some far-out, self-described "aesthetic auteur." You may, at times, run some of the equipment yourself or may have to teach volunteer novices some of the technical ropes. At the no- to low-budget level, [your knowledge] becomes an essential asset.

While in school, don't make a bunch of shitty half-assed films. Let the jerk-offs jerk off in school, don't get sucked down with them. You can't make up for that lost time. Once you're out, you're out. Build a team among your peers of ambitious, determined, hardworking people. The more you do, the more support you'll gather. And it does take a community to make a film for the most part.

You'll need something viable to show potential associates, crew members, actors and, possibly, investors. They'll take a look at your work and know right off the bat where you're coming from. Provide a good solid body of work. Your films from school might not be perfect but it will show your potential.

How important is your script? Don't jump the gun and start a production without a proper script. Make sure that this is the story you want to devote an incredible amount of time and energy to. Be confident of the direction it goes in and its dramatic structure.

The idea of just winging it on the set can prove disastrous. You may have a scene fall apart right in front of your eyes and, embarrassingly, in front of the cast and crew. You have a responsibility to your film and to the people devoting their time and energy into it.

On the other hand, improvising can be an incredibly enlightening experience. Wonderful things can happen that you could never have imagined while penning the script. Still, it is wise to have a funda-

mental understanding of how each scene should work. It's true that miracles can happen—you may see the light in an improvisational situation—but don't count on it.

Don't make your particular society an excuse not to write. Don't let people rob you of your time and creativity. Turn off the phone and find a quiet spot to work. If people have a habit of unexpectedly showing up at the door then find a bar or coffee shop to do your work. Even a park works well if there aren't too many distractions.

Don't *accept* your finished script. Be confident that this is the material you want to film and that when you hand it to someone you won't be embarrassed by it and have to make some sort of lame explanation for every other page.

When you are confident of your script, show it to some reliable people who can realistically critique it. Don't be insulted if they see things differently; they may have some valuable insights on how to

The crew of *Coven,* **preparing the camera car.**

improve your script. But don't waste your time showing it to a bunch of goofballs without an understanding of what you're doing and who will only serve to use it as a vehicle to denigrate your hopes and dreams. On the other hand, people without experience in a particular field can provide a gut instinct evaluation that comes from the heart and can be quite helpful.

Writing can be a bitch because there isn't any [one] way to do it. It's not a linear process like digging a ditch: It can take any turn at any time. The script at times can seem like an unfathomable mess, but you can't give up. You have to see your way through it. Every writer experiences this.

What equipment/format do you use and why? I use film because it is a beautiful and unparalleled format, the original medium of the cinema. For *Coven* I used 16mm black and white reversal film stock from Kodak. For my next film, *Northwestern*, I'll use 16mm black and white negative, a professional film stock.

For a camera I bought a used CP16 for $2,000. I purchased it from someone working at a production house that switched primarily to video. I recorded my sound with a Sony TC-D5M with crystal sync. Crystal sync is used exclusively for filmmaking and is what precisely controls the tape speed, [making it] "in sync" with the camera. The camera must also have a crystal sync mechanism to control the film speed. The Sony TC-D5M utilized regular ⅛" audio cassettes and I purchased it new for $1,240. It's a simple device to use and that helps if you get into a bind using a sound recordist without much experience. It's basically a glorified cassette recorder, but it does the job.

Keep in mind that for approximately the same price, or even less, you can purchase a digital tape recorder, which by its very nature can keep sync for at least a few minutes per take.

Production or rental houses can be a valuable source for used equipment. Invariably, they will upgrade their equipment and the other pieces will end up on the shelf collecting dust. Either it will continue to sit there or be donated to a university.

Cost/Budget/Funding: I think *Coven* came in at around $13,000. The bulk of the money went to film stock and the university, which I basically used as my rental house and post-production studio. For *Coven* I begged, borrowed and threw in whatever money I had. I cashed in my IRA and some savings bonds. I delivered papers and used that paycheck. When you first tell people you are making a film they look at you like you're nuts. But when you actually start doing it and there's a trail of tangible evidence, they may even be inclined to invest. I never followed a strict budget because the production itself was so across the board. But if you're going to approach serious investors you had better have a detailed and realistic budget to present them with.

How did you cast your actors? I ran audition notices in the local papers, which is a free service. For my first film I used rooms in the university to hold auditions, which provided a professional atmosphere. Also, most people knew where the university was located, so I'm sure that alleviated many wild goose chases and apprehensions about going to some unknown location.

With *Coven* I used a blend of theater actors and just "regular" people. Even though it's true that some theater actors have a tendency to be overtly dramatic (projecting to the audience) it worked in that respect in my particular situation because *Coven* had overtly dramatic fantasy

Filming *Coven*, shooting with an Éclair 16mm camera. Mark Borchardt, left, and Mike Shank, right.

situations. In other instances, people off the street lent an air of naturalism that worked well for certain scenes.

No one was paid, but they believed in the project and knew that they weren't wasting their time. They could see my persistency and knew I would follow through and complete the project. It's many people's fear that they are putting a lot of their valuable time and effort into something that will never see the light of day. You have to show them that you mean it, and they in turn will give you their best.

How did you get your film's music? Again, it was through notices in the papers. I was really blessed meeting Patrick Nettesheim. He's an extremely talented composer/musician with a great attitude. He puts in long hours and is determined to see a project to its completion. I cannot

stress how important attitude is. It's what makes a comfortable working atmosphere, and that's crucial. His work ethic is extraordinary.

How long did it take you to make your first film? Three years. Scraping up money had a lot to do with it. Also, more precise preproduction would have made things much easier. Shooting on weekends stretches things out.

What is your experience with dealing with special effects at this level? Hershey Syrup for blood. Simple but effective. I've made very realistic axes with balsa wood, you wouldn't know the difference. There are many up-and-coming makeup and special effects artists who want their work exposed. Most are very happy to contribute to a film for free or at low cost.

Coven **main publicity shot.**

Any production tips for the novice filmmaker? Study film. Learn how to frame your shots professionally. Amateur movies suffer from such painfully simple things as too much headroom over the actors. Record the best sound possible, as this is the pitfall of many low-budget films. Don't get involved in a bunch of little projects that will only serve to spread you too thin. Focus on your personal life in as much order as possible; this will have a definite affect on your ability to focus.

The more confident, determined and practical you are about your project the more likely you will get the cast, crew, services and equipment that you will need. Mount the production as professionally as possible.

Last but not least, feed your cast and crew well. They may tolerate the idea of not getting paid but if they start to go hungry...

How important is publicity for your films? Unless you're going to be the only one watching your films, publicity is key to developing a film career. There are endless film festivals out there. Get interviews in local papers. Send them a copy of your

film and tell them of your struggles to get it made. Send the same information out to the countless fanzines that review films. Word of mouth spreads. There are many underground screening programs that will show your work. Subscribe to film magazines which have this information on festivals and screening venues.

What about distribution? There are good books available on self-distribution. If it's a viable film, there are markets for it. Distributors haunt festivals because they're in the business of acquisitions. There are also many, many independent video distributors. Contact them with any publicity material you have and send them a copy of your film.

What's in store for the future? Three features. First, *Northwestern*, which is about a junkyard worker and his relationship with a writer out in the sticks. Then I will do a remake of *Coven*. *Toronto Blues* is about a successful but alcoholic writer who goes to Toronto to try and get away from it all.

It's important to have goals because it keeps you focused. If you're too open-ended you can get waylaid by other people's projects and suddenly realize that you're not doing what you really want to do.

Anything you want to add? Stick to your guns; you only have one life to live. Don't let people or situations intrude on your work. You'll be the only one sorry in the end for wasting your life. Take people's opinions with a grain of salt. You're putting your heart out there, and people are ready to crush it. Develop a thick skin. Only you know what's right for you.

(Six months after this initial interview, the documentary *American Movie* was released in theaters around the country. I saw it at the Film Forum in New York City. It was released on DVD and home video in May of 2000.)

How has **American Movie** *helped you?* It's helped financially and it has helped in terms of people knowing who I am. Because of those two elements it will help make the next film smoother. Filmmaking will always be a difficult process but some of the elements in getting personnel to help and finances will be easier. But I'm sure the mechanics will be just as tough as usual.

As far as you're concerned, do you feel that **American Movie** *is a good representation of how it is to make a low budget film?* I think it is. I was very happy with the movie. I'm now being cast in the *American Movie* character role, by life. Which is only one slice of my pie, it's not all me.

But you're able to use it to your advantage. Absolutely.

As far as independent film, publicity is the thing. I noticed sales of **Coven** *have really jumped on your Web site since* **American Movie** *came out.* Yeah, I'll be working on them today. That's an ongoing thing.

How many have you sold before and how many after **American Movie**? I sold less than a 100 before and [since *American Movie*] came out, I've reached around 2,000. So you definitely see the jump there. I have a house do the dubbing, but I send the tapes out myself. I work from about 9 A.M. to midnight everyday, so that's the routine.

You mentioned your getting cast in the **American Movie** *role?* Yes, you get stereotyped by the press as the guy in *American Movie*, which is again only one slice of my personality, one slice of my existence. So that sometimes seems odd when you read it back in the paper.

It's almost like a character unto itself. There you go.

What other television shows have you been on besides **David Letterman**? *Letterman* was great, short and sweet. I was on twice. (He asked me back.) This is a little-known fact now. Regis Philbin was not his last guest, it was me. I was his very last guest before his heart surgery.

Is Sony, the distributor of **American Movie,** *the one setting up your publicity appearances?* Yes and no. Sony does a lot of it. People independently get a hold of Sony to contact us. We were just invited to the Playboy mansion by Roger Ebert. Both *American Movie* and *Coven* are playing in his overlooked film festival. So we'll encounter him a few times in the next months.

How often have you been traveling? This weekend I have to go to the Museum of Contemporary Art in Chicago. They want me down in Gurney, Illinois; they want me in Australia, in England. I have to go to the George Eastman House in Rochester; they want me to speak at Harvard and at Cornell. Roger Ebert's film festival, host a thing on Milwaukee TV about the Academy Awards—instead of dying down, it's not ending.

Are you working on **Northwestern** *now?* It's very hard to do. My hands are very tied with business, each and every day. Yes, I am working on it. The weekends are extremely precious to me. I've got

Filmmaker Mark Borchardt, shooting *Coven*.

a black and white flick, about a writer drinking in a junkyard who writes his way out of it and meets this writer chick out in the sticks. If you tell that to Hollywood, they'll have a heart attack at the other end of the phone. Yeah, I have offers of money. But I'm an adult who sees the other end, sees where I'll loose control. They'd make the movie in color, change things, because they have to make money. I'm making an aesthetic investment from the heart. The worlds do not integrate. In fact, a big Internet company wants to do business with me, but want their hands into the next film, and that's where I'm drawing the line. I know other people would be jumping up and down waving that check, but I know the consequences of that. So screw that.

What about working as an actor in someone else's film? That I would do. I think something legitimate and nice will come up. I'm confident that will happen.

John Bowker

PRODUCER/DIRECTOR/WRITER/ACTOR

Filmography: Director/co-producer, *Beyond the Lost World* (2002); Writer/Director/Producer, *The Evilmaker* (2000); Writer/Director/Producer, *Dreamwalkers* (2000); Actor, *Crimson Heather* (2000); Actor, *Lust of the Vampire Hookers* (2000); Actor, *We Need Earth Women* (1999); Actor, *Vamperissa's Velvet Vault of Horror* (1999); Actor, *Monster in the Garage* (1997)

Biography: I was born on January 12th, 1968, in Martinez, California. When I was two, we moved up to Oregon, where my dad had gotten a job in construction. I have pretty much lived my life here in Oregon, not truly happy until I found my passion, moviemaking.

Influences/Aspirations: I guess my biggest influence directing-wise was John Carpenter. I loved every one of his movies that came out. I think my favorite was *The Thing*. Other influences were of course Steven Spielberg, John Landis, George Romero and George Lucas. From the get-go, after I saw my first movie when I was a kid, I knew that's what I wanted to do. In high school my friends and I would take a VHS camera and make short movies on the weekends with it. I moved away for a while and when I came back, one of my old friends (Joe Sherlock) had made a video movie while I was gone called *Dimension of Blood*. That thing rocked, in my mind, and it got me pumped up to get back into movie-making after several years of trying to lead a normal life. I discovered that a "normal life" wasn't for me. Movie-making is where I belong.

What is your take on film school? I have mixed emotions on that. I think that film school is great in the sense that you can make tons of contacts. You never know who's going to make it and who will remember you for projects. On the other hand, they give you the textbook format on moviemaking (which vary rarely works in the independent and B-movie scene). I'm a firm believer in going out there and just doing it. I had taken some classes at the Northwest Film School in Portland, and I will never forget this: We had a guest speaker talking about lighting, and the teacher left the room for a moment. While she was gone, the speaker said to us, "Don't tell her I told you this, but film school is a waste of time. Go out there and get involved in as many projects as you possibly can. Volunteer, do coffee runs, move cables, do *anything*. And when the sixteen-hour day is done, ask if there is anything else you can do, because if you moan and groan about going home, you can bet that the director or company will never use you again. The only way to learn is hands-on." I have always remembered that.

How important is your script? The script is very important to the movie. Sure, you can have an hour and a half of babes running around covered in blood, but that gets old after a while. You need a solid foundation and story line if you want to have a well-rounded movie. Growing up in all of the writing classes I have taken, it's always been the same. Story, story, story! I agree.

Equipment/Format: Right now I make my projects on Hi-8 (the Sony CCD-TRV43 NTSC) and have them film-looked afterwards. I plan eventually moving to digital and from there into 16mm, and then hopefully 35mm. The reason right now as to why I am using video is budgeting. It's about the cheapest way you can go. Once I get a couple of more movies under my belt and people see what I have to offer, I plan on advancing. But right now, the video is great.

Cost/Budget/Funding: A lot of people think that they need tons and tons of money to make a movie. Not so. If you approach things right and get the right kind of people who are dedicated to the project, you have it pretty good. My first feature, *Dreamwalkers* [which was in final edit when this interview was transcribed], only cost me $300, and that was mainly food for the people. *The Evilmaker*, which was

my second feature, jumped in cost to right about $10,000. That's what happens when you try to advance and take more risks. It also cost more because I put a name actress in it and I tried paying people wages.

The budget is everything. That's your guideline on how the money you have raised is going to be spent. Always try to stay within your budget, if possible.

I funded *Dreamwalkers* by myself. For *The Evilmaker* half was funded by me and the other half by a private investor. Getting funding from investors is a double-edged sword. It's nice in a way because you are not gambling with your own money. But, on the other hand, since it is someone else's money you are playing with, they usually have say on how things go, unless you contract it otherwise. I was lucky in that my investor trusted me completely with the money and opted out of not having a say, because she really didn't know that much about moviemaking. For me, it works both ways. I like to fund a project myself and find investors. You just have to remember to tell whoever is investing it's like stock options: You may never get your money back. But, hey, at least they get their name in a movie.

How do you get your actors? *Dreamwalkers* was all cast locally through people that I know. For *The Evilmaker* I got a little ambitious and contacted Stephanie Beaton (she has starred in over sixteen movies) and sent her the script. She loved it and wanted to do it. I cast the rest locally by placing ads at the colleges and [by] word-of-mouth. You would be amazed at how many talented people out there are just dying to get into a movie.

How did you get your film's music? You know, that's one of the hardest problems I had. Luckily, a couple of people I met through friends were musicians, and the rest, as they say, is history. Another friend

Video box artwork for John Bowker's *The Evilmaker*. Box art designed by Joe Sherlock. Courtesy Pipedreams Entertainment.

of mine (Joe again) is also very talented when it comes to writing music. He can look at a scene and just go with it. He has also composed for me. There is also the non-copyrighted stuff you can find at libraries. Another option is, there are companies out there that sell their music for a small fee, but the problem you have with that is you take the chance of someone else using the same music. I found that out the hard way.

How long did it take to make your first film? Eight months filming. We did it all on weekends and whenever we could. True dedication from people on that one.

What is your experience with dealing with special effects at this level? Fortu-

nately, I have a really good special-effects and makeup man (Rob Merickel) who knows what he is doing. I usually hand him a script and, within no time at all, he has broken it down into makeup logs, special effects logs, budget and so on. *The Evilmaker* had a ton of special effects and makeup. Some of the scenes were shot days apart, but you couldn't tell. If someone had a bruise for a scene and we weren't going to shoot with them again for a couple of days, we would take Polaroid's and Rob would make it look the same again. Special effects are a lot of fun, but they are also a lot of hard work if you want to get them right. And sometimes, no matter how much you plan for things and rehearse them, it doesn't always come off the way you had

Director John Bowker (left) with director of photography Joe Sherlock (right) on the set of *The Evilmaker*.

envisioned them. Sometimes they come out looking better.

Any production tips for the novice filmmaker? I always suggest [you] make movies within your means. Write for locations you know you can get. Start small, but *start*. Don't put it off until the next day or next year, just do it. If you are not sure of how to do something, ask questions. There are people out there with knowledge and expertise that would love to pass on their information. And when a day goes terrible, don't give up and throw it in the can. Keep working at it. It may take awhile to get your first feature completed, but when you do, oh man—what a feeling!

Publicity: Publicity is just about everything for your films. Word-of-mouth, posters, press releases, articles in the local newspaper, flyers, radio, TV, Internet, reviewers, any means possible. If people don't know about it, how are they going to see it?

Distribution: This area is new to me. You want to get your movie to a distributor who is going to get it out there for people to see. I think distribution is very important, for any movie. It's a ton more stressful when you try to do it yourself, plus you don't have the contacts. I'm not saying don't distribute your own movie; I'm just saying it's tougher. Try to get a deal with someone who will best represent your movie and what you expect to get out of it.

What's in store for the future? This summer I start on my third project, and I have many more waiting in the wings. I am in the process of casting it and am looking forward to getting behind the camera again. These past eight months or so have been taken up by post-production. I plan on making at least one movie a year, if not more. As long as the ideas keep forming in my head and I have the desire to get behind the camera and create, I will keep making movies.

Anything you want to add? Follow your dreams. I know that has been said a million times before, but it's true. Three years ago I would have never thought I would be in the position that I'm in. It's so awesome when you reach a goal that you set for yourself. If at first you don't succeed, try, try again. Never give up. Keep writing, keep making. And don't forget, watch movies. Study them. Observe how they made them—camera angles, scenery and so on. Believe me, it helps. Support your local B-movie maker. And most of all, believe in yourself!

Director John Bowker ready to be axed by actress Stephanie Beaton. Photograph courtey Pipedreams Entertainment.

Mark Burchett and Michael D. Fox

DIRECTORS

Filmography: Vamps: Deadly Dreamgirls (1995); *Evil Ambitions* (1996); *Live Nude Shakespeare* (1997)

Biography: Mark Burchett and Michael D. Fox have been friends and collaborators for over twenty years, having met while students at Lakota High School, just north of Cincinnati. They went on to study broadcasting and film at the University of Cincinnati. At UC they worked on their first feature film, director Bruce Weiss' *The Last Witness.*

At first glance they are a study in contrasts: Mark is big and tall and Mike short and wiry; Mark is laid-back and seemingly introverted, and Mike is fast-talking and hyper-kinetic; Mark is married, and Mike is single. Both love movies, though Mark is probably more gonzo on the subject, having worked in the movie exhibition business for Sumner Redstone's National Amusements for twenty years. The two creative partners have found that their differences in personalities and outlooks have been a considerable plus.

In 1993, along with Mark's wife, Denise Roland Burchett, they formed B+ Productions (motto: "It may be a B-movie, but it's better than average"). Two years later they shot their first feature, the vampire stripper epic *Vamps: Deadly Dreamgirls,* and followed it up the next year with a *Night Stalker* homage, *Evil Ambitions.*

In 1997 Mike formed his own distribution company, Independent Edge Releasing, and joined with friend David Levy in producing a parody video titled *Live Nude Shakespeare.*

Influences and Aspirations: We're both life-long movie fans, though Mark's tastes are probably more wide ranging. He enjoys things as diverse as the latest big-budget Hollywood extravaganza to the most obscure blood-and-breasts camcorder epic. Mike's tastes are a bit more selective. He gravitates toward smaller, grittier, more personal stories. Both of us are devout *Monty Python* fans, and we think some of that off-beat sense of humor is evident in our work. We both admire Roger Corman.

We're both writers who love the idea of storytelling. We're also very visually oriented, so making movies has always been a major dream of ours.

Our aspirations are somewhat different, though they tend to work pretty well together. For Mark, the simple act of entertaining a viewer is an art form. Mike's desires are to emotionally engage the viewer. Simply put, if each was given the chance to make the next *Star Wars* or the next *Rocky*, Mark would choose *Star Wars* and Mike would prefer *Rocky*. Our different outlooks have added greatly to our finished products. Mark makes sure that the lovers of the genre get what they are looking for out of the feature, while Mike works to give the characters greater depth.

Film School: Though both of us studied film in college, we both feel that the most valuable thing we took away from it was an appreciation for the history of the medium and a few contacts with kindred spirits. Even Mike, who has taught college classes at Miami University, Northern Kentucky University and Southern Ohio College, feels that even at the most prestigious film schools, like NYU and UCLA, the contacts you make are probably more valuable than the technical training. Technology changes rapidly and can be studied independent of school, but if you make friends with the next Spielberg—well, you get the picture.

The Script: The script is God. We're both writers first and foremost, so we both place a premium on the importance of the script. It's where your characters become real and where you stand the best chance of minimizing the most grievous continuity errors. We try to be open to ideas on staging and dialogue from our cast and crew and have utilized quite a few great

ideas. Still, our writers' egos are just strong enough that we require that the new idea or line be better than what we wrote.

The script, particularly at our level, is definitely influenced by our budget. We're unlikely to write a scene where we have to show the Space Shuttle crashing into Mount Rushmore, for example. We usually try to write just slightly above the budget level we think we are going to have, while keeping in mind a lower-cost backup plan for some scenes. However, if we find we have access to a particularly cool piece of equipment or location, we're going to tailor our script around it. For example, in *Evil Ambitions*, we were approached by Kineticvision, a local computer graphics company that wanted to add a feature film to their resume of commercials and industrial videos. They donated over $10,000 worth of computer time to our production, so we added scenes with really cool CGI [computer-generated image] effects that we wouldn't have dreamed of otherwise.

Equipment and Format: Both *Vamps* and *Evil Ambitions* were shot with a Super VHS camera and then recorded on ¾" videotape. While *Vamps* was edited in Mark's home using a portable off-line editing system, *Evil Ambitions* was put together in a full on-line editing suite at Cincinnati's Quest Motion Pictures. The reason for going with video instead of film (we had access to 16mm film equipment) was, quite simply, money. While we might have just been able to produce one 16mm feature for the cost of doing *Vamps* and *Evil Ambitions* on video, we knew that we would have been stuck with a pitifully low shooting ratio of no more than one or two takes per scene. By shooting on comparatively cheap videotape, we could do the same scene ten times if we felt the need. The end result was far more professional as a result. All that being said, we still hope to move to 16mm for our next project.

Cost/Budget/Funding: Even a "no-budget" production costs a lot of money. With our first feature the entire production was financed with our own money and that of friends and family. Mike took his life savings and Denise delayed her dreams of owning a house for a few years so she and Mark could put money towards the dream. Mark's mother contributed heavily, and our lead actor, Paul Morris, came up with much needed post-production funds. On *Evil Ambitions*, while there is a significant amount of our own money involved, we were able to find outside investors, the very patient and generous Linda Brown and George Colonel.

Actors: We've been constantly amazed by how much untapped talent there is out there. One wouldn't normally think of Cincinnati as a mecca for actors, but there are a lot of them out there working in local theater, commercials and such. A casting call for *Vamps* in the local free press brought us a wealth of talent, including our leading lady (and current *Femme Fatales* spokesperson), Jennifer Huss.

We also sent out the word to our friends and people we had encountered over the years. Paul Morris had been a friend for years and was quite a talented actor. We were thrilled when he came out to audition, and while we think we were pretty impartial, we were quite happy that he tested well enough to portray our male lead.

Given our emphasis on pretty images (and pretty women), and the expectation on the part of the B-movie audience that there would be a certain level of nudity in their low-budget fare, we were faced with how to cast some of these "key" roles. As we needed women who were physically attractive and who were comfortable enough with their bodies not to balk at nudity, we networked with local models and exotic dancers. We were lucky that many of them harbor desires to be actresses. We were even luckier that some of them could act.

How long did it take to make your first film? After several years' worth of false starts, we changed plans, and attempts to raise a large budget, *Vamps* went into production in 1995. From the time the first draft of the script was finished in April till the movie's premiere in December was eight months. Actual shooting began in July and was completed seven weeks later, at the end of August.

Publicity: We took the time to do this interview, didn't we? Seriously, it's impossible to overstate how important publicity is. Even though both of our movies are being sold nationally and internationally, it's local interest and local sales that gave us our initial boost towards profitability. We invited newspaper and television reporters on the set and chose carefully what days we had them out. We wanted to make sure that something interesting would be happening when they were there. Sure enough, several reporters from the largest daily paper, as well as several TV stations, showed up and gave us great coverage. We also approached the genre publications such as *Fangoria, Draculina, Scream Queens Illustrated* and *Femme Fatales* with press releases and photos from the production. As a result, we created at least a mini-buzz. We also take our actresses to conventions, like the Chiller Theatre, as much for the publicity as for any revenue it might generate.

Distribution: For *Vamps* we had started distributing it ourselves, through magazine sales and convention appearances. We then met Mike Raso at E.I. Independent Cinema, who offered to distribute our child for us. After working out an agreement that allowed us to keep doing the conventions and such while E.I. would market to video stores and handle international sales, we signed. Although we have been happy overall with how E.I. has pushed the movie, Mike Fox (who is making his living as a salesman) wanted to try his hand at distributing, so he formed Independent Edge Releasing, with *Evil Ambitions* as his first product. Mark, who never fancied himself a salesman, opted out of the new venture to devote his time developing the next B+ Productions feature, *Virgin Blood*.

Advice: As with any complex venture, it's the people that make the difference. The best advice we could give any aspiring movie makers would be to surround yourself with as many talented people as you can. Don't be afraid of people who may do things better than you. Include them.

Our cinematographer, Jeff Barklage, is the most sought-after director of photography in the Midwest. He's shot thousands of TV commercials and music videos. He had a commercial premiere in the 1997 Super Bowl (for Bud Light). He also shot *The Naked Man*, a movie co-produced by the Coen brothers for October Films. He is also a good friend and an incredibly valued member of the team. Meeting him was a major stroke of luck.

Neither movie would have been possible without Mark's wife, Denise. Aside from inspiring Mark to work towards his dream, she kept the productions on track as production manager and offered Mike use of their guest room for the months of production and post-production. Her organizational skills, patience, hard work and creative suggestions were priceless. We also were very lucky to land our makeup effects artist, the Savini-trained J.D. Bowers, after he read about us in the local press. J.D.'s effects are things of beauty. He also gives us Hollywood caliber effects on an ultra-low budget.

Elisar Cabrera

PRODUCER/WRITER/DIRECTOR

Filmography: Demonsoul (1994); *Virtual Hell* (1995); *Witchcraft: Mistress of the Craft* (1998)

Biography: Elisar Cabrera has been working in the film business since the age of 17, when on a trip to Los Angeles he worked as a production assistant on the set of the low budget feature film *Cool Blue*, a love story starring Woody Harrelson in his feature debut. After working as a production assistant on several more feature films (both high- and low-budget) and learning more about the filmmaking process on the way, Elisar was soon working as a producer's assistant on two feature films, the fantasy thriller *Soulmates* and the romantic drama *Love Is Like That*, under veteran indie producer Matt Devlen.

Returning to London, Elisar hoped to bring his American experience with him and stimulate commercial low-budget filmmaking in the U.K. Looking to the States to kick start this drive to low budget filmmaking, Elisar teamed with Vista Street Entertainment, a production and distribution company based in Los Angeles who for several years had been making action and horror films for the U.S. and Far East home video market.

The product of Elisar's collaboration with Vista Street was *Demonsoul*, a vampire thriller that was the first film that Vista Street has chosen to involve itself in outside of the United States. The film was premiered at the Edinburgh Film Festival's New British Expo and has since played at the Manchester Festival of Fantastic Films, the Stiges International Festival of Fantasy Films and at the Raindance Film Festival.

In 1995, Elisar went on to follow *Demonsoul* with *Virtual Terror*, an anthology of three tales of terror told by Balthasar, the Internet's first mutant child. Working as producer, Elisar found four young British directors, each of whom directed a story segment within the film.

Between 1995 and 1997 Elisar was the head of development and acquisitions at the London-based film and television sales company High Point Films & Television, where he instigated company acquisitions of programs such as U.K. cable operator Live TV's daily soap opera, *Canary Wharf*.

Since leaving High Point, Elisar continues to collaborate with fellow producer-writers on screenplays and has been developing numerous TV and feature film projects. Recently, Elisar wrote, produced and directed *Witchcraft: Mistress of the Craft*, a horror movie for Vista Street Entertainment which was released in the U.S. during the summer of 1998.

Producing aside, Elisar has been a reviewer for the Sci-Fi Channel Europe's *SF Scene*, a magazine show, and is the 1997 Cartier "Oh Hell" Champion (an annual card game tournament championship sponsored by the jewelers Cartier).

Film School: I never attended film school, although after I left the equivalent of Senior High School I did some crew work on a few student shorts to keep myself busy. I think film school is important to learn the technical aspects of filmmaking. I myself do not operate a camera or ever light a film as I don't have the training to even load film into a camera. Certainly it's useful knowing as much as possible about how a set operates technically so you are in a better position to catch anyone out if they are asking for more money for their department when you know with the equipment they already have they can function perfectly. I don't regret not going to film school because I knew what I wanted to do straight away. I guess the best thing about film school is you get to make a 16mm or 35mm short at someone else's expense.

Script: The script is all important. I don't know how anyone could ever begin filming a script they weren't confident in. It can't be *okay*. It has to be *great*. You have to believe in your script 100 percent and so do the people you are working with. If no one thinks it's ready to film, why are you going to spend the money filming it? Besides, it's hard enough raising finance for independent films these days, so you have to know you are trying to raise finance for a shit-hot script. Otherwise you are wasting your own and your writer's time. I think it was Alfred Hitchcock who said that the three most important things you needed to make any film was: the script, the script, the script.

Equipment/Format: So far I've used three different formats: Hi-8mm, DVCAM and 16mm. My anticipated next project will probably be filmed in Super-16mm, which I think is really the most ideal format for non-theatrical low budget films. For me the format to shoot on has always been determined by the budget and the end user market. What can you afford and where is it going to be shown? If it's for television, then you need to be shooting on digital or film (although from what I gather in the States it needs to be film). Television has very high standards—any foreign buyer can back out of a deal at the last minute by just stating he thinks your film is not [up] to their broadcast standards—so you need to make sure that option is not open to them. That includes presenting them with full M and E tracks (dialogue on one track, the music and effects on the other). *Demonsoul* (1994) was shot on Hi-8 because it was being self-distributed on video by the company who financed it, and their budget would only allow for a format like Hi-8 video. Of course, we made sure we used the most professional Hi-8 camera available at the time. Nowadays, with DVCAM, DVC and Digi-Betacam available, I don't think I would touch Hi-8 or S-VHS.

Actors: So far my casting has been done through either personal contacts or through A.C.I.D., a casting service here in the UK which sends out a weekly newsletter to over 150 professional actors. I am usually reluctant to do huge casting calls and prefer more intimate one on one meetings with actors. As far as casting the parts I go mainly with instinct—is he or she able to be the character you wrote for?

Music: Music for film is very important. I got the music for my films the same way most people would get the music for their low budget films. Ask a composer that you know and believe could create a great score. Make sure beforehand that everyone understands the situation—got no money and need you to sign away certain rights in perpetuity—and there shouldn't be any problems. A word of advice with regards to music. Always know what rights you need and make sure you get a release signed before releasing the video.

How long did it take to finish your first film? *Demonsoul* was filmed in twelve days (two weeks with two days off). It went surprisingly smoothly considering the amount of locations we crammed into those two weeks. The last three days were night shoots, which are always tough. Editing took about ten months. This was due to the availability of the U-matic off-line suite it was being edited on. Getting freebies usually means getting in at downtime, which sometimes means you don't get to do any editing for weeks at a time. Still, once we had a cut we were pleased with the on-line (three-machine Betacam SP). Although it was being paid for it was still a low rate during downtime, which again was sparse but not as bad as the off-line. I think we did about four or five sessions in the on-line, adding effects and sound editing as we went along and then laying the credits and music down in the last session.

Advice: Every film you make will be a unique experience and every film you work on or make will be an education. I worked on the crews of several low-budget films before making my own films and I certainly would recommend it. The experience is valuable, plus you do make contacts. The important thing is to remember what it is you want to do. I would also specify working on low budget features rather than commercials or pop promos. Once you start working in another field you end up being stuck there—the money is so good you become reluctant to take the leap into independent films, as the money is so poor in comparison. Certainly if you are making low budget films you are not going to get rich. Believe it or not none of the cast, crew or production personnel on *The Full Monty* has earned anything other than the low wage they received during the production. This is the reality of low budget films—you get paid your wage and that's it.

When you actually get down to making your film the best advice is, again, make sure the script is the best you believe it can be. After that, it all comes down to planning. Do you know how to break down a script, do a shooting schedule and a budget, how long it will take to shoot this fight scene? If you don't know the answers you have to ask someone who does, or make sure your production team does. On the subject of teamwork—make sure you are accessible to your cast and crew. They are always looking to you as the person in charge. If you're directing it then they are looking to you to tell them what it is you want. Make sure you know the answer—there is no value in being vague. It will only lead to screw-ups.

The almost universal reason why most people think micro-budget films are bad movies is because the sound is always bad. Bad sound equals bad movie. Your sound should never be an afterthought. You should strive for the best possible sound when you are filming. Shoot another take if your sound is no good (especially if you are shooting tape). Use professional sound equipment and never the camera microphone. Don't believe that everything can be fixed in post production because inevitably it can't and you can't afford it even if it could.

Treat everyone right. Feed them lunch, occasionally buy some beers—don't work everyone to the bone. Plan the best days to have off so everyone can get a good day's rest and do their laundry. At the end of the day the best advice from all this is to be practical and run the show with a lot of common sense. Don't be a jerk. And don't forget to say thank you for a job well done.

Distribution: So far all my films have been made with pre-attached international distribution. During the production of *Mistress of the Craft*, the MIFED market was on and I read in the trades that the film had been sold to Russian home video—and this while we were still filming. To me distribution is all important. I can't conceive of making a film independently without any thought about how the film is going to get distributed. Sometimes you fail to sell to your expectations, but this is the reality of independent filmmaking. Most sales agents will talk to you and give good advice. I used to work for a television distribution company and the experience has influenced me a lot in how I perceive the international marketplace. It's a huge world, and with some foresight and clear thinking you can make a film that should be commercial enough to sell to some territories and hopefully make you some profit. I study the trades and the market editions carefully. You need to spot future trends, understand what sells and what doesn't and why.

Future Projects: I'm currently reading some script submissions for future projects as well as developing my own ideas. Recently I inked a deal with a Canadian production company to co-produce a horror movie for television, which I anticipate will go into production within the next twelve months. It's based on a concept of mine, and I'm working with two other writers in putting together a screenplay, which will be an anthology. My aim this year is to get another film off the ground, whether it's this one or any of the other projects I have in development. Right now there seems to be a real international interest in British films, which I hope I can utilize to raise financing for my various projects. Also, the market for television is growing at an amazing rate and I am also looking to explore various avenues for getting into television production.

Dennis Devine

DIRECTOR

Filmography: I have directed or co-directed and edited the following features: *Fatal Images* (1989); *Dead Girls* (1990); *Things* (1993); *Haunted* (1998); *Things II* (1998); *Amazon Warrior* (1998); *Vampires of Sorority Row* (1999); *Merchants of Death* (1999); *Vampires of Sorority Row II* (2000)

I wrote or co-wrote *Club Dead, Bloodstream, Chain of Souls, Hell Spa, Sorority House Vampires, Body Weapon* (optioned by Vision International and then by RPM), *The Leveler* (purchased but unproduced by Kamin & Howell), *Valance* (purchased but unproduced by Kamin & Howell). I was the director of photography on *Hatrix, Vampire Night, Vampire Time Travelers, Decay, Blood Games, Vampires of Sorority Row.* I co-produced, directed, DP'd and edited the children's videos *Babies Make Music* and *Kids Make Music, Too.* I have produced, directed, written, shot and or edited four national commercials, several local commercials, over 50 medical videos released by the Academy of Orthopedic Surgeons (four of which have won AAOS awards), several sports videos, including films for the Los Angeles Dodgers and California Angels, a comedy pilot for HBO entitled *Take No Prisoners*, and two music videos.

Also, I teach a production class and a directing class at the Learning Tree University in Chatsworth, California.

Influences: Ever since I was a small child I have had a passion for movies. This passion was actually fueled by my family. We went to movies often. Every kind of movie. My father loved horror films and took me to just about every one that came out. He died when I was nineteen, so many of my fondest memories are of spending time with him—which meant either going to a baseball game or a movie. To me there was always something special about a dad who would take you to the latest Vincent Price film, something all the other kid's fathers would frown upon.

Horror is magical in that it can be dramatic, funny, fast, slow, moving, and scary—all at the same time. With this in mind, I would say my greatest influence in films was seeing *The Exorcist.* I was only eleven, and my Dad took me to the theater to see it. I don't think he knew exactly what to expect, and I'm sure he was a little embarrassed, but, wow, what an experience. Two teenage girls went screaming from the theater halfway through the picture. People were gasping and shrieking. I had never seen a film hit an audience like this. Right then and there, I knew I had to have something to do with movies.

While attending Eastern Michigan University, I started writing movie reviews for the school paper in my sophomore year. The paper served the local town of Ypsilanti, so it had a decent following. By my senior year, I was the entertainment editor and was seeing six movies a week—and getting paid for it! Some of the local movie theaters even posted some of my reviews. It was a real kick. So I figured this was my calling. Until I saw a film called *20th Century Oz*. My brother Mike was visiting and we, of course, went to a movie. This movie. Being true Devines, we couldn't walk out on a movie, no matter how bad it was. And this movie was *bad*! He and I have seen thousands of movies in our collective lives, but till this day neither of us has ever seen a movie that comes close to being this bad. But it was my next great influence.

I reviewed it for the paper. A short review. A negative review. But I kept thinking about it. I thought, if I got a camera and made a movie right now, it would be better than this. In fact, I had seen a run of bad movies and was feeling that maybe my true calling isn't to review movies but rather *make* movies. It's the I-can-do-better-than-this syndrome.

By the fall, I was attending the graduate film program at Loyola Marymount University in Los Angeles.

Film School: If you grow up in a city where filmmaking is accessible, and making movie contacts is an obtainable goal, then film school is not necessary. I grew up in Detroit, where there was next to no filmmaking going on that I could see.

When I moved to Los Angeles, I knew no one. Contacts are everything—if you believe only one thing I say, believe this. Almost every film I work on comes from some contact. I have had many close calls with a higher level of success. I have been attached to direct films with budgets over one million dollars. I have had scripts optioned that could've been made with well-known stars. They were hard-fought deals made without contacts. And all of them fell through. You must have seen a film that is so bad that you ask out loud, "Why did this film get made? They must've known it was horrible from the start!" It is my theory that "they" do know it. But the film gets made out of loyalty to some contact. Probably passing over some project already in pre-production, some project that carries no loyalties to the filmmakers. Sour grapes on my part? Maybe. But my experience is that many people in the business, people with no personal contact with me, no loyalty or desire to help me, have read and liked my scripts or director's reel. They have expressed interest. Started deals. Then suddenly, stopped returning phone calls. In December of 1998, I was linked to a deal by an agent to direct a five million dollar film, written by Mike Bowler, called *The Healer*. Great script. Would've put us both on the map. First, the agent stopped calling me. Then he [Bowler] stopped returning my calls. Why? Something else came along. Something with a stronger tie. Or a stronger attachment. This has happened to me at every level, so I know what I am talking about. Even in the cheapie budget field, I have been turned away on projects for no known reason. By someone who goes on to make another project, or use another director. This doesn't happen with your strong contacts. That's why they are so important. At every level.

There are many stories of deals that fall through, and of course they aren't

Director Dennis Devine (middle) on the set of *Dead Girls*.

always because an agent or producer isn't good friends with you. It's part of the business. You have to deal with rejection and brushes with success that go sour. But I would not have been able to deal with the many setbacks without the contacts I made, many who came from my film school. Others have come from work. An actor I directed became a producer, then hired me to direct. Some of the students in my film class hire me for projects and we begin networking. I feel lucky to have a solid support group. A group that has grown together, through the good and the bad. Steve Jarvis and Mike Bowler are two fellow students I met at film school who I still work with routinely. Keith Davis has become a hugely successful development guy, having worked for Mel Gibson, the Zucker Brothers and Dawn Steel. He helped me get my first agent. Jason Stephens, one of my students, hired me to work as director of photography and editor on *Decay*.

All right, so you get the idea: Contacts and a support group are important. But what else do you get from film school? Well, if you don't know the nuts and bolts of filmmaking, it's one way to gain the knowledge and experience you need to get

started. At Loyola Marymount, one of the best film schools, you get to do everything there is to do—write, produce, direct, edit. The more rounded you are, the more prepared you are to make a film. No one should walk onto a set with no idea about the process. You must learn some things first. Film school is an excellent way to do this. Some people can learn things on their own. I'm not going to say you can't be successful without going to film school. Just that it helps. John Ford was one of the greatest filmmakers of all time; he was tutored by other directors. Same with Alfred Hitchcock. No film school. He got his start in production design. And he learned that way. These opportunities aren't readily available. If you are reading this book because you want to get some idea of how to break into films, then you probably don't have many contacts. You probably can't just walk into the employment office and Warner Brothers and say, "I want to work on films." Well, you can, but unless your uncle is the president of the studio, or you have an impressive film school degree, they won't take you seriously for even the beginning mail room position.

So if you can afford the time and money, film school is a great way to get started. The schools that will help you the most:

1. American Film Institute. Hard to get into, and expensive, but if you make a film here, you're in. And you don't have to get a "rounded" education—just take film classes. It's the quickest and most certain way to go.

2. USC. Which is really, really expensive and very competitive, but lands you with the best contacts and the next best chance of getting a film job upon graduation.

3. UCLA. Similar to USC, only slightly less prestigious, less expensive. But contacts not as strong.

4. Loyola Marymount University (Los Angeles). A great program to learn in. Each student has the opportunity to do more in this program. Only a select few get to direct projects at USC. At Loyola, everyone who wants to can. Also very expensive.

5. San Francisco State University. A good program in a city that has a lot of production.

There are other schools in California with good programs, but I rate these at the top. Who doesn't? I have heard some schools in New York are good; NYU has the best reputation and tradition. But I am not familiar with the East Coast schools. There are also good programs in other states, but if you really care about contacts, and I think you should, then you need to go to film school in Los Angeles or New York.

My personal take on film school is that it gave me an understanding of techniques. How to cover scenes. How to write in three acts. Three point lighting. The basics. A place to start. My first film, *Fatal Images*, which was shot on four weekends, tripled my knowledge of film. In ten days' shooting, and ten days' editing, I learned more than my two years in film school. But while *Fatal Images* is no work of art, it is much better than it would have been had I not attended film school. Making this film was an extension of my education.

My second film, *Dead Girls*, was my advanced learning session. Everything that could go wrong did go wrong (the bit of Murphy's Law that filmmakers love to recite). I had a much larger crew than I ever had in school or on my first film. It snowed—snowed in California!—while we were shooting a summer scene. I was trying to direct *and* worry about when the food came *and* when I would call the actors to remind them about the call time for the next day *and* et cetera, et cetera. I learned that delegating work is the first thing you need to do on a film. If you want to direct, then just direct. Get other people to do the other jobs.

I've learned you always need a Plan B. If one actor shows up late, have something else ready to shoot. If you are making a low-budget film every hour of every shooting day is precious. You can't stand around waiting for someone.

I could fill a book with what I learned on *Dead Girls* alone. If the weather is bad outside, shoot inside. That's the general philosophy. If this offends your artistic integrity, then you shouldn't be making low budget films. Hold out for the millions so that you can take a few magnificent shots each day, like Stanley Kubrick used to do.

Most people who have seen all of my films believe that *Dead Girls* is my best film. While I believe it is a very good low-budget film, I know many ways (now) I could've made it better. Made it into a

Dennis Devine and werewolf friend in *Things 2*.

calling card film that would have brought me to the next level.

So for me, it took film school plus two features to get to a level where I knew how to make films that maximized the skills of my crew and cast, and maximized the budget I had to work with.

Script: I used to think you can't have a good film if you don't have a good script. But I have found that is not always the case. For example, I thought *The Thin Red Line* was a good film, but not a good script. Many felt the same way about *Titanic.* A very stylized director, with great actors and visuals, or in the case of lower budgets, lots of gore, nice-looking talent and quirky action, can make an inferior script entertaining to watch. On the other hand, with a good script, the film can often succeed despite bad or mediocre efforts by cast and crew members.

To me, a script brings structure and dialogue. If you as a viewer want to know what happens next, if what the characters are saying reaches you, then the script is working. Obviously, the actors will make the script float or sink more than anyone else. Make Jim Carrey the lead in *One Flew Over the Cuckoo's Nest* and the script looks different, doesn't it? On the other hand, put Jack Nicholson in a badly scripted film, maybe Burt Reynolds's part in *Striptease,* and no way does he save it. In my value system, the script is as important as anything in the process. To me, it is tied with acting and editing at the top, followed by the music and the director (who is important, but often given too much credit for the success of a film). I have directed five films written by Steve Jarvis. He is excellent at structure and knows how to write for the budget. These are the considerations you make when choosing a writer or script.

I have also directed some of my own material. This allows you more free-

dom to control the outcome of the film, but it also puts blinders on you, as well. It is much easier to be objective about another writer's material. So there are advantages and disadvantages to writing your own script.

Equipment/Budget/Funding: Many of my features have been shot on Beta SP format, with the video then going through a "film-look" process. A few of my features have been shot on film, usually 16mm, although some of *Amazon Warrior* was shot on 35mm.

Whenever I shoot on video it is because of budget restrictions. I have yet to find many cable avenues for video features, aside from *Mystery Science Theater 2000.* And cable usually gives the filmmaker the largest and quickest financial return. But just because you shoot on film, it doesn't guarantee a cable sale. Foreign buyers will usually take any exploitation feature shot on film, but few will handle video. Since I have my own video equipment, camera and editor, my costs are extremely low. With Beta, you get 750 horizontal lines of resolution, and less generation loss in transfers then the lower end video formats. This allows for a more professional looking final product (than S-VHS, which has 450 horizontal lines, and VHS, which has 250 lines). Still, no matter how good your video looks, it is not film. Film has more contrast, more range in the blacks and whites. And there is grain. The look is different. With the film-look process, you can fool some people with certain shots and at times even complete scenes, but you will never find a knowledgeable viewer (or buyer) who can look at a tape of a feature and be fooled into thinking a film-looked video is really film. You would be surprised at how many people show me video and try to tell me it's film. An actress friend invited me to the set of a film she was working on recently. She said it was being shot on 35mm film. They had a video camera with a cardboard façade of a film camera taped to the side of it. I guess they were getting the jump on this fake film format.

Now digital video seems to get more respect, but presently, not much more. Some successful documentaries have been shot on digital video and transferred to film, then shown in theaters recently. But please understand that they are using high-quality digital video cameras, not the one-chip low end home-use units you find at the local camera shop. A decent digital video camera will run you over $4,000. A good one will cost over $7,000. A sensational one goes for over $100,000. I'm talking the kind George Lucas uses. He shot the next *Star Wars* movie on digital video the same time he shot it on film and he plans to release it in four theaters using the digital video format. Now you can tell this to the cable buyers, or the foreign dealers, and right now, it doesn't mean a damn thing to them. But with George Lucas leading the way, the Force may be with us video users some day soon.

If you are just starting out and you don't have a lot of money, video is the way to go. Even if you shoot something with your camcorder, and then edit it and add some effects and music, you are at least learning the process. You will probably not have something that you can sell, but you will have a valuable learning experience. And who knows? I've seen a lot of video crap people are trying to sell as entertainment—some of it looks like it was shot on camcorders by guys who never took a film class.

The least amount of money I spent on a feature was $2,000. It was for a film called *Vampires of Sorority Row*. Shot on video. I paid $180 for the film-look and $500 for the music. One-pass Beta tapes can be found for about $12 per thirty min. tape. I used about twelve of them. Other expenses included having fangs made for the vampires, limited special effects, makeup, a few costumes and food. It is critical to feed the cast and crew—always—but especially when they are working without pay, which was the case here. The feature was shot in four days. I was the DP, my co-director was the star. We had one person to light and one to do sound. There was a makeup artist each day, and a special effects guy a couple of days. Our art director lasted for one day—until an actress didn't show up and the art director was forced to make her screen debut. Despite what the final credits might suggest, we never had more than four crew members working on any given day. The four shooting days never lasted more than eight hours. I knew a filmmaker who claimed he made a film in eight days, but the days averaged over sixteen hours. That's like a sixteen-day shoot to me. I like nine- or ten-hour days. I have no problem with some twelve-hour days. You often have to maximize talent and locations.

But when you shoot fifteen-hour days or more, you become counter productive. I've heard some filmmakers brag about it. I'd like to see the footage they got after fifteen hours. I've been there. It isn't pretty. A cast and crew need sleep and relaxation time. Without it, especially on a low budget shoot where everyone is doing more, the film will suffer.

On the other end, I had a budget of around $100,000 for *Dead Girls*. This feature was shot on film. We rented all of the equipment, purchased the film, which was processed then converted to video for editing. We paid all cast and crewmembers. Our locations cost money. And needed permits. And insurance. The special effects alone cost us $6,000. We shot for fourteen days. Often feeding thirty very hungry people. This film was made in 1990. If we made it with the same size cast and crew today, it would cost over $250,000.

While video costs have been going down, film costs have been going up.

I could make a feature shot on 16mm film today for about $50,000 that would have the same basic production values as *Dead Girls*, but some of the subtle contributions would be lost. I would like to have these contributions. Who wouldn't? But spending $100,000 on a 16mm direct-to-video feature doesn't make sense in this market. You'll never see the money back. So you have to streamline your locations, cast and crew. Like the corporate world of today, it's all about streamlining, baby. Who needs a DP *and* a camera operator? Just another paycheck. Just another mouth to feed. And find a DP with his own equipment and you save a ton. While it is noble to pay actors, you don't have to pay them a lot. If an actor is starting a career, then you are helping him by giving him a credit and a tape for his reel. It is critical that you feed the actor well, treat him with respect, and *Give Him the Tape* when the film is completed. In my opinion, if you are not making a lot of money on your film, and you rarely will on a low budget film, then you are not exploiting cast or crew members who agree to work for little or no pay. So why *pay* two grips when you can pay one experienced grip and get a student to work for free? The student gets valuable experience and contacts, and you get a reduced budget. You get the idea. So do I—now.

By now you should be asking, "Where does the money come from?" You may be able to scrape together $2,000 to make a quickie video feature like *Vampires of Sorority Row*. This film is being released domestically next month. Between one deal I made domestically and a sale to France, I have already made back the budget. By choosing to make a film with a well-defined market like this, and delivering the proper elements and a basic minimum of professional filmmaking, I suc-

ceeded financially. But this isn't a film I want to speak for my skills as a filmmaker. So if you really want to get noticed, you need to push the envelope. You need to make something that is going to cost some serious bucks.

Where do you get these bucks? The $50,000 to make the next *Clerks*? Or *El Mariachi*? Or *Brothers McMullen*? Something that puts you on the map. First, remember that these guys had access to equipment, too. So what you read about being $8,000 or $25,000 budgets were really $50,000- to $100,000-budgets that called in a lot of free favors. All right, already. So where do you get the $50,000? There's no easy answers from me. A producer raised money for *Dead Girls*. There were several uncomfortable meetings in which he would tell me to show up and tell everyone how important this film could be. He did the rest. Lied, I imagine. I didn't really want to know. When the producer of *Amazon Warrior* began raising money for the film, he had a lot more bells and whistles. He did some telemarketing, I believe, to find people interested in investing in films. Then I made a pitch video including highlights from all the people attached to the project, scenes from my films, some of the actors, the stunt man (Johnny Martin, who's worked on a lot of impressive films). Once, the producer rented a theater and staged a scene with Amazons fighting. He gave a speech, another producer gave a speech. They served food. It was all very exciting. Finally, he gathered up enough money to start shooting. But since he raised considerably less than was originally budgeted, I was met with several creative challenges as a director. Still, of all of my films, *Amazon Warrior* is my favorite. When you make a low budget film, and you edit, and put in the effects and music and make copies and, well, do everything, you see it many times. *Many* times. I never got sick of watching this film. But it probably is because I know what I pulled off with what I had to spend. Unfortunately, all viewers won't know this. You can't sit there with them and explain how you made a scene out of nothing or how you had this great design in mind for a mutant or a cat creature, but got stuck with a two dollar mask instead. So if there is anything you must strive to do in low budget filmmaking, it is to get the most production value out of the least amount of money.

Actors: In Los Angeles, there is an incredibly valuable magazine called *Dramalogue— Backstage West*. It comes out every Thursday and has many interesting articles about films and theater—and it has a classified section. It is in this section where I have cast the large majority of my features. Now, I have worked with casting directors who have handled the scheduling and calls, and that is a terrific luxury. But on many low budget shoots it is a luxury one cannot afford. So on most shoots, I advertise in *Dramalogue* (they do not charge for a notice) and have the actors submit resumes to a PO box. The response is outstanding. Now, I can only speak for Los Angeles, but I am always amazed by how many outstanding actors are available. I mean incredibly talented people who have not (and sadly never will) make it big. I like to think of these people as soul mates. That we have talent that manages to go unnoticed by Hollywood decision makers for years. I can't say for certain that this is in my case. I may just be over-evaluating my skill or

maybe I'm just confident. But I have no doubt about some of the actors I have worked with. Peter Tomarken from *Haunted* is incredible. Angela Eads (*Dead Girls*) was gifted and good looking. She could've had Sandra Bullock's career. But didn't.

I don't know why these people get passed over, all I know is that they are available. Sometimes for $100 per day. Sometimes for just a credit and a copy of the tape. I believe J.J. Rodgers, who stars

Box art for *Haunted*, directed by Dennis Devine.

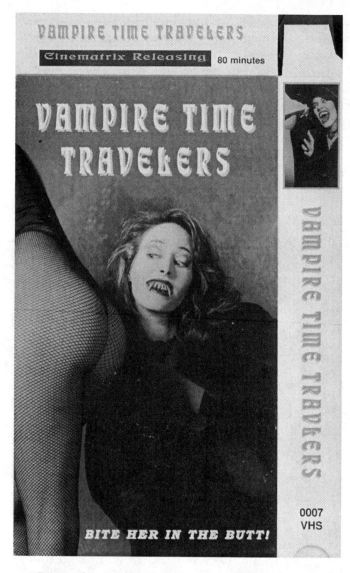

VAMPIRE TIME TRAVELERS

Cinematrix Releasing   80 minutes

VAMPIRE TIME TRAVELERS

BITE HER IN THE BUTT!

0007
VHS

Box art for *Vampire Time Travelers*, **written and directed by Les Sekeley. Courtesy Cinematrix Releasing.**

six of my films. So has Raymond Storti. Christine Lydon has been in five. Why? Because these people are not only talented, but hard working and responsible people. They take direction. They elevate material. You do whatever you can to work with these gems again. When you have eight days to shoot a film, who can put up with a difficult actor? Or one that shows up late? Or doesn't know his lines?

A big consideration for every feature that gets made, regardless of the budget, is who will be the star? You can't believe how many people I encounter who, when told I'm making a no-budget film, will still say, "Who's in it?" I tell them J.J. Rodgers or Robert Z'Dar and they say, "Who?" Of course if you're making a film for under $100,000, you can't get a star. But sometimes you can get someone who used to be one. I have worked with Tommy Kirk (*Club Dead*). Many people know him from *Old Yeller* and *Swiss Family Robinson*, the original *Flubber* films, etc. He was a big child star. So his name can at least illicit an "oh yeah." Robert Z'Dar (*Decay*) is the guy with the big chin from *Maniac Cop* and *Tango and Cash*.

in *Amazon Warrior* could be wildly successful with her own sit-com. The first film I worked on with her, *Vampire Time Travelers*, she did for copy and meals. She gets paid now, but is still in the low-budget price range. Why, I can't tell you. But at least the low budget film world benefits from what Hollywood overlooks.

Anyone who has seen a few of my films will notice many of the same actors popping up. Jimmy Jermain has been in

Of course you have to pay these people more. Some actresses will get you certain publicity in some of the genre magazines like *Femmes Fatales* and *Draculina*. If you read these, you know the names, J.J. North, Debbie Rochon.

Music: As I stated earlier, the music is as important as the director, in many cases. I grew up playing in bands and have always had a strong musical background.

I strongly believe that each scene in a movie has a rhythm. The actors must know this to play it right. Hopefully, the director has staged it right. Now the music must complement the rhythm. Imagine *Halloween* without the music. What was scarier, the cheap William Shatner mask or John Carpenter's music? Turn down the sound and watch that film and see just how important the music is.

So if we all agree that music is important, how do you get it? I run an ad in *Dramalogue*. That's where I found Adam Karpel, who wrote the excellent music to *Things II*. In some cases, I ran an ad but didn't like my choices. In one case, I then turned to a contact and ended up with the sensational music to *Haunted*, by Michael Barrow and RB. As I have said, I am ecstatic about the score to each one of my films. I feel lucky that all of my composer choices have worked out.

When Jonathan Price first responded to an ad in *Dramalogue*, he had not yet finished the USC film music program. He did his first score for me, and we simply covered his expenses. I'm hooked on his abilities to understand a scene. Then to complement it with his brilliant music. He has done two more scores, each time we pay him a little more. I hope to continue working with him—for as long as I can afford him.

Some low budget filmmakers use canned music. Some. But most know what a risk that is. You can't cut corners everywhere. Music is one area where it's not smart to cut.

How long did it take to make your first film? I have mentioned that *Fatal Images*, my first film, was shot in ten days over four weekends. I used only one dolly shot (off a rickety cart). I had two sequences in which I had access to a baby boom (small crane). Other than that, most of the camera moves come in the form of a zoom.

Yucky, ugly zooms, not the dated-but-charming Italian horror film zooms. It is very difficult for me to watch this film. In fact, I can't watch it. I like to think Steven Spielberg has some film he made when he was nine years old that he can't watch, either. The big difference is, mine got released and his didn't. So only he can watch his embarrassing cinema. Mine was in video stores. All right, so there's probably a few other big differences between me and Steven Spielberg, too, but that's another book.

Look, we all have to start somewhere. So let me stress this again, the more you know coming in, the better your first film will be. Who knows, you may never get another chance. The more you know going in, the better that film will be. Some guys know it all when they get to film school. Their student film actually gets them some major Hollywood deal. Those bastards! It happens.

Get yourself on some sets before you take the plunge. Watch how it's done. Or not done. Can't say it enough. Be prepared for as much as possible. And, hey, maybe film school's not such a bad idea, after all.

How do you deal with special effects at this level? Ironically, on my first film, *Fatal Images*, I worked with my most talented special-effects guy, Gabe Bartolos (*Basketcase 2*, *Leprechaun* films, *Frankenhooker*, etc.). He was working for Rick Baker at the time. I lucked into him, really. We had a $10,000 budget and half of it went to him. He made a severed head and a throat slash and a harpoon through the chest, among others. He was incredibly skilled and I learned tons from him about how to shoot effects. This is the real bright side of my first feature experience. I worked with Mark Case on *Dead Girls* (he came from Rick Baker's place, too) and with Mike Tristano (*Maniac Cop 2*) on *Things*. I've been lucky working with some great effects

Dennis Devine shoots a scene for *Haunted*.

guys. When the budget dips lower, I know a few tricks to simulate some effects. Things like cheating the knife penetrating into a false chest, then quickly cutting to the face reacting in horror. That sort of cheat. And, hey, if all else fails, splash a lot of fake blood around.

Do you have any production tips for the novice filmmaker? Again, try to get the most production value for the dollar. When deciding whether to spend money on something or not, ask yourself, Does it make it look like I'm spending more? For example, you think your main character should look quirky. The actor says he has a plaid shirt that looks a little quirky, but that he saw this cool shirt with a weird design that only costs 50 bucks. If you spend those 50 bucks but your film doesn't look like you spent any more, then you're hurting the business side of your film. Think business vs. art when it comes to these kinds of decisions in low-budget filmmaking.

On the other hand, say you have a stunt man who says he'll let you light him on fire for only $100 (that will cover his supplies). You jump at it because it makes

the film look more expensive. In the case of *Amazon Warrior*, this really happened. But the producer wouldn't go for the $100, so the film is without this added value.

Another tip, and this is huge, is to audition someone for each role. When I made my first film, there were a couple of actors with marginal abilities who worked for no pay. I felt obliged to use them on my next film, and pay them. They were the weakest actors in the film. I had even auditioned actors who would've elevated parts they portrayed. But I was too inexperienced to realize this.

Don't use friends as actors, not even in small parts. Your friends stink. Trust me on this. And real actors hate working with your stinky friends. If you're saying, "Not me," reconsider. I'm talking to all of you. *Don't use your friends!* They can't act. And even if it seems like they are animated, once the camera rolls, they won't be. They'll stink! Even a small part can make your film look cheesy if it is played by a bad actor. If you have to use your friends for something, use them as extras without any lines. Or you can light them on fire and save yourself 100 bucks.

Preparation and communication [are always important]. On my first film, I had shots listed, but often got slowed down modifying my coverage. Rehearse and know how much you can shoot and what you want to shoot. On my second film, *Dead Girls*, I had shots in mind, but the crew was slower than I was used to and the DP was a very dominant figure who was influencing the shot selections. Consequently, we worked long hours and got less coverage than I was looking for. From that film on, I have known what I can get and what I want and, most importantly, how to express myself to get what I want.

As I have said, I could've done so much more with *Dead Girls* if I could've better communicated to my very talented crew. I don't blame them. It was my responsibility. The DP on *Dead Girls* was Aaron Schneider, who has gone on to DP some big films, *Kiss the Girls* and *Simon Birch* to name a few. But my lack of preparation and communication kept the film from being sensational.

Publicity and Distribution: This is an area that I have only recently explored. If I had understood the importance of publicity in the early 1990s, when I was getting started, I would have had a much better chance of moving up quickly. I know it is important, but self promotion is just not something that has interested me. I will tell you this, though, if you don't promote yourself, no one else will.

As for the films, my earlier films were all released, but I had nothing to do with the distribution. Occasionally I would find a review in *Variety* or some such place, but the distributor basically ignored me. Last year, I joined up with Steve Jarvis to distribute my films with Cinematrix Releasing. Now I am active in the publicity for each film. I even make my own boxes. Now when my name gets around, I know about it. Publicity is important in this business. Start learning that early on.

Choosing a distributor is another challenge. Some are crooks who will never give you any money. But some will help you out. There is no easy answer to distribution.

What's in store for the future? I am co-producing and working as DP on a feature called *Vampire Nights*, which is scheduled to shoot in June 1999. It will either be shot on digital video or 16mm film. The shoot is scheduled for 12 days.

I am almost finished with a horror screenplay that I am co-writing and co-directing with Steve Jarvis. It will be shot in July or August on video. We are looking to cast a well known genre actress for this project, someone like Debbie Rochon or J.J. Rodgers.

There is the usual variety of projects in development with various producers, with higher budgets for film. They are searching for funding much like the producers of *Amazon Warrior* and *Dead Girls* did. But for every ten of these projects with producers looking for money, I am lucky if one gets made. So I am hopeful, but moving ahead on the smaller projects.

Tommy Faircloth

DIRECTOR

Filmography: Crinoline Head (1995); *Generation Ax* (1998)

Biography: I was born in 1972 in Aiken, South Carolina. After graduating high school, I started attending college and also began acting and modeling to get my foot in the door of filmmaking. I had always wanted to be in movies or direct movies since I saw *Friday the 13th* and the *Nightmare* [*on Elm Street*] movies. I loved horror and used to use my sister and cousins in my homemade movies I shot at home. I used to collect *Fangoria* magazines and dream about being in a cool horror movie. I also *loved* John Hughes movies, as well. This love for both will eventually morph into my style of horror films (*Crinoline Head* and *Generation Ax*).

I got my first big break on the television series *In the Heat of the Night*. I had a small speaking part with the two leads in the series. This just sparked my interest in filmmaking, and it was there I decided that I wanted to do more than just act. After that, I did tons of local and regional commercials and extra and bit parts in fea-tures. I began seeing the same people on all the commercials and movies that I had been working on, and began relation-ships which eventually led into me get-ting jobs on these movies as crew instead of actor.

After getting my associates degree in Aiken, I moved to Columbia, South Car-olina, to begin attending film school at USC. It was there I really began working on different feature films and movies of the week. I started off working as produc-tion assistant and moved in to extras cast-ing. I worked with such directors as Penny Marshall and Sandra Locke, and actors like Whoopie Goldberg and Halle Berry. I loved working behind the scenes and was taking in everything I saw to apply to my film, whenever I got a chance to shoot one. I was going to school full-time and work-ing on all these films full-time and was getting worn out! I got picked to take the test to become an assistant director trainee for the DGA while in school, so I flew to California and took the test. It was there I realized that I did not want to be an AD at all. So I took the test in a hurry and then went sight-seeing and met two very cool people who would later help me with my films as far as music, et cetera goes.

I landed the job of art department production assistant on *Die Hard 3*, which was a great job. There were tons of sets and I got to work closely with all the designers, and it was while working there I decided that I wanted to do my own feature film.

While I was working on *Die Hard 3*, at the same time I was making contacts for my movie. I was seeking music, actors, et cetera, while working on the set. It really sounded cool to be calling from *Die Hard* and asking about another movie. People took me seriously.

To make a long story shorter, I shot my first movie, *Crinoline Head*, in the summer of 1995. I had no idea what I was in for. I had way too many leads and this, on top of directing and acting and producing, stressed me out. I finished *Crinoline Head* in 1996, and it was released on video in late '96, early '97. I got great reviews for such a movie, and the top of the cake was being featured in *Fangoria* magazine!

I decided to take another crew job on a film to help raise more money for my next movie, *Generation Ax*. I got a job as a key production assistant on a big budget Tom Berenger movie called— I can't even remember! It was a great position, basically a second 2nd AD position with big actors and a pretty big budget. I got so fed up with the set and the attitude that I quit after a week. I started shooting

Video box art for Tommy Faircloth's *Generation Ax* Courtesy Horsecreek Productions.

Gen Ax in summer of '97 and finished editing in summer '98. It was released on video in fall of '99 and now its on sell-through! I'm now seeing other films to release on video through my company, Horse Creek Productions.

What is your take on film school? Well, my take is that film school can be a great

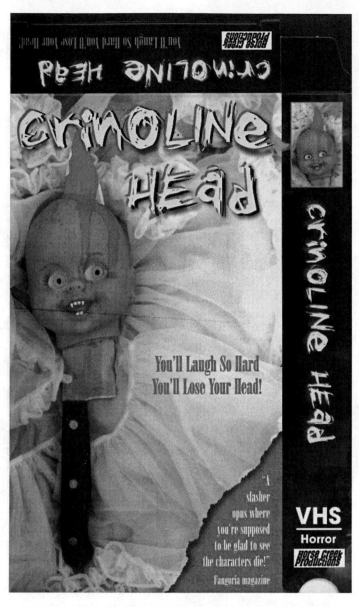

Video box art for *Crinoline Head*, directed by Tommy Fair-cloth. Courtesy Horsecreek Productions.

great actors and directors work on movie sets. As far as technical [matters] go, its good to learn how to operate sound, video, editing and camera equipment so that you know as much as possible when shooting a movie.

How important is your script? When shooting a film, the script is very important. From that, I break down every scene, every shot, frame by frame, and if you don't have a complete shooting script, then you will waste more time shooting, which adds more cost. And you don't want that.

What equipment do you use for your films? I use 16mm cameras. I love the film look. And when transferred to video, 16mm looks as good as 35mm, plus you do not lose any picture. The 16mm is closest size to TV, and if you shoot for TV frame, you keep all your picture. I believe it's more professional-looking, and when you're a first-time filmmaker, you want to look as good as possible so that people will concentrate on your story rather than the shitty look of the movie. I also learned how to use 16mm film cameras so I could shoot my films as well.

way to meet potential crew. I met all my crew in film school and had access to some great equipment. But if you don't have some goal of your own, or a little talent, don't bother. My film school was not "all that," but I met some of my best friends there who later did crew work. Working on movies was my film school. I learned directly from the source watching these

Cost/Budget/Funding: Well, with my first movie, I used my own cash and credit cards. With my second, I was able to obtain a few investors that saw my first film, as well as my own cash, and was able to have a bigger budget, and more time to shoot. I normally don't have a set budget, and just spend as needed. Usually, film labs will give you a good deal if you tell them you're a student. When buying film, you can also get a discount if you're a student. It's always best to buy more film that you need cause you can sell it if you do not use it or, or in case you need to re-shoot something later.

How do you get your actors? I always put announcements in publications as the *Hollywood Reporter* and *Backstage* so that actors will send me headshots. When I see someone I like, I'll call them, and if they live across country, I'll get them to send me an audition video. I also have local auditions by placing ads in newspapers and such and rent out a conference room at a hotel to have the auditions at.

My lead in *Generation Ax*, Marina Morgan, sent me her head shot, and I loved her look. I called her and got her to send me a video and then I flew her down to meet me and my other lead, Brian Kelly from *Crinoline Head*. I knew she was right. There are also skanky actresses that want to fuck their way into your movie, but I want a good actor, not a whore.

I love getting music together for a movie and *Generation Ax* had a great soundtrack. I was in Atlanta at a show with Crystal Method, and they had a few other techno-type bands opening up for them. One was a group called Arkarna who had a song on the *Batman and Robin* soundtrack. (I used the same song plus another one from them.) They had a new CD coming out soon on Reprise records. I ended up meeting a way cool guy that was really into the indie film scene, Howie Klein, and he is president of Reprise. He started out in the music business the same way I was in the film business. Howie had his own label like I have my own video label. He decided to help me pick out all the music for my film. I had tons of CDs

to listen to, and I picked out several songs that fit my movie great. I went to concerts to see bands perform that I used in my movie. Reprise even cut a special promotion *Generation Ax* soundtrack CD that I gave away at the premiere and in press kits.

Howie and I ended up becoming great friends and through him I have met great people. I also get free tickets to shows, but that's another story.

The score was done by a guy across country. I would edit a scene and send it to him. He would score it and send it back. I would add the score later in post [production]. That worked well and saved money from me having to fly him down to the edit studio and score the film there for days on end.

How long did it take to shoot your first film? My first film took me only nine days to shoot. That was way too fast with the number of actors I was working with. The good thing is that most of the action took place on and around this lake house. All the actors and crew stayed at the house, as well, so this saved time and money. My second film was shot in twenty-eight days. I had more money to work with and I planned out every shot and gave myself extra time. You never know what kind of trauma will happen on a set, so plan for the worst. On *Generation Ax*, we were shooting at a club with about sixty extras, and our lights set off the water sprinklers. The whole placed was in about four inches of water. Luckily, we did not get kicked out. We cleaned up in about three or four hours and finished shooting.

How do you deal with special effects at this level? Special effects on my films have not been that important. I shoot slasher films, so I mainly need fake blood. In *Gen Ax*, I had to get a head of one of my actors made which was about the only big effect

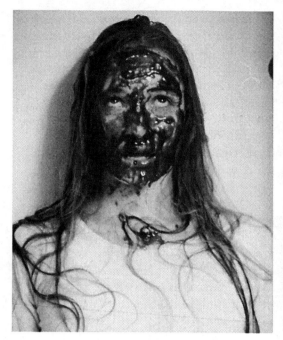

Scenes from Tommy Faircloth's *Crinoline Head*.

I had. I don't like to use too much gore because I want the audience to imagine what happens instead of showing them everything. Karo syrup and red food coloring is the best effect I use. However, in *Crinoline Head*, there was a scene where Cathy Slaminko's character was drowned in her own shit. For that, we melted a Baby Ruth candy bar and chocolate syrup together in a hot, sticky mixture for the actress to stick her face in. As it started to dry, her eye lashes were glued shut. A small problem but funny in the end. She is a close friend of mine, so I was not worried that much!

Production Tips/Advice: Plan out every single shot before you start your production. Plan the camera angles—plan the edited movie—and your shots from there. This will save you tons of time and money. I mean, shots will always change, but you need to have a storyboard of some type to keep track of what you have to shoot. Have a back-up plan for actors who may

not show up. Always have extra film. Carry a credit card with you at all times.

How important is publicity for your films? Publicity is very important for my films. Even locally. With *Crinoline Head*, we have a week showing of the film locally in the town I showed it. It did well, but I did not concentrate on local publicity, so it just did as well as can be expected. With *Generation Ax*, we did a word-of-mouth rumor about the film using everyone we could in Columbia, and we also had a small story about it in the local arts paper and we only had one showing. Over 800 people showed up and we could not even seat everyone. We had to use two full theaters and the local news came out as well. When you begin marketing your film for distribution, you need to get as much publicity as possible, especially for horror movies. I always send out screeners to get reviews in magazines and online magazines like *Fangoria, Film Threat, Shock Cinema, Rue Morgue,* et cetera. This is a

Scenes from *Crinoline Head*.

great way to get the buzz out about your movie so that people will ask for it in video stores.

Distribution: This sucks, because there is going to be plenty of people who want your movie, but do not want to pay for it. This is the main reason I started releasing my own films, but I actually make my money back faster this way. I also like having the control of keeping the rights to my movies. I have also learned a ton about the business this way, too, so unless I got some excellent offer from a distributor, I would keep releasing my own films myself.

What's in store for the future? Right now, *Generation Ax* is just coming out on video. It has done excellent so far in France and is about to be released in Germany, Austria, and the Netherlands. I have gotten great reviews here in the U.S., too, and am waiting to see how it does in sellthrough.

I am currently seeking to release a film on my label, Horse Creek Productions, from an outside company. I also may release a *Generation Ax/Crinoline Head* combo DVD later this year. I have tons of extras to include on it. I also am writing my next script. If I get the strength to shoot, it will be my next film.

Bruce G. Hallenbeck

WRITER/PRODUCER/DIRECTOR/ACTOR

Filmography: H.P. Lovecraft's *"The Statement of Randolph Carter"* (1980); *Trick or Treat* (1983); *Vampyre* (1991); *Fangs* (1992); *Black Easter* (1993); *London After Midnight* (2000).

Biography: I never had a chance. I saw a movie on TV called *The Undying Monster* when I was only three years old. It was a werewolf movie, and I was hooked.

Of course, it helped that I grew up (if you want to call it that) in a little town called Kinderhook, New York, which was where Washington Irving actually wrote "The Legend of Sleepy Hollow." The legend of the Headless Horseman is big in this town (a distinction it shares with Tarrytown, which is where Irving actually set the story), and there are a lot of "haunted houses" around, so my Halloween nature was nurtured at an early age.

I turned five in 1957, the year of the big Gothic horror revival, saw all the Universal monster movies by the time I was seven. I saw *Horror of Dracula* in 1958 in a theater, and I remember kids running screaming from the place. As for me, I was in Heaven. It changed my life. Of course, it helped that my beloved grandmother, who raised me, let me indulge my creative interests. I made comic books when I was seven or eight that were based on horror movies of the day. I discovered *Famous Monsters* magazine when I was eight, and was fascinated by the fan section in which kids wrote in about the home movies they'd made. I thought, if they can do it, why not me? I started making movies when I was twelve, with my father's camera. The first one I completed was called *Kiko, Son of Kong*—it was mostly claymation. I'd been in denial for a few years about the Son of Kong's death in the original movie, so I brought him back in mine. After that, I completed my first live-action movie, *The Creation of Frankenstein*. I played the monster through most of it (with a Universal Frankenstein mask and my hands painted green), except for some scenes when I was stunted by my best friend, Jim Leffingwell.

Numerous other films followed, including a spy movie, a science-fiction film and several vampire films—all short subjects of between three and fifteen minutes.

Director/actor Bruce G. Hallenbeck. Photograph by Kevin Lindenmuth.

And all were silent, shot in Regular 8mm film.

When I graduated from high school, I took a year off and got heavily into writing. I had numerous articles already published in journals such as *The Christopher Lee Fan Club*, mostly film criticism, and in high school I had won a top writing prize for my short story "Fear Is the Color of Darkness." When I was seventeen, I discovered the writings of H.P.Lovecraft and, inspired heavily by them, started writing my own short stories. Three of them were published when I was nineteen in a professional fantasy magazine called *Moonbroth*. I was paid very little money but I was now a "professional" writer.

I got my first Super 8mm camera around this time and started dabbling in filmmaking again, doing my own version of the Moody Blues' *Days of Future Passed* album as a kind of music video. I simply played the soundtrack album to the image. Two years later, I got into Super 8 Sound, a difficult medium to work in because the sound is always slightly out of sync with the picture. But it was another step up the evolutionary ladder. I had, by that time, taken a course called the Art of Film in college—but more on that later.

Of course, none of this stuff paid the bills. I got the occasional writing check, but by this time I had a state job. Three years of civil service drove me nuts, so I got into radio, with a job as copywriter/talk show host/production director/salesman/engineer at a Hudson, New York, radio station called WHUC. I was in radio for about fifteen years. During that time, I continued to write for magazines such as

Fangoria, *Cinefantastique*, *Monsterland* and many, many others. I also continued to make movies. My first Super 8 Sound film was called *Lord Ruthven*, based on *The Vampyre* by John Polidori. Then I did another "music video" film based on Jethro Tull's *Songs from the Wood* album.

In 1979 I traveled to England for the second time in my life (the first had been in 1975, when I met Hammer music composer James Bernard and interviewed him for *Little Shop of Horrors* magazine) and I went out to Pinewood Studios, where a script that I had written based on my short story "Fear Is the Color of Darkness" was under consideration for filming by Tyburn Productions. The financing fell through for the project, but I got to know more Hammer alumni, and felt yet closer to my dream of making movies.

In 1980, I took a video workshop at a local cable station and shot a video short called *H.P. Lovecraft's "The Statement of Randolph Carter."* It was broadcast on the local public access channel. I followed that up with a short horror piece called *Trick or Treat* and had my own cable show, called *Bruce's Bazaar*, for two years. It was a loopy Monty-Pythonesque comedy show that I hosted and performed in.

In 1983, I got into 16mm production with a project called *Cannibal Church*. It never got finished, but we shot an eight minute promotional reel that was taken to MIFED by Alexander Beck; it was deemed "too outrageous" and never got funded.

I rewrote the script and it was transformed into a more Hammeresque project called *Grave's End*. I got my Hammer friends interested in it, and by 1985 it was announced in *Variety* as a British-American co-production starring Caroline Munro, Ralph Bates, Michael Gothard, Bobbie Bresee and Russell Todd, to be directed by Jimmy Sangster. Need I add that the funding fell through? There was actually $400,000 in escrow for the production, but the investors (who were Greek) argued amongst themselves and pulled out.

The project was optioned by two other producers—William Paul and Brendan Faulkner—and fell through both times. Everyone loved the script, from special-effects ace Ed French to dear old Ralph Bates—but no one came through with the money.

Feeling frustrated by dealing with so-called "big boys," I decided in late 1987 to mount my own production in 16mm. I got together with a local filmmaker named Antonio Panetta, who happened to own his own Arriflex camera. He wanted to make art films, and I wanted to make horror films, so we compromised on a remake of Carl Dreyer's *Vampyr*—an art-house horror film.

The movie ended up being released by Panorama Entertainment in 1991 under the title of *Vampyre*, which was all very nice, but the distributors didn't have a clue as to what to do with it. It wasn't an exploitation film, it had very little dialogue, and was quite surreal. So it quietly died in its first release. But I was very glad that my grandmother lived to see it; it was dedicated to her.

After attending a FANEX convention in Baltimore, at which I met Veronica Carlson, I asked her to host and narrate an hour-long shockumentary called *Fangs*, a history of vampire movies. She hadn't been in front of a movie camera in seventeen years, since she had done *The Ghoul* for Tyburn. We flew her up to New York and shot her scenes on the same locations we had shot *Vampyre*, and everybody had a great time. *Fangs* was released by my own label, Pagan Video, in 1992. We took out full-page ads in *Filmfax* and sold quite a few copies, essentially broke even on the production.

I wrote a script then called "Raven's

Inn," based on the old classic *Horror Hotel*. I wanted Ralph Bates to star in it, and he might have—had he not passed away that year at the age of fifty from pancreatic cancer. Just one of many tragedies that I'd had to endure in the 90s, a decade of almost absurd highs and lows. My grandmother passed away in 1993, and my grandfather the following year. As a kind of therapy, I wrote and directed *Black Easter*, an anthology of mood pieces about death and the beyond. It starred Veronica Carlson and Debbie Rochon. It was the first feature that my company shot on video (with Betacam). I was very happy with the result, but a hold-up in post-production has kept the film from seeing the light of day as of this writing. A great shame, as I think it contains the best performance that Veronica has ever given. Hopefully, it will be released soon.

Meanwhile, I'm working on a project called *London After Midnight*—not a remake of the Chaney classic but an *Avengers/X-Files*/H.P.Lovecraft combination of elements that should be a lot of fun. Hopefully, it will be completed by the end of 2001.

Video box for Bruce G. Hallenbeck's *Vampyre*. Courtesy E.I. Cinema.

Along the way, I've fallen in love, gotten married, have met many of my idols (including Peter Cushing), have lost beloved family members, have seen *Vampyre* reissued (and praised in a book called *The Vampire Film*), *Fangs* reissued (and finally putting me in the black as a producer) and have fought financial problems. The tide seems to be turning now, and maybe, just maybe, the new millen-

nium will see me turning my scripts into movies on a regular basis. Will Pagan Productions be the new Hammer? That would be a hoot, wouldn't it?

Influences/Aspirations: As I've already noted, my early influences were the films of Hammer and Universal. It was a great time to be a kid; when you went to the movies you could see stuff like *Horror*

Prudence Petty as Holly Gemini and David Louis as David London in *London After Midnight*. Copyright Pagan Productions 2000.

of Dracula, Curse of Frankenstein, Brides of Dracula, Kiss of the Vampire, House of Usher, Masque of the Red Death—it was the era of classic Gothic horror. Later, when I discovered H.P. Lovecraft, I decided that it was up to me (as I had the same birthdate as old Lovecraft) to make movies based on his work. It's something I'd still like to do.

Ultimately, my dream would be to have a production company along the lines of Hammer. I rate Terence Fisher as one of my favorite directors, along with Alfred Hitchcock, Akira Kurosawa, Ken Russell and Orson Welles. I have very little interest in making schlocky exploitation; classic horror is my meat and potatoes. And I have less than no interest in making anything reality-based; I'd rather create a world from scratch.

Film School: I never went to film school, and in fact never finished college.

I took several courses related to film and media, [and it was] The Art of Film from which I learned a lot about film criticism. I made my living as a film critic for many years. But at the end of the course, the professor told me that I should have been teaching it instead of taking it. Ultimately, I felt at the time I'd rather be making movies than taking courses on them. And I do think that all you need to do to be a good filmmaker is to A) watch movies, as many as possible, and study them and B) go out and make them. Only by actually making films can you become proficient at it. I know film school graduates who are very good at filmmaking, and I know some who only spout theory and get very full of themselves. As pompousness and pretentiousness annoy me, I steer clear of the latter. There's nothing wrong with film school, and in fact it can be very beneficial. But there's nothing wrong with on-the-job training, either.

The Script: The script is all-important. Very few good films have been made from bad scripts. I think that the single biggest problem with movies today—big budget or low budget—is with the screenplays. They're either endless car chases or endless uses of the F-word. Lazy screenwriting has become the order of the day. With the exception of *Vampyre,* which has very little dialogue, I try to write scripts with good, literate dialogue. I used writers like Rod Serling as my model, to some extent; the old *Twilight Zone* shows were beautifully written. Special effects have become far too important in genre films. Look at movies like *The Haunting,* which show almost nothing but have compelling characters and situations. That kind of filmmaking takes genuine talent.

Vamp (Patricia Martin) seeks solace with a statue in *London After Midnight.* Photograph by Ted Dimmer.

Equipment/Format: I have used several different formats in my productions. *Vampyre* and *Fangs* were filmed in 16mm, and *Black Easter* on Betacam. I find both of those formats to be extremely professional, high-quality and relatively easy to work with. Of course, you need crews who know what they are doing—you can't do it all yourself. I don't usually do my own photography. As a writer/director and sometime actor, I have far too much else to think about. My current project, *London After Midnight,* is being shot on video by Joe Bagnardi, for whom I acted in his movie *Shadow Tracker.* You might say he's returning the favor.

Cost/Budget/Funding: Vampyre was filmed for about $20,000. In post-production the budget escalated, and the final cost was $60,000. Most of the money came from private investors; about $9,000 of it was my own, and about the same amount came from my partner on the production. *Fangs* was made for about $6,000, entirely funded by the producer. *Black Easter* was also funded by its producer, Lane Masterson. *London After Midnight* is, so far, funded by yours truly.

Actors: For *Vampyre*, we held auditions at a local high school, and we videotaped them. All the actors we used were local, most of them with theater backgrounds. I like to use stage actors, as I find it much easier to tone them down than to bring low-key film actors up. I also like the more theatrical, British style of acting. For *Fangs*, of course, we used Veronica Carlson; the script was written for her. *Black Easter* was cast both locally (after a series of auditions) and out of Manhattan. I cast Debbie Rochon because we had just done a photo shoot with her for *Raven's End*, which ended up not being filmed. I cast Veronica again in a key role, and Arthur Lundquist (who had been campaigning for roles in my films for some time) and Cheryl Hendricks, both of whom had appeared in *The Regenerated Man* for Ted Bohus. I think that *Black Easter* is the best-acted movie that I've directed. *London After Midnight* was cast after a series of taped auditions; the actors are locals with stage backgrounds and some movie experience.

Music: The score for *Vampyre*—which is exceptional, I think—was composed by Edward J. Kilgallon and produced by Robert Bengraff. It's entirely original and was produced at a now-defunct studio called Sidestreet Productions. Kilgallon was eager to get into film composing, and is now based in Nashville. The sound and music track were the most expensive aspects to completing *Vampyre*, and those involved in it were among the few people on the production to be paid up front.

How long did it take to make your first film? The bulk of *Vampyre* was shot between April and July of 1988. When we obtained a distributor, they asked that we shoot more scenes, which we did in March of 1989. In November of 1989 we shot one more additional scene—the teaser—and that was it.

Special Effects: Special effects at the low-budget level of filmmaking are important, but as it's impossible to make *Titanic* for $20,000 (or less), low-budget films should not rely on effects for their success. I feel that independent films should rely more on character, atmosphere and story than their studio counterparts. Effects on *Vampyre* were minimal, consisting of simple double exposures, blood squibs (including the old trick of filling up a condom with fake blood), smoke and fog and a few fangs and scars along the way. *Black Easter* had some gore effects, but mostly it was atmospheric stuff like making rain that kept us busy. *London After Midnight* will feature some animation effects that should be fun.

Production Tips: If you want to make a movie, then make it. Don't let anything stop you. If you don't have the money, find it. Borrow equipment and get as many freebies as you can. Tell your actors they may have to brown-bag it. Above all, be patient. If you're directing it, bear in mind that your actors are (probably) not being paid, so don't act like a tyrant. Work with them, not against them, and you'll find that they will reward you with the best performances they can give. Don't raise your voice on the set; if the cast and crew feel that you're acting like an idiot, they may take a walk and not come back. And thank everybody at the end of the day's work. They've earned it, and much more.

Publicity: Publicity is very important to the success of any film. *Vampyre* was not publicized enough on its first release. It was dropped by the distributors into a pile of exploitation films, where it did not belong. The reissue by E.I. Independent Cinema has finally, I feel, given *Vampyre*

Holly (Prudence Petty) dances for her life in *London After Midnight*. **Pagan Productions 2000.**

the kind of marketing that it needs. It has been packaged as classic horror, not exploitation, and an excerpt from a favorable review is being used on the video box cover. Perhaps it will at last find the audience that will understand and enjoy it.

Distribution: Obviously, if your film isn't distributed properly, it won't reach its intended audience. I was not at all happy with the initial distribution of *Vampyre*, and it was made worse by the fact that the distributors kept us, the producers, in the dark about everything and claimed all sorts of expenses against the production. I can't imagine what those expenses were, as I never saw any kind of publicity whatever from them in a single magazine or book or newspaper. Be careful when you choose a distributor; there are many who are waiting to take advantage of your naïveté.

Future: I hope to continue making movies on a regular basis. I also hope to make somewhat bigger productions, although I have no interest in being a mainstream filmmaker. I would love to establish a production company that could turn out small films at a profit. I'm greatly encouraged by a lot of new interest in my work, and by the efforts of E.I. to market my films.

Additional Comments: To be a filmmaker, you have to love movies. You have to be willing to put up with sleazy distributors, working long hours for little or no money, and sometimes getting no financial rewards in the long run. But if you've completed a film, you've done something remarkable that relatively few people are able to claim. I applaud all independent filmmakers who, against all odds, complete and release movies that are in some cases better than those of their Hollywood counterparts.

Andrew Harrison

Filmography: The Blaxorcist (1990) A ten-minute short spoof of *The Exorcist* using an Asian friend as the exorcist. I did everything in it as far as behind the camera goes, but that's not saying much. If you ever get to see the film you'll understand why.

Weirdo in the Woods (1990) Thirty minutes. A group of mates go for a drinking session in the woods and all get killed by a weirdo. I think every independent does a slasher flick—it's required. Again I did everything apart from the music which was composed by Darryl Sloan.

Zombie Genocide (1991–1993) Sixty-five minutes. Well, you know this one. I co-directed with Darryl and another guy who's no longer with the crew, Khris Carville, who also did the camerawork. Darryl did the first half of the film's soundtrack, the second half was written by a guy called Clifford Mitchell. He was in a local band called Joyrider, they did a cover of the old Jane Wiedlin song "Rush Hour," had some success over here and in England, broke up. All the editing was done as we filmed apart from the last couple of minutes which was done using a video with editing equipment. I also did the SPFX.

The Wages of Sin (1998) Nineteen minutes. Again, you're familiar with this one. Did almost everything behind the camera, apart from the music—again that was Darryl—and we directed it as a team, myself, Darryl and Paul Barton.

Dark Light (2000) To date we've about 60 percent of footage filmed. This time I'm directing, Darryl's the music-man and Paul PR as well as one of the main stars, as is Darryl. I'm in it myself, just a couple of scenes.

Influences/Aspirations: I think that one of my most strong influences has got to be George A. Romero and the whole zombie thing. You only have to look at *Zombie Genocide* to see it. It was the love of zombies and that whole genre that got me into making movies. The thought of directing my own movie with complete control is very appealing, more so now that our films are starting to get noticed to a point. I hope that the future holds something exciting for Midnight Pictures and I really think it will, especially with all the positive feedback we've got recently. It's strange to read what people are saying about *Zombie Genocide* and *Wages* on the internet at *Homepage of the Dead* and other mag/reviews. It's been with us for so long as a very small thing and to see all the talk is, well, welcome.

Filmmakers like Spielberg and Cameron always amaze, as well as the likes of Peter Jackson and Akira Kurosawa, to name but a couple.

Film School: Film school to me seems a very American way to go. That's not to say that it's wrong or mind-shrinking—the opposite if anything. As far as I'm concerned, if you can get into film school go, look at some of the great directors et cetera that have come out of them, but at the end of the day don't let it worry you if you haven't; life is a great teacher, and so is sticking both hands in the pot and seeing what comes out. Everyone's a critic, and it's so easy to criticize something without actually thinking about all the hard work that some person has put into a film.

Script: Script is important to an extent. If we're shooting a scene according to script and we see a better way to shoot it, we do it. I have no problem changing the script, in fact nearly everything we've shot for this new film is different in some way from the actual script as is. I think the script is the perfect shoot, the way we'd love it to be. But when you go to shoot it it's not always practical. That's why we never storyboard any of the sequences.

Equipment/Format: At the moment we are just using ordinary 8mm home video cameras, previously we did use full size 16mm video tape cameras but they're too big. In the future, if the tide turns, we'll probably go digital, but only if it seems that some money is coming our way. The 8mm is cheap and easy to use and for a group of guys doing this because they enjoy it, that's the way it has to go. Sure, we'd love all the gear, but like I said, until the horizon looks brighter that's the way it's going to be. Also editing 8mm is easy and now even more so, as we've got a kick-ass editing program for the PC.

Cost/Budget/Funding: What's that? What we need, within reason, we buy between us. We don't really have a budget. As for funding, not yet but who knows what the future holds.

Actors: Normally it was just ourselves and friends, but we've seen the need to expand. A local newspaper did an article on us and we asked for anyone interested to contact us. We got a good response and organized a small interviewing session and got some good actors, to boot—well, you can let us know when you see the new film.

How do you get your music for the movies? For *Zombie Genocide*, the music was composed using a Commodore Amiga 500 computer, which had a primitive (by today's standards) sound chip allowing only 4 musical notes to be played simultaneously. For *The Wages of Sin*, the Amiga was connected to a Yamaha MU-10 sound module, providing a much more professional edge to the music. For *Dark Light*, the forthcoming film, the music will be composed on a high-spec PC running Evolution Soundstudio software, equipped with SoundBlaster Live, one of the most highly rated soundcards. The PC is also connected to a Technics P30 digital piano for composing and a Sony MiniDisc unit for recording. All of the equipment mentioned is part of Darryl's gradually expanding bedroom "studio." Composing music has been a personal hobby of his for a long time, and he naturally has charge of the music side of things for Midnight Pictures.

Special Effects: I'll try and throw together things for the effect that I have lying around. I try to pick things up now and again that I think may be useful. I do buy some latex and stage blood, but in some scenes we need a lot of blood, so I've

The crew of *Zombie Genocide*, Andrew Harrison, Darryl Sloan, Chris Carville, Clifford Mitchell.

got my own recipe for blood which looks and flows pretty well. Usually I look at the effect that I want and think of the easiest way to do it, and whether that's using the camera or blood, it just depends.

Production Tips: Well, I would say don't be afraid to try anything. You can do wonderful things with a camera at a strange angle and some moody lighting. I'm still learning as I go and that's a great way to gain experience.

Publicity: Paul Barton usually handles all our PR, but it has become apparent to us lately that publicity is very important, especially for independent movie-makers. And the Internet does and will play a big part in it. All you have to do is look at all the hype surrounding *Blair Witch* to see how important it is. If you can plug it, do it.

Distribution: Well, we did try Screen Edge but we got no response, so for a start we got some local video shops to rent our films, but that's just really for fun. Any real distribution has to be looked at seriously for our new film, but at the minute we're just not sure how to proceed. We have some small distribution in the U.S. at www.leatherface.com. They sell our last two movies for a couple of dollars, nothing in it for ourselves but publicity, which suits us for the moment.

Future: Who knows? When we finish *Dark Light* we'll do another film as of yet undecided. We do have a kick-ass script for a zombie one, kind of like a sequel to *Genocide*, but it would take some time and money, neither of which we have at the moment. My personal view is that we keep on going maybe get some of fame, maybe some money and just keep on shooting.

How is filmmaking in Ireland, as compared to the U.S.? There are two types of films made in Ireland. They're either comedy/romance or about the Troubles. We're trying to change that with the horror type, which Irish movie-making falls short on; but at the end of the day, like most high-budget movie-makers, they're aiming for the safe markets of comedies and action genres. Who can blame them. Since we have complete control, we can afford to try something different. Censorship lately in the U.K. and Ireland has been relaxed somewhat, but being down where we are, censorship doesn't really matter. It's only the further up the chain you go that it starts to play a bigger part. We're not really aiming for lots of blood and guts, only if it's necessary. Then we try to make it as real as possible. Sometimes showing less adds more.

Marcus Koch

DIRECTOR

Filmography: Blood Junkie (to be produced 2002–2003); *Pack .44* (in pre-production); *Bad Blood* (1999); *Rot* (1998); *Mousetrap* (on hiatus)

Biography: Marcus Koch, born on March 18, 1977, grew up in Pinellas Park, Florida, and started using his father's camera when no one was home, experimenting with special effects consisting of papier mâché and clay. When he was nine years old they caught him with the camera—and bought him his own. By the time he was thirteen he had more than seventy-five short movies, all having some gross or disgusting effect such as severed heads, arms, legs, guts. Little creatures were also a common sight about the house. He started getting serious about making movies when he was fourteen years old. Marcus is also editor of *Sub-Genre*, a horror fanzine.

Influences: It's my parent's fault. From day one I was exposed to horror films, never once subjected to *Mr. Rogers* or *Sesame Street* (thank God), or else I may have grown up following in the same footsteps as Gein, Fish or Berkowitz. However, I do have a twisted obsession with watching people die in nasty ways on film. I had an incredible fascination with the illusion of death as a child and I made it my quest to discover what kind of movie magic it took to create such horrific images.

As early as first grade I was well aware of my artistic abilities and also had a knack for card tricks and other assorted magic. It wasn't until the third grade that I found out about special-effects makeup. I read an article on a man by the name of Tom Savini and it was then that I realized that this is what I was going to do—create illusions.

Two other great forces that drove me to make films are Tim Ritter and Peter Jackson. There was this great little video store where I lived that carried hard to find movies, one of which was *Truth or Dare: A Critical Madness*, which I watched at the age of seven or eight years old. A year later a film called *Bad Taste* came out and gave my world a swift kick in the ass! I've been a big fan of Tim Ritter and Peter Jackson ever since.

Film School: My outlook on film school is probably much different from most people. I went to art school and that sucked enough. However, having hung out at film schools and with the people who attend them, I decided I didn't like the whole mind-set that everyone had. They were all trying so hard to follow what the book said was right, not do what the book said is wrong. If one single creative soul did things against the grain he or she was used as the prime example of how not to do things. Film school will teach you how to properly care for your camera and equipment but the only way you're really going to learn how to make movies is by getting out and doing it on your own. Trust me, spend a year making a movie and by the time you're done, you will have experienced more rights and wrongs than in two years of film school.

Scripts: I think scripts are very important, the true backbone of the production. However, I believe good movies can be made from bad scripts and bad movies can be made from good scripts. It all depends on how successful the director is translating those images from page to screen.

Equipment: I started out with a VHS camcorder then moved to a Hi-8mm Handycam and Sony Editing decks. Now I shoot on digital video and use non-linear editing gear. I also own an Arriflex 16mm camera, a bunch of tripods and a fourteen-foot boom crane.

I really like working in video, mainly because it's the equivalent of a Polaroid—instamatic! It's also much less expensive than film. Video looks great if you really learn how to use it to your advantage. Film is more likely to find a good distributor, as video is still looked down upon in this industry. It makes me sad to know that popular opinion still rules. It should be that content is what makes a film, not what format it is shot on.

Budget/Funding: Budgets and funding in my films have been little to nothing. I've never had to go to any investors for money to finance the movies. My film *Rot* was shot for damn near nothing because it was shot on video and the main cost of the production was makeup, blood and beer. I will be re-shooting *Rot* on 16mm this summer, and it has been a nightmare trying to find investors! So I've been writing up business proposals and sending them to people with lots of money. Now, the hard part is convincing these people to believe in my work and trust in me to make their money back.

Actors: For my movie *Bad Blood* I was lucky with actors. I cast my friend Karl Bereberich, who had been doing musical theatre since he was very young. Our parents were friends, and it just worked out that he was always available. I cast him as the lead vampire. Karl looks very much like actor Bruce Campbell, when covered in blood.

For *Rot* my choice for actors was simple; I needed punks, and who better to play punks than real punks, such as Billy Scam and Tiffany Stinky. Billy Scam and I have been friends for a really long time and I knew that he could act. He prefers to play with his band, the Scams, but is up for doing any movie. He recently made a cameo in the movie *Attack of the Killer Manatee*, directed by Wes Horn. Tiffany Stinky, also one of the squatter punks, really had the look I was going for and was able to do just about anything that I asked.

I've also been a fan of Joel D. Wynkoop for some time now, because of Tim Ritter's movies, and knew that Joel would be excellent for the role of the mad scientist. Lucky for me he had faith in my script to take time out of his busy schedule working on *Truth or Dare 3: Screaming for Sanity* to play the part.

The best advice I can give about

Poster for Marcus Koch's *Rot*. Courtesy Undead Entertainment.

have to deal with copyrights and other stuff like that. Talk to local bands. Most of these bands will be more than happy to write soundtracks because they know it's free exposure. If there's a song that you feel you need and you have the money to pay royalty fees, go for it. On *Bad Blood* everything was written for the movie by local bands and musicians. The soundtrack for *Rot* was a mix of punk bands and stuff a friend and I wrote. *Mousetrap* also has a soundtrack written and played by local musicians.

First Movie: With my experience of working on numerous short films and winning several short film competitions, I decided it was time to make my first feature. *Lunchmeat*, which ran an hour in length, started out as a test run for a new effect involving an eyeball and an exacto knife—and everyone was so excited about it that we just kept shooting, making up the plot as we went along. Next time, I want to focus more on plot and character development. *Lunchmeat* was

finding actors is that you should go with who you know. You'll be surprised at how people who have never acted before will do amazing things in front of a camera. Also, check out the local stage theatre or call or write an actor or actress you're interested in. The worse thing they can say is no.

Music: It's better if you have original music for your productions, so you don't

so boring and the characters were less than believable. I wrote *Bad Blood*, a movie that would have an elaborate story and characters that were interesting. Unfortunately, I bit off more than I could chew. I was only thirteen years old at the time and trying to do something really big. It took another seven years to finish the movie.

The biggest problem was the actors not showing up. The only reliable actors were Karl Berberich, ShoShannah Smith and Kevin Kovacs. Everyone else had better things to do, which forced many script rewrites and creation of new scenes. The finished movie is close to the original script but it's still a patchwork of all the useful footage. The new story is tied together by a new character, Margo Brant (played by Marge Andrews), a washed up romance novelist whose new story is the movie. Now, granted I could have just chucked the whole project, but I was determined to finish the movie. By the sixth year into it I gave up, defying the very words I live by. I was so sick of changing things, sick of actors changing their hair, failing to show up when they set the times and dates—and most of all, I was sick of the word *vampire*!

I was eighteen years old and ready to move on to the next project rather than beat a dead horse. So I wrote *Rot*. In the middle of working on *Rot* I showed actress Marge Andrews the footage of what could have been a cool movie. It had some really nasty effects and even a cameo by Conrad Brooks. It was her idea to tie the whole movie together using her as a tie—and damnit, it worked! Granted, the film is dark and it has a few continuity problems, but the acting is decent and the effects are disgusting. So, I am pleased with how the movie turned out. From this hard lesson I've learned how to deal with the actors, how to plan and organize and how much work is really involved in making a movie.

Distribution: When the movie is in the can, it's time to prepare for the bumpy

Actor Joel D. Wynkoop (left) and Marcus Koch with the mutant alligator head, on the set of *Alien Agenda: Endangered Species*. Photograph courtesy of Twisted Illusions.

road of distribution. *Rot* was easy to shoot compared to my attempts at finding a distributor. Many distributors are very interested in my film, but I've found a lot of politics to be involved. I've also been told horror stories from many people who have been screwed out of their money from some distributors. Some people say the best way is getting out there and doing the footwork yourself. If your film is good enough it will spread by word of mouth and those buyers will come flocking to you. But don't count on it. Do the work yourself and self-promote the movie until you're blue in the face, and then do it some more. If you are looking for distribution, be well prepared to shop around and see what they have to offer you. Everything is going to sound great, because they [the distributors] want you to choose them. But there will be strings attached. If you can, talk to other filmmakers who have worked with distributors to see what their opinion is of them and how they were treated, et cetera. This will help you.

Publicity: Short, sweet and to the point: You need publicity. I've found out that it isn't cheap. *Bad Blood* had no publicity, primarily because I was lacking the funds. It was a hard lesson learned, and no one has really seen it [*Bad Blood*]. With *Rot* I set aside money for advertisements, called newspapers, screened it at a local movie theatre and wrote to magazines. Publicity pays off, even if it's bad publicity. It's better than no publicity.

Special Effects: Shooting at this level of moviemaking is rough as it is. By making a movie with a lot of special effects you could wind up digging yourself into a deep grave. But inexpensive effects can be achieved. I did a little looking around and found a marine store that specialized in fiberglass and mold-making materials and

Marcus Koch (left) shooting Billy Scam on the set of *Rot*. Photograph by Mitzy.

also carried rubber latex and A/B foams as well as other useful supplies needed for effects work.

I have been playing with effects since I was seven years old and have found, through experimenting, how to make an effect look its best. As with any illusion, it's how it's perceived. In my movies panty hose become intestines, Knox gelatin becomes open wounds, blocks of foam become mutant alligators. I'll do whatever it takes to pull off an effect. However, I would really like to do effects with a budget and proper supplies. One day.

What the Future Holds: I'm finishing *Mousetrap*, which is directed by Mike

Independent director Marcus Koch. Photograph by Stacy Pickhardt.

Becker, Sunny Faulhaber and myself. Soon I'll be re-shooting *Rot* on 16mm film. Other future projects include *The Clique*, which is about murder, suicide and coffee, and two films, without titles, that will be the same story from two different points of view. There may also be a medieval fantasy movie involving puppetry.

Tips for Novice Filmmakers: Here's a bit of information that will be useful if you ever run into a problem regarding permits. Let's say you're out shooting one day on the street and "Johnny Law" steps in and asks for a permit. You don't have one and he gives you a fine for shooting without a permit from the city. Don't panic. You see, there's a loop-hole in this law; if you are shooting a movie on video this law doesn't affect you because you are using video. "Johnny Law" will disagree and tell you you're making a movie, and you need a permit to shoot any movie. Well, if this law is true Mr. Law would have to bust every last tourist, videotaping their exciting family vacation adventures! And if families all over America are allowed to play up to the camera in an attempt to win *America's Funniest Home Videos*, why should we video-filmmakers be any different?

Jeff Leroy

DIRECTOR

Filmography: Crack-Up; The Screaming (2000); *The Hunting Season* (2000)

Biography: I was born in 1964 in Butler, Pennsylvania. My father was a steel worker, now retired.

Influences/Aspirations: I always had a fascination with film and television. In the first grade I remember making a film on tissue paper, punching sprocket holes in it and asking the teacher to run it through the projector. In 1972, when I was in the second grade, I saw the *Poseidon Adventure* and fell in love with any movie with disaster and miniature destruction. This included Godzilla films and *War of the Worlds*. As a kid I wanted to be an astronaut, loved watching the NASA moon stuff. And I loved a TV show called *UFO* that aired on Saturday nights. *UFO* featured great visual effects by the late, great Derrek Meddings. That was where I developed my love of blowing up miniature models. I also loved the Hammer horror films and Ray Harryhausen films. I got my hands on my dad's 8mm film movie camera and within five minutes my brother broke it! I bought a Super 8mm camera in 1979 and have been making home movies ever since.

What is your take on film school? I went to the University of California at Santa Barbara—a great place. It's right on the ocean. I got exposed to a lot of films I normally would not watch. I found film school a pretty good experience but more theory than actual film production.

How important is your script? First I fall in love with an idea. I feel strong about the LA riots and the news coverage (*Crack Up*) or New Age cults (*The Screaming*), then I write a script. Then I have a bunch of people whose opinions I trust read it. I rewrite the script based on their criticisms. I don't believe in writing in a vacuum. Other people can judge your work and point out holes in your plot faster than you.

Opposite: **Video box art for Jeff Leroy's** *The Screaming*. **Burning Moon Home Video.**

What equipment/format do you use and why? I have some 16mm Bolexes I used to shoot *Crack Up*. A lot of people say you can't shoot a feature film on a Bolex. It's noisy and tough, but you can do it. For high speed miniatures I have a 16mm Bell & Howell that runs 150 frames per second. For video features I use Betacam SP because the colors look great and the picture has depth that I don't find in the digital formats.

Cost/Funding: My first film, *Crack Up*, cost about $25,000 and sent me to bankruptcy court. I didn't have a budget. I just ran up my credit cards until they shut me down. Then I started writing bad checks. My third film, *The Screaming*, shot on Betacam SP, ended up costing less than $800! I'd prefer shooting on film.

How do you cast your actors? In LA if you throw a stick you hit three out-of-work actors. I go through *Backstage West*, get a bunch of photos and have an audition. Usually I find who I want in the first reading. Usually I try to use people that have done a good job in previous productions and are dependable.

How did you get your film's music? In LA if you throw a stick you might hit an out-of-work musician or two, as well. My score for *Crack Up* I paid for. I found a guy in *Backstage West*. For *The Screaming* and *Crystal's Diary*, I did favors for the musicians on their projects. I hardly ever use needle-drop music. Those places, like Network Music, are a big pain in the ass.

How long did it take to make your First film? Over three months to shoot.

Jeff Leroy working on the rocket base miniature for *Planet of the Living Dead*.

Over six months to edit. I kept running out of money for the post-production and writing bad checks. Finally, I owed them so much money they gave me a job running the stockroom while I edited at night.

What is your experience with dealing with special effects at this level? I love miniature effects and the stop-motion animation of Ray Harryhausen films. The digital effects can be really powerful if they have something to do with the story, like in *The Matrix* or *Starship Troopers*. Usually they are just big, cartoonish and lame, like *Lost in Space* and *Jurassic Park II*. I can't believe the effects in *Lost in Space* could capture any kid's imagination the way effects of *War of the Worlds* or *UFO* or *20 Million Miles to Earth* did for me. I'd love to try and recreate a shootout from *Straw Dogs* or an explosion I saw in *Journey to the Far Side of the Sun*—with no money, of course.

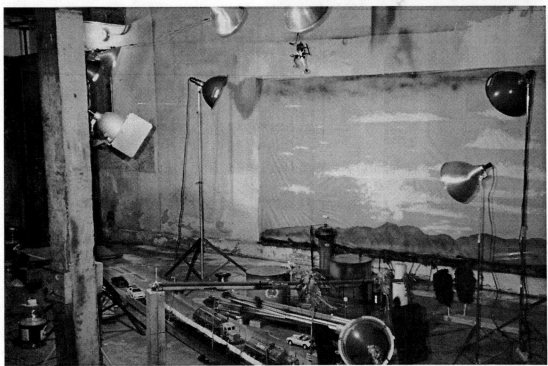

Top: A victim from *The Hunting Season*, directed by Jeff Leroy. *Bottom:* Miniature set from *Crack-up* (1996).

Any production tips for the novice filmmaker? Start on video. Don't shoot on film unless your parents are rich.

How important is publicity for your films? Since so few people have ever heard of my films I guess I should work on that a little more.

What about distribution? Since I have been working with David Sterling, usually the films have a distributor before they are made. The tough part is getting money out of these guys. For the last few years the markets have been really lousy. But that seems to be changing.

What's in store for the future? A film like *The Thing* that takes place on Mars. A mummy movie. A *Deliverance* type thing. A movie about a killer robot. A sequel to *The Screaming*. Does anyone want to see a big budget remake of *Day of the Triffids*? I do!

Anything you want to add? When I was making *Crack Up*, running up debt, doing a bunch of terrible things I never dreamed I would do, I lay awake at night asking myself what the fuck I was doing. No matter how bad it gets, follow your dreams and finish the job.

Santo Marotta

DIRECTOR/PRODUCER

Filmography: Creature Comix: Dracula's Quest for the Blood Gems (1997); *Knight Beat* (1998); *Rage of the Werewolf* (producer/co-writer/ actor, 2000)

Biography: I grew up reading and collecting comic books and watching the old Universal monster movies. I started drawing my own comic strips and drawing whoever would pose for me. I had decided early in life that I would become an artist. Little did I know at the time that I would later transfer this love to filmmaking.

I attended the School of Art and Design in Manhattan, majoring in cartooning, where I participated in an internship program at Marvel Comics Group. This was a great experience for me because in between doing the grunt work of copying artwork and scripts, answering phones, filing and getting coffee for the staff, I learned a great deal of first hand knowledge about the business that I would never have learned in a classroom.

Later, I went to college at the Pratt Institute. It was there that my interest in filmmaking began to spark. I was majoring in graphic design/illustration but I seemed to be enjoying my minor classes in animation, filmmaking and Shakespeare more and more. Filmmaking became more fascinating to me as I learned how I could give movement and the illusion of three-dimensionality to your subjects. I made a few short animation projects, the favorite of which was one with two dinosaur characters I created. I also did some Super 8mm film short projects. I was hooked. I loved filmmaking. It was an extension of my artwork and ideas on paper. I felt a little like Dr. Frankenstein must have felt; I could now make my own creations come to life!

Influences: I'd have to say that my biggest influences on filmmaking were the old black and white Universal monster movies. After college I found a renewed interest in them and began buying them, building a video collection of the classics I loved as a kid. They seemed like the Greek tragic hero stories of old. Most of the monster characters seemed to be afflicted by some sort of curse, a botched experiment or were simply misunderstood, which led to some interesting stories. The acting, makeup, lighting and props were amazing, even by modern standards.

Film School: I think you should take the classes you need. Film schools cost a lot of money and you may not need to take all the classes. If you're looking to come out with a diploma, then it's a different story. But if you're looking to learn what you are missing I think there is nothing better than first-hand experience. Working with a small film crew is a great start. You'll be surprised at the amount of knowledge you'll come out with after working on your first project. Learn from your mistakes.

Script: It's like the blueprint for a building going up. Without it you won't know where it's going, how long it's going to be or how many people it's going to take to make it happen. The more people involved, the more detailed it should be. For example, if you're going to have a director, several actors, someone shooting the film for you, someone in charge of music, lighting, costumes, et cetera, then you'll need to fill them in on the game plan. The script enables you to do this so it's clear and understandable to everyone involved what it is you want to convey on film. The director knows what to direct, the actors know the lines you want them to say, the cinematographer knows the angles, time of day and lighting you are after. Now, if this is a solo project or you're going to be doing just about everything except the acting, then your script need only contain the lines the actors will need to study. If it's going to be a spontaneous shoot then you don't need a script. The bottom line is you should always have an idea of what you want in your head, even if it's not on paper.

Equipment/Format: There are many different types of equipment, film and video formats available to the independent filmmaker. For my short film projects I did in college I used Super 8mm film and learned how to cut and splice the film by hand, then use a clear tape to join the scenes together. By today's standards, this is a primitive form of editing. By using Super 8mm and editing it myself, it gave me the feel of how the larger, more expensive films of old were done. I supposed this is where the term "ended up on the cutting room floor" came about. The problem with Super 8mm film is that not many people use it anymore and it's hard to get it processed without sending it out to Los Angeles.

In making *Creature Comix* and *Knight Beat* I used a Sony Hi-8 video camera. I chose this format for budgeting reasons. The quality is also very good. (Try to get the non-metal particle drop out tapes— they are a little more expensive but worth it in the long run.) Also, by shooting in video I could see the shots I took that day without sending the film out to be developed. In the future I'd like to shoot 16mm film or use a digital camera.

Budget: I kept the cost down by making or finding my own props, costumes and any artwork needed. You'd be surprised at how much money you could save by making your own special effects. Many of the cast members were also skilled as carpenters, makeup artists, et cetera, and other cast members were willing to help out in other ways such as cooking, driving, holding the microphone, and just plain helping out with odds and ends. At the end of *Creature Comix* we rented space on a computer editing system called D-Vision. *Knight Beat* was edited on an Avid. That's where most of the project's budget went, but the results were amazing. We were able to add many needed special effects and embellish the film in other areas.

Producer/actor Santo Marotta as reluctant hero Jake in *Rage of the Werewolf*.

Raising the budget for your film can be one of the toughest chores. I raised the money for my first two films by selling a lot of the comic books I had saved (I kept four boxes of my favorites, of course), working odd jobs and two of the cast members contributed some small amounts. Since the films were horror based, it was hard to get funding from an outside source. If you're looking to get funding for a project you'll have more luck with a documentary piece. There are many organizations that are willing and able to contribute funds towards a project that fits their criteria.

Actors: In casting my first two films I used friends who are aspiring actors and others by means of a casting call. If your friends are serious about acting and filmmaking I think it's a great idea to work together. But a word of caution: Making a feature film or even a short is not all fun and games. A lot of hard work is involved, and you don't want to choose people who are going to run out of steam before the project is completed, especially if they are key players. Because my projects were made on an ultra-low budget, the actors were not paid. Instead, they received copies of the films with a screen credit, a copy of the comic book version of the film (which I made) and meals. When the project was completed a cast party and screening of the films were held. If you can't afford to pay your actors it's important to keep them happy and share a mutual respect.

Music: For the music in *Knight Beat* I first laid down some existing music I thought would be good for the film, then later put down all original music. My editor introduced me to a musician who had some previous experience with low-budget movies. He listened to the music I had down already and came up with original music that had the same mood I was after. We then replaced the old music with the new music and the result was much better than I had hoped.

How long did it take to make your first film? Creature Comix was a monumental effort on my part, as well as for everyone involved. It took about nine months to shoot and another three months to edit, primarily because everyone, including myself, had full-time jobs. We were like weekend warriors, trying to get as much done with the time we had to work. Also a lot of that time was spent building rubber costumes, finding and creating sound effects, drawing the comic book art that appeared in the film, casting, and revising the script. It's tough to make a feature film when you are working another job, and it's even tougher when everyone else is doing the same thing. I suppose another reason for the lengthy time involved is that this was a new experience for most of us involved. We had never made a full-length movie before, and there were many things we wound up doing over in an attempt to make it as good as we could. I learned a great deal from that experience and came away with a lot of good memories.

Special Effects: I created most of the special effects in my films. You'd be surprised what you can do by altering some fake skulls and rubber masks, adding clay, smoke bombs, flaming dummies, and some neat sound effects. Computer editing also allowed me to enhance some of these effects as well as creating new ones. My suggestion to a new filmmaker on special effects would be to experiment and see if you or someone in your crew can create the effect. This will save you lots of money and may even look better than what a computer program might accomplish. If you look at many of the new movies, they often rely too much on computer graphics, and the result is a stiff or unrealistic-looking shot. The computer effects are only a tool and should not be thought as the end-all of special effects.

Production Tips for the Novice Filmmaker: As I stated before, try to make as many of the props, costumes and effects yourself to save money. They will also look like you want them to look. Make sure that the cast and crew are reliable, responsible people to work with. Don't just pick people because they are your friends or neighbors. Try to figure out a budget for the film so that you know what you are getting into. Have regular production meetings with your crew—fill them in on any new developments before they get to the shooting location. Make out a shooting schedule so you know what scene or scenes will be shot on what day and which actors you'll need. Be prepared for the dreaded "X" factors: It rains the day you are shooting a sunny day, the actor leaves for L.A for a beer commercial, the batteries go dead in your camera, you run out of tape, and so on. Try to be as well prepared for the shoot as possible, and try to anticipate upcoming problems as much as possible. Be strong—your cast and crew will look to you for leadership and guidance.

Publicity: If you are serious about becoming a filmmaker as a means of living, then you want to get noticed. Shooting in a small town like we did for *Creature Comix* got us in a few middle-town newspapers. We aired both *Creature Comix* and *Knight Beat* on public access in New York City and we got a few responses. We also entered a few contests and sent copies of the tapes to several magazine distributors. These are just some of the avenues of publicity. They weren't the best for me, but I feel good that I tried, and it's important to try and get your work out there. The right publicity can lead to distribution, and distribution will lead to money. I am still exploring that area myself.

Future Projects: I don't know what's in store for me in the future. I do know that I'm going to continue making low budget movies and comic books until someone notices my skills and gives me a bigger budget or a solid job where I can utilize my creative skills. I'd like to see if I can get future projects distributed so I could start making a living at what I love doing.

Alexandre Michaud

Filmography: Noir (1998); *Punitiae* (1998); *Madness* (1996); *Urban Flesh* (1997); *Le Dernier Noël* (2000); *Desire* (2001).

Biography: Born in Rimouski, Québec, Canada, in 1977. Graduated in finance from École des Hautes Études Commerciales of Montreal in 1999. Studied for one semester at Helsinki School of Economics in Finland in 1998. Actually working as an accountant for the Montreal Transit Society. Created Helltimate Studio in 1995 to produce a movie called *Bound in Blood* that failed because of financing. Made two short films in college called *Noir* and *Punitiae* that got the public raving. Went to Manitoba in 1996 to co-direct with Preben Lunding an anthology called *Madness.* Produced and directed *Urban Flesh* starring Marc Vaillancourt in 1997. The movie was released in 1999 as a preliminary editing, and the final version, edited by Karl Knight, will be available in 2001. Co-directed *Le Dernier Noël* (*The Last Christmas*) with Jef Grenier in 2000. I'm actually working on a short movie to be shot on film in the summer called *Desire.* It will be part of two anthologies to be released in 2001.

Influences and Aspirations: I'm very influenced by the Italian horror cinema. I love Dario Argento, Michele Soavi, Lucio Fulci, Umberto Lenzi, Sergio Martino and Mario Bava. Outside of Italy, I'm influenced by the movies of Ringo Lam and John Woo. I'm also inspired by the music of Danzig, Manowar and Soulfly/Sepultura. I got into movie-making to express all the images that are haunting my dreams and my waking hours. Making movies is some kind of liberation as well as a means of expression. Another reason to make movies is simply because it's the only job where you can attend work meeting and get drunk for the good of the company. Making movies is fun. It's tough but it's fun. In my opinion, becoming a full-time director would be a pretty good achievement and a very decent way to make a living.

What do you think of film school? It's probably very good. I took all the classes I could without going to film school, and that helped me a lot. Directing a movie is a job. You need to learn it somewhere.... Talent, that's another thing. One thing for sure, you need to know the basic rules of movie-making before calling yourself a movie-maker.

The cast and crew of *Urban Flesh*. Last row, from left: J.F. Lamarche, Dany Fortin, Anthony Pereira, Martin Dubrevil and Alex Michaud. Middle: Marie-Eve Petit, Whatsisname, Marc Vaillancourt. Front: Jef Grenier.

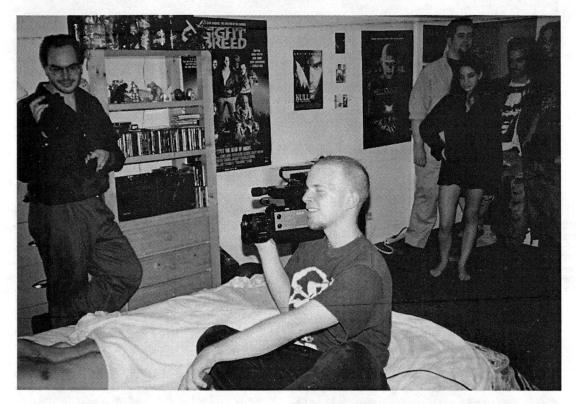

Left to right: Director Alex Michaud, J.F. Lamarche and the cast of *Urban Flesh*. Photograph courtesy Helltime Productions.

How important is your script? Depending on the project, the script can become quite secondary (just like with *Urban Flesh*). Sometimes, the images and the actions in the movie are enough to deliver your message properly and entertain the audience. Sometimes, you need a solid script to build your movie around. I don't think the Godzilla movies have great script, but they are great movies. Same can be said for the kung-fu films and some of the slasher films.

What equipment/format do you use and why? I used S-VHS for *Urban Flesh* simply because it was cheap and because we had access to a camera. With good lighting, you can get pretty good results with it. If I had the choice, I'd rather work on 35mm or 16mm because of the different look film has. My next movie, *Desire*, is going to be on 16mm. I like to edit on the PC because you don't have to count the studio hours and because you can move back and forth into your movie before going to print. It's also cheaper and you can work in your own bedroom with a beer and a cigar in your hand.

Cost/Budget/Funding: In the underground movie business you basically have to fund your movie yourself and then try to make as much money back as possible. That's why it's so hard to make a first movie (and the second if the first isn't successful). I believe somebody without many contacts in the business (just like I was) can make a very decent video movie with a budget around $1500. If you want very good gory special effects, you can ad another $1000. The editing is the most expensive part. If you can get a free editing room or if your computer can do video editing, well, you're in business. To make a movie on film that will look good with the big guys, I think you need as low as $150,000 or $200,000. Forget the bullshit about *The Blair Witch Project*. That was not a movie. That was just some cool video footage that people enjoyed a lot. It is impossible to make a good-looking movie on 35mm with less than $100,000.

How did you cast your actors? You have to be very serious with the actors at the auditions. You have to make sure that the guys and gals you are gonna meet are really interested in doing the movie [under] your conditions. You need a shooting schedule to present them, and you have to show that your are ready. Then, you can choose the most serious and professional people available. If you see that somebody has no acting talent, don't cast him for anything even if you think this person would fit with the physical description of the character. Bad actors are bad for a set. They slow you down and are bad for the morale of the troops. Also, don't believe too much in yourself. You cannot make a bad actor good simply because you are a magnificent director. If somebody is not so good at the audition, he is very likely to be not so good in the movie, even if you are a magnificent director. Finally, if you see that an actor sucks in his first scene, fire him. Don't stick with bad actors for the complete shoot. It's always better to re-do a scene than to re-do a movie.

How did you get your film's music? The music is very important for a movie. There are plenty of young musicians and bands out there that will let you use some of their songs. You would be surprised by how cool some musicians are and how willing to help you they can be. (My favorite musicians are Danny Elfman and

John Williams.) Like everybody, I think that some good rock/metal songs in horror movies can fit well. Punk music is also great. It helps render the trashy feeling of a movie if that's what you are after. One thing for sure, if you don't have a big budget on music, don't try to imitate Williams, Elfman or Silvestri. These guys are very great composers and not many people can get close to what they are doing.

How long did it take you to make your first film? It took three full years. We started writing the script for *Urban Flesh* in November 1996. We made the casting in June 1997. We started shooting in July and we ended up in September '97. We then got some problems with the editing room we were supposed to have for free. We finally started editing the movie in May 1998. The movie was ready for presentation as a preliminary version in November 1999. The premiere for *Urban Flesh* was held on November 6, 1999.

What is your experience with dealing with special effects at this level? If you want to put some SFX in your movie, you have to know about it [special effects], simply because you'll have to help the effects guys in pre-production and on the set. I have many friends doing special effects for Hollywood so I learned a lot about it over the years. If you want your effect to look good on the screen you have to know perfectly how you'll do it and what it will mean for the crew on the set.

Any production tips for the novice filmmaker? Face the problems. Solve the problems and get on with it: No shooting is perfect. You have to roll with the punches, as Jerry McGuire would have said. I once came up with the rules of indie moviemaking with a young French director about a year ago. If I remember well, the rules were as follows:

Left to right: Martin Dubrevil, Alexandre Michaud and Marie-Eve Petit in between scenes on *Urban Flesh*.

RULE 1: Make a movie. (That means, do it and finish it.)

RULE 2: Make a good movie.

RULE 3: Express yourself in the movie.

RULE 4: Make money with it so you can make a better one.

You have to follow the rules in order. If you get to one, that's pretty good. If you get to 2, that's better. If you get to 3, you'll be pretty proud of yourself. Finally if you get to rule number 4, you'll be a winner.

How important is publicity for your films? These days, publicity is everything. A movie with bad publicity or without any publicity is a movie that will not be seen by the crowd. If the movie is not seen by the people at whom it's aimed, the movie won't be enjoyed. People choose the movie they're going to watch at the theater from a list of about 30 movies (if you live in a big city). They have very little info to make their choice—the title, the poster and the publicity. If people start seeing your movie, then word-of-mouth [might lead to] more people seeing your movie.

What about distribution? People don't like to order a movie they have never heard of from the mail. That's why a good distribution channel is awfully important. Most people need to look at the cover and actually hold the movie in their hand before they really want to see it. To get many people to see it, I think you have to get into as many video stores as possible (even if there is only one copy in each). Once some people have rented your movie and loved it, they will tell their friends and then these persons (and the one who told them) are more likely to buy it by mail or by the net.

What's in store for the future? I just finished co-directing a new shot-on-video feature in French called *Le Dernier Noël* (*The Last Christmas*). It's a funny zombie flick with a lot of special effects and gore. I'm also working on a short movie on film called *Desire*. This movie will be part of two different anthologies by directors Karl Knight and Marc Thibault. It will be an art film about the lust for flesh and the devil. After that, I'll come back with another short film on 16mm. I'm also preparing a comic book anthology called *The Dark Chronicles*. I'll be publisher and editor of the mag. That should go to print in 2001. Finally, I'm working on my B-movie website, The Asylum. The site is updated every month, and it features full reviews and news about old and new B-movies from all around the world.

Ted V. Mikels

Filmography: *Strike Me Deadly* (1963); *One Shocking Moment* (1965); *The Black Klansman* (1966); *The Hostage* (1966); *Agent for Harm* (1966); *Cataline Caper* (1967); *Girl in Gold Boots* (1968); *Up Your Teddy Bear* (1968); *The Astro-Zombies* (1969); *The Corpse Grinders* (1972); *Blood Orgy of the She Devils* (1973); *The Doll Squad* (1974); *The Worm Eaters* (1975); *Ten Violent Women* (1982); *Space Angels* (1985); *Naked Vengeance* (1986); *Angel of Vengeance* (1987); *Dimension in Fear* (1997); *Corpse Grinders II* (2000)

Persistence and perseverance plays a major role in the creation of a B-movie. Without the huge budgets of your typical Hollywood production and with the shooting schedules more often than not determined by the availability of actors and crews, the director, who in fact may also be the producer and the writer of the movie, faces an almost insurmountable wall of problems. No one knows this better than veteran filmmaker Ted V. Mikels, who in the past thirty years has produced over twenty independent features of his own and dozens more for other companies.

Recently, Mikels has been working on two more movies, *Dimension in Fear* and the long-awaited sequel to his infamous *Corpse Grinders*. Mikels had first used the title *Dimension in Fear* when he was trying to get a bank loan for a movie twenty-five years ago. Mikels explains, "I was dealing with a bank on a loan for a picture. They had decided not to go with me on a different title for a different script so the next morning, before they gave me an answer, I said 'Just a minute. I want to do *Dimension in Fear*'—and on the strength of that title they OK'd the loan. But I changed the name of the film to *Doll Squad* after I got it going. So I consider *Dimension in Fear* my magic title." This time around, *Dimension in Fear* is about an escaped serial killer who is pursued by the authorities across the country. Unlike your somber, "Henry" type killers, though, this character has a rather odd trait—before he kills someone he bites the back of his hand and slaps his face, covering it in blood. When he encounters the main character, a young woman he picks up hitch-hiking after her car breaks down, he gets more than he bargained for. Before he can kill her she rakes his face with his car keys and escapes into the nearby desert. The next day, he is at the quick care center where he has his injured eye attended to. Coincidently, he runs into the unconscious girl who was brought into the center for revival by a group of dirt bikers who found her in the desert. As soon as night falls, he breaks into the hospital and unsuccessfully tries to kill her again.

"A detective takes her under protective custody," Mikels continues, "And she stays with him until they get to Las Vegas." The killer catches up with them, knifes the detective and pursues the woman through the basement of a casino. "It's real cat and mouse," Mikels adds. "Meanwhile, the killer's good twin brother is trying to find him, and when the police close in on him the woman is screaming that the twin is the killer—and the men shoot the brother, believing they are shooting the serial killer. The next morning, after she says goodbye to everyone, a hand comes from behind her, covering her mouth. The next shot is in the desert—we see her purse, a picture of her and her mother blowing in the wind and we see one shoe and lipstick. We don't know what happened. You're the first to hear the whole story."

Mikels will finish shooting for *Dimension in Fear* in June of '97. "I'm dependent on when I can get people together. I'm also DP Cameraman on this. If I don't have any help, I do it alone. With luck, I use a minimum crew of six. Sometimes a crew of thirty is a disadvantage because you have to feed them and shelter them—it's like having a big tail on a little dog."

As for *Corpse Grinders II*—it's a movie that Mikels has wanted to do for years. "I've had people trying to buy the rights but I rejected all offers because I

Director/producer Ted V. Mikels.

wanted to do it myself." This sequel, which starts off on a war-ravaged alien planet, concerns the descendents of Atlantean cat-people who return to present day earth in search of food. Ironically, the only food they find palatable is Lotus Cat Food—which contains ground up humans. "So they make a deal with the government to ship a load of that back," Mikels explains. "Meanwhile, the nephews of the original corpse grinders are being investigated by the MIBs and the CIA. I play a part of a professor who pretends to be a bird watcher while listening to the strange sounds of the spaceship as it lands. He

Video box art for Ted V. Mikels' *The Corpse Grinders.*

I've ever done has enjoyed the financial success and rewards of *Corpse Grinders*, and this is probably due to several things," says Mikels. "When we made *CG* we had a fantastic campaign—we had ambulances in front of the theaters, flashing lights, a nurse on duty checking blood pressure and everyone had to sign a certificate of assurance that they were of sound mind and good health or they couldn't come into the theatre." It worked. People came in droves. "We created a triple bill—*Corpse Grinders, Undertaker and His Pals* and *The Embalmer*—that knocked them dead and wiped out all competition." Today, the whole industry has changed. There's no longer any regional distribution. "Unless you're doing blanket promotion, where you have 2000 prints released at the same time across the country, you don't stand a chance of making money. Now, with home video, everyone mistakingly believes that you get part of the rental fee from the video stores. You don't get a nickel of it. The only reason I'm forging ahead is because I think the industry will bring about its own change. I'm not sure what that is but I've always been ahead of the direction that production was going."

The state of current distribution aside, Mikels is still enthusiastic about moviemaking. "I love my work so much—I have a ball. I make sure everyone has a lot of fun. That's why we all do it. If I keep going I'll build a library of films—maybe someone will want to buy them all and I can go to the Bahamas. What can one say?

ends up on the spaceship going back to the planet Sita to continue his research."

So far Mikels has gotten a small deposit against a $500,000 budget. He has started building the gravestones, gone to Hollywood and found the inside of a spaceship for the cat people and also begun designing the spaceship war that will be done via digital computer effects.

But why make a sequel to a film that was made over twenty years ago? "No film

If I was doing it for money I'd probably be doing something else."

Spoken like a true independent.

Biography: Born in St. Paul, Minnesota. Moved with family to Portland, Oregon, at age seven. High school and part college in Portland at University of Portland, more at the University of Oregon at Eugene, Oregon. Grew up doing magic tricks, age five, later played accordion, did magic, ventriloquism, acrobats on stage, had a two-and-a-half hour show, then a one-man show entitled *Open Sesame.* Wanted to put it on film, thus began shooting with 8mm, then 16mm. Prior, had shot still film developed in bathtub (as a very young kid). Worked with film cameras (movie) since a late teen-ager, developed first 16mm film in a leaky tank in the bathtub, lost it all, then found the un-soldered seal. Spent ten years in Central Oregon where the sun shined constantly, shooting films, casting my players from the community theater, writing my story outlines on the backs of envelopes. Then, same day, took the players assembled, went out and shot. Got the film back, edited, and for ten years, these were my textbooks.

Did my fist 35mm feature, in Bend, Oregon, 1959, outdoor action. There were no such things as genre or cult films then. My first was an action-adventure called *Strike Me Deadly.* Took me three years to finish the final edit and answer print. Had to keep selling things, and work to pay for the progress.

Film School: Film school has its extreme limitations. Hands-on is hard to get enough of. My thinking was the best school is the school of hard knocks. Get out and actually do it, instead of theorize.

How important is your script? Script is important mostly to let everyone involved know what you have in mind to accomplish, and to follow progress. Its important to have only an outline if you are doing improvisational filming, which I now really love. The script usually serves to help one find backers, supporters, and to find out everyone is a director, telling you what you should do.

What format do you shoot on? Up until two years ago, my only format was 35mm, since I own all of the cameras and post-completion gear. However, with the way things have changed, and changed so drastically, why bother? Some of my current BETA SP actually looks just as good, if not better than my 35mm. And after a few generations, who knows the difference?

The industry has changed so drastically in the last few years that it seems to boil down to any money that you can put together then becomes your budget. Add to it deferments, credit card debts, dollars borrowed or promised, and you have the total cost of your film project. Then comes the distribution, release, promotion et cetera.

Funding: When it comes to looking for money, I have always stated that the only money you can count on is the money you hold in your own hands or bank account. You have the money [to spend, the money] promised to you, when you are actually spending it. Many times filmmakers have told me they want to attend to other production problems because they "have the money." I ask them if they are spending it yet, and nine times out of ten, they don't have it in their possession. And nine times out of ten, they never do get it. Funding is close to impossible to find. Another myth is when you believe after you show the world you can make a film, funding will become easier the next time. Not so, it never becomes easier. Ask those with many years of successful films behind them. They will tell you that funding is just as hard as ever to find.

Casting Actors: When dealing with low- or no-budget films, your casting is of deadly importance. Dedicated performers are hard to find. Even though they might love the script, they often have obligations and priorities that might keep them from committing to a locked-in schedule. I constantly face the difficulties in scheduling performers in the same scenes at the same times. I usually write my scripts so that I have the fewest [actors] required at any one time. Unless you are paying well, performers' priorities take precedence, and you wait.

Some actors read well, and often are not able to improve their performance as they may be locked in to a specific delivery. These have to be given special consideration to help them through and beyond, to help you get what you need from them. I like to test their ability to be turned up or turned down, as it were, according to my directions before locking them in to specific roles. I have said that [an actor's] temperament is almost as important as talent, and that applies to the crew also. With the proper temperament, actors and crew can be helped to mold into what is required.

Music: Music comes in many forms. In Hollywood, for years, I had more composers offering to do scores for me for free than I had actors to work for money. The reasoning behind this is that you only have one composer for each film, and require maybe hundreds of performers and crew people. Often composers never have the opportunity to do a film score, and the challenge can become obsessive. I have had the pleasure of [having] the accomplished composer-conductor Nicholas Carras to do my scores for forty years. I don't think I have had outside composers

other than once or twice. I have even sent Nicholas to Europe, where he composed, conducted and recorded a large symphony doing original music for me. Of course budget always comes into play. You must remember, however, that music comes in two basic forms. One is "source music," seen or heard from a known or visible source, and "underscore," which involves the emotions desired for the film. The mood of the music can make or break a film.

How long did it take to make your first movie? My first film was over three years in the making. I had such tiny money for a 35mm outdoor action-adventure film that it became stretched out. I had to keep earning money as I went, also sold my home, car, drums and musical instruments. Unless you've done it, its hard to appreciate what it takes. Then, as you continue to work on your film, you want to make changes or additions, and these take extra time and money. I have never believed in seven-day wonders. Its takes a solid five to eight weeks or more of constant filming to put together sufficient acceptable footage. Proper coverage takes time, and includes creative lighting, sound recording, et cetera.

Special Effects: For special effects, you need to be creative. In the *Doll Squad* I wanted to utilize effects that I had never seen before. And in *Mission: Killfast*, I created some exclusive effects of my own. Since all of my films were 35mm until just recently, the cost of special effects was prohibitive. Nevertheless, I hung out with laboratory printers, and talked them into experimenting for me. Everything then on film took a lot of time. Sometimes two or three weeks for matting, blending, et cetera, then color timing so the effects could be cut into the 35mm negative without jumping. Now, with video, its an entirely different story. Effects sometimes can be created within minutes that would have been impossible on 35mm film. Recent filmmakers have some advantages we didn't have. For example we had to dolly on tracks because we didn't have zoom lenses. How things have changed! I love shooting my films myself now, as I have a lot of fun making my camera "float."

Any tips for the novice filmmaker? Production tips can be given by the thousands; however, the best tip I can give is always believe that you can do it. I have only enjoyed doing "impossible" things. I used to say anyone can do possible things, its the *impossible* things that take a little longer. Another thing: Check out your prospective film by running your story line past a number of people. Get their reactions to the subject. You're not looking for directing advice, but how they like or dislike the subject matter. If five out of ten people give you a hard time, and do not carry on the enthusiasm you have, be careful. You might be wasting your time.

How important is publicity for your films? Publicity is paramount. If you don't tell people about what you have made, you will "eat it" all by yourself. If you have a gimmick that people will talk about, or remember well, you are ahead. You cannot buy the publicity you need; you must generate it. Word of mouth is too slow. Think of something unique that can be picked up by the press or talked about in reviews.

Video box art for *The Doll Squad*, directed by Ted V. Mikels.

Distribution: Distribution is tough. I have had dozens of my films distributed by outside companies, but a viable contract is hard to get; in fact, I usually draw them myself, as I was a distributor in Hollywood for seventeen years. *The Corpse Grinders* made so much money because I was the distributor. Of course, I had seven full-

Video box art for *The Astro Zombies*. Copyright TVM Global Entertainment LTD.

time employees working for me that I had to pay with the proceeds, but it was worth it as they watched over all my theater dates [bookings] reports, collections, et cetera. Someone really has to believe in your film in order to possibly spend more on distributing it than you have spent making it. Naturally they want their money first and are in the position to get it.

What's in store for the future? The future holds a heavy uncertainty. Changes are ongoing. One thing to remember, however, is that there will always be a need for entertainment. In all times, good or bad, the world at large relies on it. Everyone has their own idea of what the future will bring. (Remember, we haven't even touched seriously into holograms and the like yet.)

Future of low budget films: Low budget filmmaking must change drastically in the next decade. There will be thousands of films made that will never be seen by anyone except those who make them. I did that for ten years prior to my first feature. However, I used many, many films for my "textbooks" until I felt ready to wade into the stream, and I think since every video manufacturer, both digital and linear keeps telling move-makers how easy it is to make their own movies now, there will be the greatest glut of film projects that never see the light of day in the history of the movie industry. You must be strong and totally determined, and have the right stuff to survive.

Brian O'Hara

DIRECTOR

Filmography: Fare Games (1996); *Rock 'n' Roll Frankenstein* (1999)

Biography: A couple of years after being expelled from college I was lucky enough to get a job cutting porno films (an ex–film teacher got me the gig). This was back in 1982. The films were being produced by a company called Avon Productions, located in the Times Square area. The movies themselves were extremely low-budget hardcore bondage and discipline affairs made by a guy named Phil Prince. The funny thing is I've recently discovered that these movies have a bit of an international cult following. For the record, I was picture and sound editor on *Tales of the Bizarre, Dr. Bizarro, Kneel Before Me, The Punishment of Prunella* and a few shorts. Before the shot-on-film porn industry died, I was able to cut a few of the bigger budgeted x-rated flicks. These include *Lady Lust, Brooke Does College, Super Girls Do General Hospital* (my personal favorite), *Pussycat Galore* and maybe one or two others, but who can remember. This period of cutting fuck-and-suck movies lasted a little over two years.

Eventually I moved into the world of legitimate film (whatever that is). I did a fair amount of sound editing: some of the episodes of *Tales from the Dark Side*, a horror movie called *Spookies*, [and] two independents for the same producer-director— *Small Time* and *The Messenger*. The feature films I was picture editor on are: *Rock 'n' Roll Frankenstein, Poisoned Kiss, Fare Games, Def by Temptation* (re-cut), *Caged Fury* (associate editor), *Posed for Murder, Escape from Safe Haven, The Rejuvenator*, and *Tusks*.

I used to write scripts in my spare time and in 1988 sold my first to a producer who I had previously done editing for. The movie was released by Sony Video as *Underground Terror*, and it was pretty much an embarrassment. Desperate to direct a feature, I more or less made a pact with the devil and in 1995 was hired to write and direct a movie for the owner of a taxi cab company here in New York who had dreams of becoming a big-time producer. The film which came out of this association was a disappointment titled *Fare Games*. The biggest nightmare about shooting that picture was I didn't see eye

From *Rock 'n' Roll Frankenstein*. The monster's first publicity shot.

to eye with the director of photography the executive producer had hand-picked. Things got off to a bad start when I attempted to strangle the DP on the second day of shooting. As the crew pulled me away from him, he was able to take a rather large bite out of my arm. Needless to say, getting through the rest of that shoot is not a memory I cherish.

In 1997 I decided to literally go for broke and make a film I could be proud of. So I started living off credit cards full-time and went about getting the ball rolling on *Rock 'n' Roll Frankenstein*. I actually tried to shoot on DVC Pro but gave that up and assembled a real crew and we shot on

Super 16mm. Principal photography began in January 1998. I didn't have a finished 35mm print until about May or June of 1999. Doing a blow-up is a long and expensive process. By the way, I went through bankruptcy proceedings to the tune of $175,000 in November of 1999.

Influences/Aspirations: When I was younger I suppose the filmmakers who I most admired were Sam Peckinpah, Martin Scorsese, William Friedkin, and George Romero. I was sixteen years old when I came to the realization I'd like to make movies. It was at that age that I got involved with still photography because it was accessible. I setup the obligatory darkroom and all that. I did mess around with super 8mm film a bit, but being a loner, it wasn't feasible to shoot narrative stories, which is all I've ever really been interested in.

Film School: You have to start somewhere and if you're totally green—without contacts and a working knowledge of film—then film school seems like a reasonable choice. Of course, if I knew then (at the age of eighteen) what I know now, I would have done things differently. If I had a son who wanted to get involved in filmmaking I'd advise him upon graduating from high school to work as a PA on film shoots. There are numerous short term courses you can take to get hands-on experience making short films. So between the contacts you can make working as a PA (not to mention the knowledge you gain) and the directing and hands-on-camera experience you can get from one of the four- or eight-week intensive filmmaking programs, you can get better than what a film school would give you for a fraction of the cost.

The climactic finale of *Rock 'n' Roll Frankenstein*. **At the Gerbils 'R' Us Warehouse, the monster struggles with himself.**

Of course, I come to this conclusion using twenty-twenty hindsight. My two years in film school introduced me to a life-long mentor, Bruce Speigel, who's advice I still seek out to this day. He was the person who got me my first film job, the aforementioned porno editing gig. Not to belabor the point, but if you're eighteen years old, have parents with money and yearn to be some big-time Hollywood hotshot, then your best bet is to apply to one of the well-known California film schools—USC, UCLA, whatever.

Script: The script is paramount. If it doesn't work on paper, it'll never work on film. It's obvious why 90 percent of the films made today suck so bad: they sucked on paper. The bane of independent films in the past decade has been the twenty-something auteurs who think so highly of themselves that they can't wait to commit

their little semi-autobiographical masterpiece to celluloid. The most egregious example of this being the films made about making a film. What a crock. These people have nothing to say and no story-telling technique. It's all about ego. And since filmmaking is so expensive, it's an unfortunate consequence that many (if not most) independent films are being made by good salesmen/hustlers who convince investors (or relatives) to give them the cash—all so that they can see their name before the head titles with the obligatory "A Film by" credit.

As for Hollywood, the reason nearly all the scripts coming out of that gold-plated shit factory can be explained by the old adage, "Too many cooks spoil the broth." They may even start with a good treatment or book, but then they go about hiring writer after writer to work and re-work the material until they "get it just

right"—a formula for disaster if ever there was one. You can't create a worthwhile or meaningful story by committee—especially when the committee is staffed by a bunch of no-nothing nabobs who live in the Hollywood hills.

Equipment/Format: We shot *Rock 'n' Roll Frankenstein* in Super 16mm. I did try the DVC Pro format but was disappointed in the look of the test transfer to 35mm. I have seen other examples of stuff shot in PAL digi-beta transferred to 35mm which looks quite good. But if you're going to go the route of shooting on video and transferring to film, you really need an experienced camera person. If you're shooting a documentary as opposed to a narrative feature I think the new video formats are great. Of course now *Blair Witch* pops up in everyone's mind, but that was a very unique project which could get away with looking the way it did. And don't forget, it was transferred to film using the best process available.

Cost/Budget/Funding: If you know at the script-writing stage that you're basically doing the film on your own, then of course you write-in locations and props at hand. After you have what you think is a feasible-to-shoot script for the money at your disposal, then it's time to break it down and see how wrong you were. The two biggest factors being shooting days required and locations you'll need. Each shooting day has a bottom line figure that it will cost: crew salary, food, equipment rental, vehicle rental. So naturally you try to limit the shooting days. As for locations, that's what's going up on screen behind your actors. I can't stress enough the importance of locations and set dressing. If you've got bare walls you'll cringe when you see it on the screen. And unless you're

shooting in the woods (*Blair Witch* again), good locations can be a bitch to get.

As for funding, good luck. I went the credit card route, although I do have one main investor, someone I knew prior to doing the project. I really have no advice here. No one's interested in giving me money, and I don't like to ask.

How did you cast your actors? The standard ad in *Back Stage.* I also put up notices on bulletin boards at acting schools. And I did make use of an eccentric casting agent who ended up referring me to one of the leads in *R&R Frankie.* The movie was cast non–SAG. Using a friend's office, I held casting sessions where actors would read "sides" and I'd video tape them. One of the strange things that happened during this process was the number of actors who turned down lead roles in the movie after reading the entire script. The material disturbed or offended them.

Music: We have a couple of original rock 'n' roll tunes (hey, it's *Rock 'n' Roll Frankenstein,* after all) that the band formed by the Monster plays in the movie. I wrote the lyrics and a friend, John Klann, wrote the music. Luckily the actor playing the Monster, Craig Guggenheim, can sing and play guitar. We recorded the songs in a studio and shot to playback when filming.

As for the scored music to the film, most of it is classic music—from Beethoven to Brahms. There's something like twenty-two different classical pieces in the film. It's great music, it works in the movie and it's free (we re-recorded all the classical music so symphony performance rights wouldn't be a problem).

There's also some other scored music done by a good friend who has a music

Opposite: **Director Brian O'Hara supports his friend Jesus in** *Rock 'n' Roll Frankenstein.*

Frankie revitalizes a severed cow head in *Rock 'n' Roll Frankenstein.*

production company, but he preferred to go uncredited as he works on TV cartoons and was afraid the controversial nature of *R&R Frankie* would come back to haunt him.

How long did it take you to make your first feature? Well, the first film I officially directed (unfortunately) was *Fare Games.* That was shot in twelve days. It was a 35mm shoot and four of the days were done in a studio, which made things move much faster. Nearly a quarter of the movie takes place in taxi cabs, and we shot all those scenes in two days in the studio using front screen projection.

The *Rock 'n' Roll Frankenstein* shoot was originally supposed to be twenty-two or twenty-three days. It got extended to twenty-five days. And then a couple of months later we had to shoot another five days due to some out-of-focus footage which was caused by a defective lens. I

ended up having to sue the company in small claims court to get the money refunded on the camera package we returned halfway through our shoot. Fortunately for us, the insurance company actually paid for the five days of re-shooting, classifying it under negative damage. We're talking about $30,000, so getting that money saved the day.

Special Effects: In *R&R Frankie* we had a fair amount of make-up effects which were all handled by Craig Lindberg and his small crew, which he calls General Mayhem. The only thing I know about special effects and make-up effects is that they're usually time consuming to implement, which is of course a real drag. There are a couple of old-fashioned optical effects (no CGI) in *R&R Frankie* which due to my background as a film editor I didn't find too hard to orchestrate.

Advice/Production Tips: You can never be thorough enough in pre-production. *Be prepared* should be your motto. If you waste time on set/location, you waste money, you waste resources and you may never finish, or get what you had wanted in the can. If you're on a low-budget and don't have an experienced line producer and AD, mistakes will be made. It's inevitable. Hopefully the mistakes won't sink the production. Fortunately there are a ton of books on film production available out there which can provide invaluable information from experienced veterans. Buy them and read them.

The other thing novices usually never understand is what hard, back-breaking work making a movie can be. It's basically a blue-collar job (for the crew, that is), yet so many of these little fuckers who somehow get a chance to direct a movie think everybody should eagerly hop on board and be grateful to help create their "vision." (For no pay!) It's those types of egomaniacal pukes who make me ashamed to be called an "independent filmmaker."

Publicity: Nothing is more important than publicity. Without it, no one knows about your film. No one will see it. Of course the first step is trying to get a distributor to notice your movie, and for independent productions, film festivals can help you get their attention. In the case of *R&R Frankie* though, this was not to be.

Before committing *R&R Frankie* to celluloid, I knew it would never be what you'd call a festival darling, but it really galls me that the so-called "underground" festivals have shunned what could very well be the ultimate underground movie (in my humble opinion). *R&R Frankie*

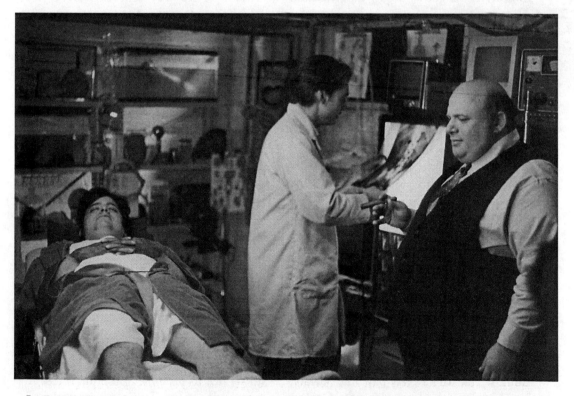

In *Rock 'n' Roll Frankenstein* the monster lies unconcious while Bernie and Frankie decide his fate.

was given the pariah treatment by the New York Underground and Chicago Underground festivals (and others I won't bother mentioning). But the final straw was when the IFP refused to grant *R&R Frankie* a screening slot at the 1999 Independent Feature Film Market. That's a market, not a festival. At that point I knew it was war. Basically my movie was facing the very real possibility of languishing in total obscurity. Desperate times call for desperate measures. I showed up at the New York Underground Film Festival with a battery-powered TV and set it up on the sidewalk in front of the theater's doors. I played the *R&R Frankie* trailer ad nauseum and stated my case to people going to watch movies at the festival. The response I got from festival goers was tremendous (and made up for freezing my balls off out on that sidewalk). But more importantly I got some media attention. That little stunt got the ball rolling for *R&R Frankie*.

I think the best resource for promoting an indie film without distribution is the Internet. A Web site is a must. It should start as a basic electronic press kit and then it can build from there. The Internet is the world's first real democracy. Even the little guy has a voice, and you really can get quite a bit of attention via the web. What's more, the cost is minimal.

It was through the *R&R* Web site that I was first contacted by the Helsinki Film Festival. This opened my eyes to the prospect that perhaps *R&R Frankie* would be better appreciated by more open-minded, European film festival directors, as opposed to the types who program American fests. Thankfully, a number of foreign film festivals have invited *R&R Frankie* to screen at their venues. The great thing is that these fests pay your airfare, hotel and meals. Nice deal. So far I've taken the movie to Finland, Sweden, Spain and Brazil. Coming up, it's Portugal and Brussels.

Distribution: Hey, I'm hoping to get some. Think you can lend me a hand?

In my case, where festivals in the U.S. gave my film no exposure, I need press (and more press). Self-distribution is a possibility, but I'd rather avoid that long, hard road. The only way a distributor is going to pay a film any attention is if that film has created what they like to call "buzz." If you get enough press, you've got a buzz going. And of course the easiest way to attract the press is if your film has some kind of controversy swirling around it. One of the controversies (yes, there are more than one) *R&R Frankie* is embroiled in has to do with animal rights violations. During the shooting of the picture there was a—let's call it a mishap, with a gerbil. After a letter was sent to PETA, the American Humane Association got involved. At this point the ASPCA is investigating and I'm told I face felony animal abuse charges. But who gives a shit. It got me a headline article on the Page Six gossip column of the *New York Post*. I find the whole episode rather amusing (and I must confess that I more or less did instigate the whole thing).

What's in store for the future? Taxes and death. If somebody would cough up the money, the next film I'd like to direct is from a script I wrote called "The King of Porn." I was so disgusted by that piece of festering shit, *Boogie Nights*, I'd like to see a decent film made about the porn industry. But I've got other scripts too. I just don't have money.

Anything You Want to Add? I'd like to piss on IFP and all the other[s] who pay lip service to promoting unique voices in independent film. They're full of shit, total hypocrites. (What else is new?)

Andrew Parkinson

DIRECTOR/PRODUCER

Filmography: I, Zombie: The Chronicles of Pain (1999); *Dead Creatures* (2001), Fangoria Films.

In *I, Zombie*, Mark, a botanist, is bitten by a sick woman while on a field trip. He is infected with a virus that makes him crave fresh human meat. On returning to London, he takes a new flat and lives a life of isolation where he can satisfy his need for flesh. Repulsed by his own violent behavior, he takes a series of victims, eats them, and disposes of their remains the best he can. As his illness progresses he becomes weaker and more disoriented.

His girlfriend Sarah is shattered by his vanishing, but slowly rebuilds her life with the support of her friends.

Mark is obsessed with Sarah and determined to see her again. He anaesthetizes and kidnaps her taking her back to his new flat. He starts to hallucinate and, aware of his own volatile condition, returns her safely to live her new life. He is getting weaker, and after dragging the body of one of his victims, his leg breaks. Unable to seek medical help, he screws a metal plate onto the side of his broken leg. The boundaries between reality and his increasingly disturbing hallucinations become more blurred. The flesh on his face is starting to ulcerate. He can no longer leave the flat.

All that remains is to attempt as dignified a death as possible.

Biography: The thirty-seven-year-old director of *I, Zombie* has been making short films in Super 8mm film and 16mm for fifteen years. Seven years ago he moved from the north of England to work for the BBC in London. There he started work on more ambitious projects. *I, Zombie* is his first feature film and took four years to make. Made on a minute budget, it brought together a cast and crew of professionals and semi-professionals, who all contributed to the project over many weekends.

Influences/Aspirations: I grew up in the north of England. As a child I became fascinated with films and horror films in particular. I was fortunate enough to have parents who would let me stay up late (after many hours of pleading) to watch the late night horror films on TV. The old Universal horrors were the first films I saw, then the Hammers and Corman's Poe

Andrew Parkinson (right) directs *I, Zombie*.

cycle of films. As a teenager I desperately wanted to make films but this was before there were any film colleges in the area, so like any healthy teenager I got a guitar instead. I became a fairly good guitarist and got the usual bad grades at school to go with it. Around this time I bought an old Super 8mm film camera and started making short animated films.

I left school and became a trainee X-ray tech, which was a job I did for the best part of ten years. It allowed me to play in various bands and make my little films. By now I had switched to making Super 8mm Sound films, mixing the sound tracks on a four-track cassette recorder. Now this felt more like filmmaking. In 1990 I managed to get a job in television post-production in London. This gave me a more technical background. I shot some films on video and used 16mm film for the first time.

I felt that it was a case of now or never: If I didn't stick my neck out and have a go at making a feature I would never do it. I dug out an old outline I'd written a couple of years earlier and started making *I, Zombie*. I made the film purely for my own satisfaction; I didn't see it as a project with any commercial potential beyond fringe horror film circles, so I didn't make any concessions to mainstream sensibilities. I was blissfully happy.

Film School: Film school is a good place to get your hands on equipment, meet people, drink beer and be broke. In the UK they vary widely in terms of the course content, and some have a very strict theoretical approach to the subject. They're not interested in helping you get your B & W cyberpunk road movie off the ground.

If you do want to go, it's worth doing some research before you decide on a college. A qualification from the right college could get you a job in the media, but make sure the college covers your area of interest. On the whole, when it comes to getting a job, the industry seems to be more interested in practical experience and initiative. I know quite a few people who have been to film school and very few of them have picked up a camera since.

If film school isn't an option and you want to get into filmmaking, my advice would be: Join your local film or video-making club—a good source of equipment, crew and advice. Join your local amateur dramatics society—a good source of actors, props and lights.

Both of these will cost very little and will get you circulating around the right sort of people. You now have no excuses.

Equipment Format: Most of my early films were shot on Super 8mm film, which I continue to use on occasions even though it's increasingly difficult to get the stock. I wanted to shoot *I, Zombie* on film. Many of my favorite horror films are on 16mm,

and I've always liked the look of film, the grain, texture and colors.

The down side was the expense of the stock, processing and telecine. This meant the film had to be shot on a very tight ratio, I think it came in at around three to one. This was a huge disadvantage in that it meant we couldn't do several takes, multiple angles or improvise, all of which added to the tension of everyone once the camera started rolling.

The equipment used on the film was rented and borrowed from various sources. The main camera, an Arriflex SR2, and lights were rented from a filmmaking workshop. There are a few of these in London. They rent equipment and run courses. The gear is much cheaper than a professional rental house, but it tends to be a bit battered and abused. If you are going to use one of these, it's worth hanging around, getting to know the people and

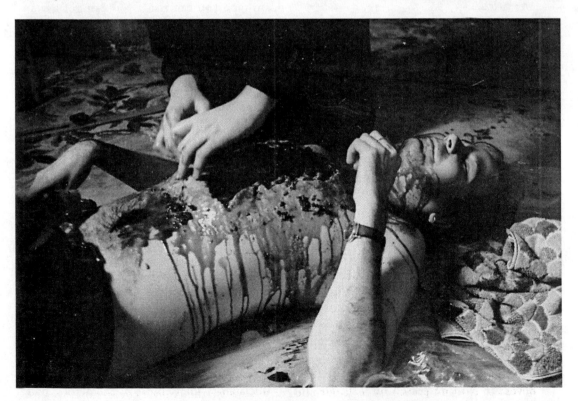

A victim gets a chewing out in Andrew Parkinson's *I, Zombie*.

helping out. That way you learn which bits of equipment you need, what works and doesn't, and you can get discount or even my favorite price, for free.

If you are shooting on film it's also worth having a small backup camera, a Bolex or something similar. This will stop you having to rent out the big camera if you only need a couple of pickup shots. It also makes you less conspicuous in public places, always a good thing. The best camera to use to learn about filmmaking with is the one you can borrow for free. Try to get to know other filmmakers and help them out. If someone has an old camera tucked away, they probably only use it for a couple of weekends a year, so they'll probably help you out. If I was starting out today, I would certainly be experimenting with video. The domestic formats are cheap and easy to use, and the new DVC cameras produce amazing results for the price.

Cost/Budget: One of the big decisions facing the low-budget filmmaker is how to finance the project. If you put up all the money yourself you could end up broke, but at least you are in charge of the project. If the financing comes from other people, be they friends, family or collaborators, they have a say in the project and they need paying back. You're not in charge anymore, but at least you're not broke. The choice is yours. Some people seem to be able to get grants for their films. In my experience, they tend to be given to projects that deal with what can best be described as worthy subject matter. If you're making a genre film you might as well save the stamp.

Balancing the budget will make the difference between finishing your film or having a half shot story that you can't afford to edit. If you get it wrong, the cast and crew will be pissed off with you for being incompetent. You now have the problem of finding extra funding mid project, and you have a great deal of stress at a time when you really don't need it.

It's important to remember that no one format is better than another. Choose one you are comfortable with technically and can afford. An unfinished 35mm epic is of no use to anyone. Many people opt to shoot on hi-band video; you can buy your own camera and have a simple edit set up at home. This takes a lot of stress out of the equation.

If you do shoot on film, the costs are equipment rental, film stock, processing, telecine or rush printing, editing and the sound mix. If you have your rushes telecined instead of printed, you can then treat it like a tape edit and have a tape to show people. This is how many TV programs are made, and [it] saves on the negative cutting and final print stages, which are very costly. When the film is finished on tape you can see if you can get a distributor interested so they can pay for the negative cut and print. If you contact all the facilities houses near you and ask as politely as possible, explaining your plight, sooner or later someone will appreciate what you are doing and give you a good deal.

Whether you pay your cast and crew a small wage or expenses will really depend on how much money you have. Not paying people is actually quite stressful, because you're never sure if they will turn up or not. But if you have no money your options are limited. When I made *I, Zombie,* I was broke and couldn't even pay traveling expenses. I really regretted this at the time and hope in the future to be able to pay expenses and even a small wage.

How did you cast your actors? At the time of casting I was helping out a theater group by doing the lighting for their productions. I knew most of the actors, had seen them in various roles, so I knew what

From *I, Zombie*. Actor Giles Aspen (left), director Andrew Parkinson (right).

people were capable of and who I could get along with.

I'd already worked with Giles Aspen and Dean Sipling on a short film and most of the other actors were interested in being involved, which was great for me. The nice thing about having seen these people in different roles meant that I didn't have to go through any auditions, with all the "thanks, but no thanks" that goes with it. I'll probably have to do that next time.

I was very fortunate with the cast, who were very tolerant about the endless overruns and reshooting. Giles Aspen and Ellen Softley turned out to be excellent leads. Giles took an awful lot of physical abuse in the lead role, covered in makeup for hours on end and performing his own stunts. Good thing he has a sense of humor.

If you need an actor there are stage publications and casting newsletters where you can advertise. Don't be surprised if you get lots of interest: Most actors work on the stage and are very interested to do any film work, especially if they can get a good show reel out of it.

How important is music to your movies? The soundtrack was extremely important to this film. It's a rather intimate film with very little dialogue in places, so the music really sets the tone and pace. I've always been interested in music, so writing the music for the film was something that really excited me. Before we started, I knew the tone I wanted to go for, and as I was working on the final drafts of the script, I started playing around with different ideas and themes. All the music was performed by Tudor Davies, who can play the piano in more than one key, and myself, who can't. Tudor was also the sound recordist, music producer and engineer, and co-dubbing mixer. It's okay for people to wear more than one hat.

We were very fortunate to have an excellent dubbing mixer, Andy Hewitt, who adopted the film as a project to try out his new dubbing theatre. We transferred the analog eight-track master tape onto a digital mixing system, which meant we had maximum flexibility to move tracks around and blend the music with the sync tracks. We sat in a dark room listening to the same scenes for days on end, only stopping to eat piles of junk food and drink endless cups of coffee.

How long did it take to make your first feature? The film took four years to make, a fact I find rather depressing. The biggest problem was the script, which was not structured properly. The film was shot and edited in about eighteen months when I realized we had a problem, which was a great pity because everyone thought we were finished. Up until then it had all gone very well. I started rewriting, shooting and editing, and it took another eighteen months to get the structure to work. No one actually fell out with me, but some of the working relationships became a bit strained, which was not surprising, really. Fortunately, everyone stayed with the project and eventually we got there and the post production started, which took about six months. When you're starting to make films everyone tells you the script is the most important thing. I learned the hard way that they are right.

Special Effects: When I was writing the film I knew I wanted there to be as many effects as possible, mainly because I like special makeup effects. In the script the protagonist gets bitten by a zombie, then turns into one himself, slowly going through various stages of decay. In the meantime, he eats numerous people, his leg breaks and he repairs it with a metal

plate involving a power drill, et cetera. All the stuff horror film fans love and other people find unwatchable. I rang around various makeup schools and finally got in touch with Paul Hyett, who was keen to take the job on. He was eighteen years old and it was his first feature. He brought a lot of enthusiasm and inventiveness to the project. He now works in mainstream films, TV and adverts.

The problem with effects is they take so long to set up, so it's bad news to have people waiting around for their scene. Bored people have a tendency to wander off and when you need them, they are nowhere to be seen. It's not always possible, but for effects work it's a good idea to do a second-unit shoot where there are minimal cast and crew hanging around waiting for the head to explode.

Production tips for the novice filmmaker: Before you think about filming

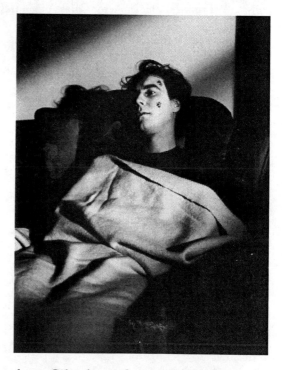

Actor Giles Aspen deteriorates both physically and mentally in *I, Zombie*.

anything get your script as polished as possible, show it to as many people as possible and listen to their feedback. Some of the advice will be good, some bad. Look for any recurring comments people make which might highlight problems. An idea is to meet other writers and bounce ideas off each other. This is quite good for exploring story avenues you might not have gone down on your own.

Before production begins, plan everything in as much detail as you can. This way you have less worries when you get on the set. I tend to storyboard everything. I can only just afford to work on film, so unfortunately there's very little room for on set spontaneity.

Don't have too big a crew if you don't need one. It's possible to work with a cameraman, sound man and production assistant to do the clapper board. For simple scenes, you could do the camera or sound, an actor could do the boards, so you don't have to have too many people standing around on your tiny location.

However broke you are, always feed people. People won't mind seven days on soup and sandwiches. They'll appreciate the fact that you're broke and making an effort.

Finally and most importantly, if you don't know something, ask. There are no stupid questions—it's only stupid not to ask them.

Publicity: Without publicity no one knows you've made a film, so they won't watch it. The good thing about making a horror film is that there is a fan base out there publishing fanzines, putting things on the internet, organizing festivals, and they are interested in new films and filmmakers. When you've made your film you contact people, do a bit of networking and they are happy to publish pictures and articles.

The people who like horror films appreciate that many of the edgy, confrontational films are produced by low-budget indies, so they are not as prejudiced as fans of mainstream film when it comes to unknown filmmakers. They are also more likely to actively seek out new material that might be of interest to them. During shooting it's important to get as many photographs as possible, production shots of people stood around the camera and shots of scenes within the film. On *I, Zombie*, Christopher John Ball lit the film, took the stills, put together a Web site and acted as unit publicist. Keep people as busy as possible!

Distribution: I'm relatively new to the problems of distribution. *I, Zombie* is about to be distributed on video in the U.K. by a company that specializes in low-budget horror, sci-fi and thrillers. As the publicity of the film spreads, I'll be approaching similar companies in other countries. It's a relatively slow process and not particularly profitable in the short term. So, if you're making a film don't spend too much money thinking you'll get rich quick. It might not happen.

Future Projects: At the moment I'm writing a couple of scripts that are in a similar vein to *I, Zombie*. I'm not going anywhere near a camera until I'm completely confident the script is finished. One of these (probably the cheapest to produce) will go into production early next year. In the meantime, I'm helping a friend out doing the camera work on his low-budget film. One thing about getting people to help you out means that there is never a shortage of people asking you for favors.

What do you think is the biggest difference between independent filmmaking in the United States vs. the U.K.?: The size of the U.S. and the censorship laws. The size issue cuts both ways. Because it's bigger there are more people making films, more fanzines and more distribution possibilities. The only benefit of being in a smaller country is you stand out more, which can be useful from a publicity point of view. The oppressive censorship in the U.K. means you can't sell a copy of your film without it being classified by the censors, which is an expensive process. This means low-budget filmmakers can't self-distribute without the compulsory services of the censor, which many filmmakers can't afford. So, in a way, I think it's harder over here.

What is your take on censorship? I'm heavily in favor of categorization. I wouldn't want to offend anyone by accident. But on balance, when we're talking about films made by consenting adults for consenting adults, I'm against censorship. Society needs to protect the young, and certain material should not be available to them, but for adults I can't see any advantage in censoring films. What is deemed offensive material very much depends on the personal agenda, political viewpoint and sexual orientation of the person watching the film. To have your film edited by an external body is rather sinister. It makes you realize that you are not living in a society where you are free to express yourself.

Additional Comments: Making my first feature film was a long, hard slog. It was also the realization of a long-held dream. I'd encourage anyone to do it. Something that's really important, and that most people don't talk about, is looking after yourself as a filmmaker. The process is mentally stressful and hard physically. Take care of yourself, preserve as much energy as you can and enjoy the process. If you have a story you are really passionate about it will carry you through. Good luck.

NOTE: Since this interview was conducted *I, Zombie* was picked up for distribution by Fangoria films. I had sent a copy of the movie to my friend Mike Gingold, who is managing editor of *Fangoria* Magazine, and he in turn passed it along to Tony Timpone, the editor, who really liked the movie. Six months later, when I had gone to the Fangoria Weekend of Horrors, there was a huge poster that said "Fangoria Films Presents *I, Zombie*," which was great. It was released to the home video market in May 1999 through Bedford Entertainment/MTI Home Video. Tony still owes me a lunch for making him aware of the movie! Parkinson recently completed *Dead Things*, another Zombie movie.

Brett Piper

DIRECTOR

Filmography: Mysterious Planet (1982); *Battle for the Lost Planet* (1987); *Mutant War* (1988); *Raiders of the Living Dead* (a.k.a. *Dying Day*, 1989); *A Nymphoid Barbarian in Dinosaur Hell* (a.k.a. *Dark Fortress*, 1990); *They Bite* (1993); *The Return of Captain Sinbad* (1993); *Dinosaur Babes* (1997); *Draniac* (2000)

Biography: Born in New Hampshire in 1953, bought a Kodak Brownie 8mm movie camera when I was eleven, more cameras and more movies since then while supporting myself in construction, freelance art and design, newspaper composition, et bloody cetera.

Influences: James Whale and the rest of the Universal gang; Willis O'Brien; later, Corman and Terence Fisher and (big-time) Hammer. Still later, John Huston (the only director to whom I ever wrote a fan letter—and he wrote back!) and Orson Welles.

Aspirations: I just wanna make movies, you know?

Film School: I have mixed feelings on film school. I consider most formal education a crock, but if I'd gone to film school I wouldn't have wasted so much time reinventing the wheel, and I would have gotten to play with real equipment. (I didn't know how a Steenbeck worked until I sat down to edit my first feature and taught myself how to use one.) On the other hand, most guys I know who went to film school know which buttons to push but don't understand why. Their knowledge is very superficial.

Script: The script is the blueprint. It tells you what you'll need to make your movie. But once the ingredients are assembled, the movie takes on its own life. A slavish adherence to the details of the script is possibly the worst trait a filmmaker can have.

Equipment: [Some] 16mm color negative, an Arriflex. I like their cameras; they're light and easy to handle (although I have a Bolex Rex 16mm that I've used on every film I've made and in fact shot two entire features with nothing else). Sixteen

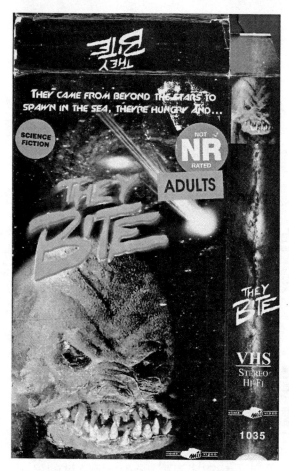

Video box art for *They Bite*, directed by Brett Piper. Box art copyright MTI Home Video.

was the only performer in the film who'd never acted before. In actors, experience counts for nothing—you've got it [talent] or you ain't. When I have the money I advertise in the New York papers (*Backstage, Showbiz*) and fly them [the actors] in (New York is only a few hours away). Otherwise, it's a long, hard search, and if you ever get anyone you really like it's just dumb luck.

Music: I used to have a guy who was really cheap and pretty good who did music on several of my films, but ... no longer. I should learn to play a keyboard and do it myself.

How long did it take to make your first film? About a year, if you don't count the

millimeter resolution is better than video and plenty good enough for the limited release a low-budget film like mine is going to get.

Cost/Budget/Funding: The bane of my existence. The worst part of making any movie is scraping up the money. It's marginally better to get some money maven to raise it for you, but then he's going to want to call the shots himself and demand an inordinate kickback for doing so. I have nothing good to say on this subject. Or maybe three words: Be born rich.

Actors: I get actors anywhere I can. The best actress on one of my recent films

Video box art for *Mysterious Planet* (1986), directed by Brett Piper.

Video box art for *Dinosaur Babes*. Take 2 Productions, 1999.

Publicity: I got a fair amount of publicity on *They Bite* before the film ever found a distributor. I'm not exactly a household name. Publicity is not my concern.

Distribution: I think for really tiny films, self-distribution is becoming more viable. The tendency of distributors to rip off the filmmaker is so entrenched nobody even notices it any more. The deals are all outrageously slanted in favor of the distributor. One distributor admitted that under the terms of the agreement he was offering me there was no way I would ever see a dime, but he still couldn't understand why I refused to sign. I have had distributors offer me no salary and no percentage of the profits and still expect me to make films for them. The attitude of people in

time spent chasing money. Except for the actors and a handful of musicians there was no one else involved, so it dragged on awhile.

Special Effects: My approach to special effects is of more interest to a historian than a contemporary filmmaker. I'm like one of those Japanese soldiers still hiding out on a tiny Pacific island twenty years after the war has ended. I'm doing special effects pretty much the same way they were being done in the twenties, before the invention of the optical printer (much less the computer). It's cool, I like it that way.

Advice to Filmmakers: It's nuts. It's hard work. I've never considered it fun. I don't know why any sane person would try to do this for a living. I don't think many sane people do.

Publicity photograph for Brett Piper's *Drainiac*.

distribution is [that] they are the pushers and we are the junkies, and sooner or later we'll have to come around.

Future Projects: Who am I, Criswell? I'm finishing up a film now, if I can raise completion money. Then I start looking for money for the next picture. We'll see.

Mark Pirro

PRODUCER-DIRECTOR

Filmography: *Buns* (1978), *The Spy Who Did It Better* (1979), *A Polish Vampire in Burbank* (1982), *Deathrow Gameshow* (1987); *Curse of the Queerwolf* (1988); *My Mom's a Werewolf* (1998, writer); *Nudist Colony of the Dead* (1991); *Buford's Beach Bunnies* (1992); *Color Blinded* (1998)

Biography: Pirromount pictures started in 1970, when a 13-year-old Mark Pirro was given a movie camera and projector for Christmas. In the three years to follow, early Pirromount produced six short films utilizing classmates, relatives and friends. The films were silent and ran between 10 and 20 minutes in length. In 1974, Pirromount Pictures moved from Ithaca, New York, to Hollywood, California, with about $1,000 and a dream.

In 1978, Pirromount made its first talkie—a 22-minute comedy entitled *Buns*. *Buns* was a comedy about a man who went on a murderous frenzy every time he saw a hamburger. *Buns* was cast with many friends Pirro made while working as a tour guide at Universal Studios.

In 1979, Pirromount produced a 48-minute James Bond spoof for $1,600 en-titled *The Spy Who Did It Better*, which was promoted on CBS-TV's *Two on the Town* and was named one of the Ten Best of the West.

In 1981 Pirromount began production on *A Polish Vampire in Burbank*, a sweet send-up of vampire films. It took two and one-half years to complete and has gone on to become one of the most inexpensive movies ever produced. The budget was $2,500.

From 1981 to date Pirro has directed six feature films, numerous shorts, promo-tionals and commercials, on budgets ranging from $300,000 down to three figures.

His 1998 feature, *Color Blinded*, his first to use digital technology, was shot on such an ultra-low budget that even Pirro and his associates were amazed. "I never thought I'd be able to make a 90-minute feature for a fraction of what I spent on *Polish Vampire*," says Pirro. "In those days I was forced to use yesterday's technology to make a film with-out spending a lot of money. Now, I'm using tomorrow's technology."

What is the advantage of working on a lower budgeted film? On a higher bud-

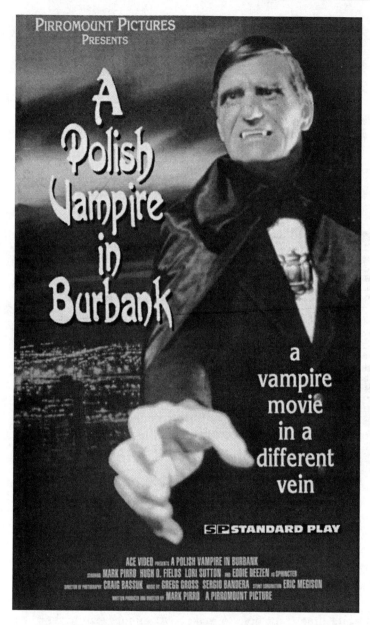

Mark Pirro's *A Polish Vampire in Burbank*. Courtesy Pirromount Pictures.

geted film, you have to get your permits, insurance, unions—even if it's a non-union film. You have to deal with more of the corporate structure of filmmaking, and I've never been one to enjoy that. I try to hire a co-producer to take that part of the responsibility away from me. I have no interest in that aspect whatsoever. Let's say you need fifteen ten year olds for a [classroom] scene—on a larger budget film you have to get [actors to play] their teachers. If you do a low-budget film, you just do it. You tell everyone working on the film to bring their kid in for one day and you just start shooting. And the possibility of getting into any trouble is remote because there's no lights, trailers, dressing rooms or catering. I think this will get more structured as time goes by because there's going to be more people with camcorders. They might start clamping down on the small projects at some point. But traditionally I've been able to steal shots and do crazy things that you could never get away with on a 35mm shoot.

On the other side of the coin, these problems are taken care of by someone else on a bigger-budgeted film. If you have the money to hire a co-producer to deal with the business side of it. You also have a lot more people, so you don't have to do everything. Your filmmaking can be much more comfortable— you don't have to be the first one on the set and the last one to leave. You do your job and leave. It gives you a bit more of a comfort zone to work with. You don't have to worry about, "Gee, if we work another hour do I have to buy them all lunch?"

What do you think of the current state of independent productions? This is some-

Pirro using homemade blimp for his Super 8mm camera for *Curse of the Queerwolf*.

Mark Pirro directs his leads Michael Palazzolo and Taylor Whitney in *Curse of the Queerwolf.*

thing I've been doing for a long time and now it's becoming very common. I think the niche that we created for our production company really isn't a niche anymore.

With *Color Blinded*, the digital movie I recently did, I did my own music and would never consider doing that before. But the computer makes it possible. I said, "My god, I can write my own music; I don't need to hire a composer." Once everything is shot, everything can be done in my post-production studio. Moviemaking has never been more affordable, especially if you can get past the film vs. video controversy.

It's nice to know I was part of this. The saying goes, "The road West has been paved with bones of pioneers." Often, the people who start these things aren't necessarily the ones who end up the most profitable. I've come to peace with the whole thing. You start realizing that Hollywood is an exclusive club and the only thing you need for membership is success. If you're not successful, no one wants you near the club. I know so many people who play the Hollywood games and do the hypes and all that kind of stuff, and sometimes it works for them and sometimes it doesn't. But it's encouraging to know that the rest of the world is catching up and people are bringing filmmaking into their own hands now.

Talk a bit about your idea of bringing low-budget films to the masses. I have an idea for a basic-cable channel I'm shopping around. I'm trying to get a larger cable company to piggyback us—you need to convince them that there's a need for this, what we're in the process of doing, which lays out the concept of the network and how programming is never-ending, how you can continue to get films. As we speak, 400 films are being produced right now, in this country alone. If these filmmakers knew there was an outlet, it would give them a realistic goal. For all these countless films, here's a place where you have a home for your film. It's extremely difficult to get a film shown on the Independent Film Channel or Bravo. How independent are these guys?

Eventually it will click, but the right person has to be there to see it. Unfortunately, the people at the cable companies who are in a position to do this don't care about the little people. It's the lottery game. But if I don't do this network, someone else will. Let's say someone is well connected, like an uncle at Bravo. They could get the jump on it. But mark my words, it has to happen. Even if it turns into a regular network show that shows clips. Somehow there'll be an outlet for all these features.

So many filmmakers are now in the same situation of there being no distribution or outlet. If there was an outlet, the public would eat it up. And it's time to put it together. So it's a struggle. Anything new is.

Mike Prosser

DIRECTOR

Filmography: The Dividing Hour (1998)

Biography: I was born and raised in the Portland, Oregon, area and still live there. I went to college in Ashland, which is a good theater town, as an acting major. Although I only took two film classes in college, I always knew I wanted to go in that direction. So, I started with art, make-up effects, and acting in my grade school years, moved into writing and directing for stage, designing and building sets, and naturally progressed into the filmmaking thing.

Influences/Aspirations: I've always been a huge movie fan. Movies like *Star Wars* and *Indiana Jones* were some of my favorite movies growing up. And of course the horror movies. What attracted me to the horror movies were the monsters and effects. Some of my favorite horror films are *Hellraiser, Evil Dead,* and *Jaws,* which are very creative and spooky at the same time.

Most of my influences as a filmmaker are Clive Barker, for his sexual undertones and tripped-out characters; David Cronenberg and his own brand of almost antiseptic psychological horror made flesh; Jim Henson, for his heart and sense of fun; Spielberg, for his power to make you laugh, cry, and most importantly, make you care about the characters, although he's sappy sometimes; Sam Raimi, who has a fun time with the camera; and early John Carpenter, hard to beat the mood and music of his finest stuff.

Film School: I think film school is a plus for people who want to network, who don't necessarily want to do it on their own or be the head honcho on a production. It's a good place for people to meet and get jobs that lead to other jobs. The main thing about film school is that if you're not generating your own material you'll have nowhere to go. All that knowledge doesn't do you any good. In some respects film school wouldn't have been that great for me, but I sure would have loved those

Opposite: **Video box art for *The Dividing Hour*, directed by Mike Prosser.**

THE DIVIDING HOUR

"A dark, vicious comedy of errors...this indie HOUR delivers on all counts" —Editor, SHOCK CINEMA

THE DIVIDING HOUR

THE DIVIDING HOUR

ALBEDO PRESENTS A PLAYGROUND FILMS PRODUCTION BRAD GOODMAN GREG JAMES MIKE PROSSER BRIAN PROSSER "THE DIVIDING HOUR" JILLIAN HODGES MAX YOAKUM AND JAY HORENSTEIN DIRECTOR OF PHOTOGRAPHY JEFF YARNALL

WRITTEN BY MIKE PROSSER AND DAVID WALKER EXECUTIVE PRODUCER JEFF YARNALL DIRECTED BY MIKE PROSSER © 1998 PLAYGROUND FILMS

ALBEDO
DISTRIBUTION

Publicity photograph for *The Dividing Hour*. Clockwise from top right: David Walker, Jeff Yarnall, Greg James, Mike Prosser. Creature by Gamut Studios.

contacts. If you're going to be a leader, you don't need to go to film school. You can just make a film. You can find the money, the equipment, the people. Just ask people, and they're usually more than eager to help. That's how I got one of my assistant editors—I called a video editing place. But he was so interested that he was willing to help out for basically nothing. You can always find someone with a camera, someone with lights. Everything was borrowed. You can get stuff you need, particularly if you're a good motivator. You have to be. It's tough, too. The motivational part runs the risk of dropping to the side after a while, when you're overwhelmed with trying to get a movie done. Try not to let that happen. When you're doing a low-budget movie, you have a hat rack full of hats, and they don't always fit. Admit your faults and ask for help when necessary. Your cast and crew will respect you all the more.

How important is the script? Essential! It is the most important thing. If you don't have a good script, you're not going anywhere. In our low budget genre, I think a lot of people rely on gore and nudity. And that's fine; there's a market for that.

The main thing for me with scriptwriting is that I don't treat any of the scripts like a horror movie. I'm not trying to distance myself from horror at all, but I think I'm doing the horror community a disservice if I say it's *just* a horror movie. I'm not leaving out the elements of a good movie. I'm making sure the characters are trying to show the whole person, show them goofing around, sad, angry. The build and the flow of that character throughout the story is very important, and it's one thing I really try to focus on. Tell a good story with the most interesting characters we can create. And hopefully you can cast someone to fill that part and make it better than what is on the page.

How much does the script change during shooting? Not a whole lot. With *Dividing Hour* we wrote it the year previous to shooting. Right before that we did a rewrite to tie some elements together, like the River Styx. I didn't want it to be *From Dusk Til Dawn* in that it seemed like two different movies. I loved the beginning but not the end of *FDTD*. I felt it was inconsistent and jarring for an audience. Going into the shoot we'd tape footage and sit down as a team—Dave Walker, my co-writer, Jeff Yarnall, cinematographer and co-producer, as well as the actors—and discuss what was being shot and what was left to shoot in terms of the relevance to the final product. Dave was able to eliminate some of the script we didn't need because he was a bit more distanced from the project than I was. Stuff that got cut wasn't integral to the plot. Then in the editing process we cut more dialogue. There was a six-page monologue, and the one-take footage of that monologue was nine minutes. We cut four minutes out of it. I would have trimmed a tiny bit more from it, but I was forced to cut around the performance. Greg was so great and [imparted] such a wonderful flow to the piece that I had to cut from emotion to emotion, sometimes leaving in less significant lines. If I hadn't, the flow would have become choppy. Luckily it is one of the audience's favorite sequences. These are things we should have cut previous but didn't have concrete script readings like we do now. You learn more about writing from the editing process as a first-time filmmaker, more so than anything. You're able to see the finished project—see what works, what doesn't, what you can cut around or can't, and what can be rearranged to keep a balance or heighten your conflicts.

Format and Equipment: We shot with a Hi-8mm consumer-grade one-chip because it had better picture quality than any other equipment we had access to at the time. It was my high school drama teacher's camera and we borrowed it until we finished the movie, bought a wide-angle lens for it to give it a little more breadth, because we always intended to letterbox it. And we used a slight soft-focus filter to make the video look less electronic. For lighting we had a three-light lighting kit. We'd rent a generator for the weekend, hide it where it wouldn't make any noise (or as little noise as possible). Everything in the creek scene had to be re-dubbed. And I'm glad we did, because it's the cleanest sound in the movie, and you don't realize it was dubbed.

We edited on a Mac with Adobe Premiere, not realizing the limitations of the computer at the time. It would hold only eight minutes of edited video and then it would stop. So we'd dump to S-VHS tape in eight-minute chunks. At the end of editing process we also lost seven scenes—due to a major computer hard drive crash—which we had to re-do. So, we put together the movie in chunks, waited to find a good enough machine to piece everything together and then dump to Betacam. We eventually hooked up with Darren Westenhaver, who edits on a Mac with Media 100 software. Did our final sound mix there and dumped to Betacam and did our dubs from that.

Cost/Budget/Funding: We thought we could do it for $5,000. We were wrong. I think we started shooting with half the money and said let's just start. We got into it and figured some of those costs will happen in post [production]. A lot of our finances went to feeding the crew. They weren't fancy meals, but a big chunk went there. The rest went to tapes, post-production, buying bulbs because people kept on knocking the lights over, and renting the generator. We spent a good chunk of money on harddrive rental, we bought elastic-reality morphing software. I was working for Pacific University at the time, so we got the educational discount. If you know anybody in the educational system you can get a lot of discounts if you know the right people. For three months, we shot on our interior sound stage (the local community theater on it's off season) on the weekends. We spent about $200 on the set (borrowed canvas flats) and paid the theatre a $50 utility fee. Still, that's dirt cheap. Luckily I was directing the first show of the season, so we could leave our setup behind the play's set and continue our weekend shoots during the day. I think we ended up spending $7,000. It is what it is. I think it benefits from Jeff having a good eye as a cameraman. My experience as a set designer and the benefit of building the set allowed the action to be played out exactly how I envisioned it.

The movie was self-funded? We sent out investment letters to family and friends. A lot of the film was financed by close family and old high school teachers who believed in us and our talent. So it was a great opportunity for us. We hope we can pay the money back, with interest. I probably spent $1,100 of my own money, bet it was a lot more, stuff I didn't keep track of, gas money, et cetera. When you say approximate there's things you don't keep track of.

Actors: Dividing Hour was real easy to cast. Casting myself was probably a mistake. I really should have just directed and focused on that. It probably would have been a lot less hassle on set. Sometimes I just didn't know my lines. Greg, who plays Dean, is an old friend since high school, and was an acting major in college. Jillian, who plays Dawn, I met in college. My brother plays my brother. I knew everyone from either high school or college. My prop lady was someone I met when I was

Before and after shots of the house in *The Dividing Hour* using Photoshop and AfterEffects. Photograph courtesy Mike Prosser.

forced to go to church as a child and she was really involved in theater. Her husband, Max, plays Louis, the father in the film. You wouldn't know it from seeing him, but he's the nicest man in the world, always smiling. It was a coup for us to get him because he worked out very well.

Sometimes it works using non-actors. Sometimes they just go way beyond what they're expected to do. For example, there was a scene where the character Peter is talking to Louis and he's supposed to be sitting in the corner, just staring at him. Well the man literally did not blink for four minutes. Because he wore glasses with a strong prescription, he couldn't really see anything, just sit there and zone out.

Did it make it easier using people you already knew? Yes and no. Because I knew them I could easily reference things from the past, and I knew many of their strengths and weaknesses as performers. The disadvantage: When you work with your friends, a lot of times they don't respect your opinion, they're used to rolling over your ideas with their own. [It's] great to have a flow of ideas, but it can get in the way of your personal vision of the film at times. My friendships are rather competitive, even antagonistic, and so it makes it hard to direct and get people who are not part of that clique to listen to you sometimes. You really have to fight to get your opinion out and understood if you have strong-willed friends. I remember one day, when we were going to shoot the scene that came right before the rape scene and I said I want this to be a one-shot. I was met with the reaction "No, no, we'll get that in two shots. It'll be easier." I knew it would be easier; that wasn't the point. I wanted to shoot the scene that way because I wanted to see the connection between the two people simultaneously before the insanity ensues, a calm before the storm which would emphasize the impact of the rape. Well, everyone finally did the scene that way and it worked out great. You think they'd respect your insights into the script a little more because you wrote it and your vision of how you want it to look is usually pretty vivid. I think you have to have that vision, to be really prepared and know how you want the scenes, and then convey that clearly to them previous to setting up the shots. It makes them reassured that you know what you are doing.

I think on *Dividing Hour* they sometimes saw I didn't have a vision for a particular scene, and sometimes they saw I was making it up on the set. Things are going to change on the set, but be prepared with something to go on at all times. On the next movie I'm having a complete set of storyboards. I'll know what we're shooting, how I want it to be played. When there's a firm groundwork, people are hard-pressed to change your vision or play director themselves.

How long did it take to shoot and edit?
Took about a year and a half to shoot on weekends. I think it was thirty-six days spread out over that time. We started in June or July 1994, shooting only on weekends periodically through October, and then went on hiatus when weather went bad. We waited until the following spring to finish. Editing was very long and drawn out. It was a five-year process all together. I'd change the movie, but I wouldn't change a thing about the experience.

Justin Brandon as one of the mysterious shadows in the woods in *The Dividing Hour*.

Special Effects: I designed the monster for the end of the film, on paper, and sent down to my friend Brian Sipe who works for Greg Cannom. He whipped up a mask and a slip sleeve arm. I think it was around $800, which is a good deal because it's a nice mask. Jeff, my cinematographer, and I both did make-up as well. The hands morphing together was nylon and liquid latex gluing the actors together; [we] then utilized the morphing program we bought. I saw this shot-on-video movie that had a lot of morphing and I thought, "I can do better than that." People froze, transformed, froze, and then moved again. So we learned from that—a lot of ones we did were static shots but we always cut before last frame of the morph so there were no still frames which read as false to the eye.

Showing the monsters for little amount of screen time helps, and that makes it scarier than what it truly is. I used to work for Will Vinton Studios out of high school as a sculptor. I worked on Michael Jackson's *Moonwalker* (the only Michael Jackson figure in the movie is the one I sculpted), "Meet the Raisins," dog food commercials, et cetera. I met a lot of great people there. One of them was Webster Colcord, who has since moved into computer animation as well. He worked on *Antz*, *James and the Giant Peach*, and currently *Monkey Bones*. But he did some animation for us for free. He built the armatures for the animation, I sculpted the figures, cut out Ken doll clothes, and painted them to look like the clothes in the movie. He painted the faces of the characters and animated them with a blue screen. He had leftover

The crew readies a shot utilizing Jeff Yarnall's homemade jib crane in *The Dividing Hour*.

film and processing opportunities from a commercial and was able to get it in on that job. Some of the blue screen stuff didn't work, and Jeff and I redid it with our camcorder hooked directly into the computer. Our opening sequence was done with Photoshop and After Effects, which are an invaluable set of tools for filmmaking.

Publicity: Publicity is horribly important. I don't have the knack for it yet. I think there is an art to it. I went on the Internet for six months on horror Web sites, talking it up. You have to hit the Web. Make a press kit with pictures, bios of the actors and head technical people of interest and get it out there. We were lucky that *Fangoria* liked it. It was favorably mentioned on a "cult video" episode of *Roger Ebert at the Movies* and that came about from the interest of Harry Knowles at

aint-it-cool-news.com. He liked it so much he gave it to Guillermo Del Toro (writer and director of *Mimic*), who gave us a quote that we threw on the Web site. Periodically he [Del Toro] and I will email each other and talk. So you have these mentors around that you can throw ideas at or ask questions about stuff. Everybody knows someone who knows someone.

Distribution: We went the self-distribution route because we heard all the horror stories. We've been offering our tape to some other distributors out there and might turn it over to someone who has a good catalog of titles and is aggressive in their publicity. We don't view it as a money-making venture—it's a resume for us. It's a foot in the door. It's a crapshoot.

Next Project: My goal is to shoot the next one on 16mm with some name people

Mike Prosser applies the final touches to Greg James for the finale of *The Dividing Hour*.

in it. It's called *Adverse Effects* and it's a monster movie. Half the cast are monsters and each have their own very unique personalities. Some funny, some bickering, one non-humanoid. That makes it unique. And that's what I strive for, to make something unique. I love my characters. I never had anybody read the script and not like it. It's a couple-million-dollar film, not a $7,000 movie. Hopefully the publicity on *Dividing Hour* will help us.

Advice to Filmmakers: Read every book you can. Go to as many movies as you can. Pick the best movies apart and find out why they did the scenes the way they did. What worked and, sometimes more importantly, what didn't and why. Cast the best actors you can. Be prepared. Be over-prepared. Love what you do.

Joe Sherlock

DIRECTOR

Filmography: Dimension in Blood (1996); *Monster in the Garage* (1998); *Vampirisa's Velvet Vault of Horror* (1998); *Crimson Heather* (1999); *Lust of the Vampire Hookers* (1999); *Trailer Park Double Wide Trilogy of Terror* (2000); *We Need Earth Women!* (2000)

Also worked on but didn't write/direct *Shadows of Dread, Dreamwalkers* and *The Evilmaker.*

Biography: I grew up in New Jersey until I was ten years old, when my family moved to Oregon. As a kid I was always into science-fiction, comic books, monsters, Greek mythology, et cetera. In elementary school my friends and I would play "Super-heroes" or "Greek Gods" (which are essentially super-heroes, if you think about it) over the lunch hour. After May of 1977, however, our lunch-time role-playing became *Star Wars* oriented. *Star Wars* made a big impact on me and further cemented my love for all thing science-fiction, especially anything with cool-looking monsters or aliens in them. I used to write and draw homemade comic books with my friend Tony, and I think that really was the first step (in effect, storyboarding) towards making movies. My dad had a Super 8mm film camera, and I was inspired by stop-motion animation work he did with his brother. After moving to Oregon, I began making stop-motion shorts of my own and continued drawing comic books. Another favorite pastime was creating radio drama-type recordings with a tape recorder or two and some friends. I wrote and recorded many an outer-space adventure, another step towards making movies. At the end of high school I began making humorous shorts using a friend's video camera, and that eventually turned into making short video adventures with my dad's camera. Finally, years later, with my own camera, I embarked on my first video feature, *Dimension in Blood.* That learning experience was followed by more like *Monster in the Garage, Crimson Heather, Eyeball of Fear, Lust of the Vampire Hookers,* et cetera. And now I can't stop myself!

Influences/Aspirations: Who got me into moviemaking? My dad, who made cool stop-motion animation Super 8mm movies; Don Dohler, because I saw his movie *The Alien Factor* on television and thought, "Hey, I can do that!"; Roger Corman, because he put out cool B-movies with the three B's in them: beasts, babes and blood; Fred Olen Ray, for the same three B's as well as his speed and creativity; and my friends Rob and John.

Film School: I took some film history in college, but I haven't attended a real film school. But I can see the value of it, to a certain extent. I have a BFA in Art and Graphic design from a state university. They taught a lot of theory, but not as much practical work. Luckily, I was working in my field while in school, and that freelancing allowed me to learn the practical stuff. In a similar vein I think it is good to have a grasp of film theory, film history, the "right way" to do things. On the other hand, this needs to be balanced with the practical aspect of what to do when your actress flakes out on you, your location suddenly is unavailable or your effects are failing. In other words, you can learn what to do when things go smoothly, but you need to know what to do when things don't go smoothly. A lot of that is learned by doing. I asked a friend of mine, a film school graduate, about going to film school and he said, "You get out of it what you put into it."

How important is your script? Sometimes it is important. Sometimes it is not. I have done projects where the shooting started before the script was finished. I have done projects where I completed the script before shooting and stuck to it very well. I have done projects where the script

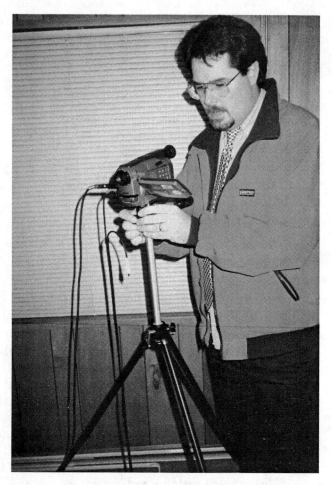

Joe Sherlock, in character for *Lust of the Vampire Hookers*, adjusts the camera before stepping into the shot.

was nearly cast aside and ad-libbing and on-the-spot rewrites did the job. Obviously it is easiest to shoot from a finished, detailed script. But sometimes, especially in the no-budget video arena, the caliber of your acting talent precludes you from getting performances matching your script to the letter. Sometimes all you can do is coax someone to improvise the basic idea of the scene. Sometimes it is better to just feed a few lines and let someone run with it. Whatever you need to do to get the performance you want is what you have to do.

What equipment do you use and why? I started using just a Panasonic VHS camera. It was a pretty souped up one, with several cool effects built in that I exploited as best I could. Later, I got a Sony Hi-8 camera with a bunch of bells and whistles, and that's what I'm using now. I got a nice external microphone that I can jack into the camera, and we rigged up a boom out of an old broom handle. I've got a few lights, as well as an audio mixing board I used to monitor sound, plus sometimes we'll hook up a television so that we can see the big picture of what we're shooting. Sometimes that set-up takes too long to move around (and it's hard to have all that stuff out in the middle of the woods or some remote location), so sometimes it's just me and the camera.

Cost/Budget/Funding: Well, I usually describe my stuff as "no-budget video," and it's true. I have never started a movie with a budget. I'll spend money over the course of a production but it's just bits and pieces of spare money or money I make from selling my movies or fanzines or comics collection. Thus far I have not paid any actors—most are just friends and everyone seems to have a good time anyway, so it's not a big deal. Sometimes I'll buy lunch or drinks or something, but most of the money is spent on tapes, lights, props and other equipment. I've bought a lot of Karo syrup for fake blood in my day, plus meat for gore scenes, cigars, plastic vampire teeth, boxes and boxes of pudding, newspapers, magazines, paint, booze, KY jelly, and all kinds of other incidental props and supplies.

Now, when it comes to duplicating the tape, that's another story. Again, the money comes from selling other stuff: movies, comics, fanzines, et cetera. I usually have to save up for a while to get a bunch of tapes copied. Add to that the cost of the clamshell cases, color inserts and flyers and mailings to help sell them, and there ends up being quite a few ex-

penses. After you give free copies to the folks who helped you the most and sent out copies to the magazines in hopes of getting reviewed, there's not a ton of money to be made. But, then again, it's mostly to have a good time and able to sit back and watch something you've created.

How did you cast your actors? Thus far, all of the actors I've worked with have been friends or friends of friends. I've actually never had a casting call. I've just asked people if they wanted to be in my movies and most say yes. It is amazing what people will do if you just ask them. I have had people covered in pudding, have fake blood spit all over them, dance around half naked, jump into streams, nearly sweat to death under rubber monster masks, shower in front of me, scream, yell, smoke, drink, make out, drive like maniacs, et cetera. And, for the most part, they loved it and would do it again! In some cases I've worked with people several times and wrote the parts specifically for them. I try to match the part to the person, but sometimes you just have to take the best you can get.

Film's Music: Most of the music in my movies is composed and performed by myself. I have an old drum set, a few keyboards and a borrowed mixing board, and with enough of the right cables and adapters, have been able to record three- and four-track songs myself. I've also been in a few garage bands and have used old tapes of that for some music as well as … one of my friend's bands. Everyone is cool with it as long as I mention the band in the credits. Besides, people usually get a kick out of hearing our old band in one of our new movies.

How long did it take to make your first film? All told, from the first night of shooting until the premiere party, it took over a year to make my first movie. The majority of the shooting was done over the course of two months but then a few scenes and pick-up shots spread out over several months. Then there was the music—all composed by me to a rough cut of the movie. Then there was editing and other post-production stuff. Remember, I do all this in my spare time, while holding down a full-time job! My second movie took longer, since my son was born in the middle of what turned out to be a two-year project!

What is your experience with dealing with special effects at this level? Most of my projects have special effects in them. For the most part I'm doing science fiction and horror movies, so there's always a need for some blood to spill or a spaceship to whiz by. A lot of my effects are in-camera effects—forced perspective, whip-pans, special-effects makeup, et cetera. My old VHS camera actually had a chroma-key feature so I was able to mess around with some blue-screen type of effects. My friend Rob Merickel often does the makeup effects for my movies. He has done everything from full body makeup for alien slave dancers to a severed head to a staked vampire to a simple bruise or scratch on the face.

Production tips for the novice filmmaker: Just do it. Use what you have around you. My movies are built around the people I know and what I know they will do, the locations I have access to, the various props I have or can get and what I am capable of shooting with my equipment. I say just keep making stuff and have fun with it. Whether it's Super 8 film or video, stop motion animation or live action, just be creative and create something. Making movies is fun, but it is also hard and frustrating and annoying and a pain in the butt, so you've got to have a real passion (or addiction) to it to keep it up.

How important is publicity for your films? Pretty important since the sales on one tape will hopefully support the costs of the next. At least that's how I hope it happens one of these days. I mean, eventually I'll run out of comics and stuff to sell! I feel I've been pretty lucky. I was doing a B-movie Fanzine, *Dr. Squid*, before I started making video movies, and that had gotten some attention in a few magazines and Web sites. I used those connections to get some coverage for the movies I was making. I've been able to get coverage in several of the low-budget B-movie magazines like *Draculina*, *Scan* and *Alternative Cinema*, as well as other fanzines. A lot of that coverage resulted in correspondence with other video moviemakers rather than actual sales, but any press is good press.

I also maintain a mailing list for my *Dr. Squid* zine and send out mailings promoting my movies several times a year.

The big thing that has helped is putting up a *Dr. Squid* website featuring my movies. For $14.95 a month I have full-color pictures, descriptions, interviews, related articles and ordering info that is all about (and only about) me and my movies, and it can be seen by people all over the world. I maintain a very large email list through my *Dr. Squid* site and use that as another avenue to promote my movies.

I've taken my tapes and a TV and VCR to several comic book shows in the area. I've only sold a few tapes but it is a crack up to sit behind the table and watch people do double takes as vampires bite victims or alien slaves bellydance on screen.

One of the actresses I work with a lot, Shannon, started up her own fanclub. She has a newsletter and a website through which she sells autographed photos and—you guessed it—my movies.

Distribution: Right now I'm primarily self-distributing by selling through

Zeon and Victoria Stone (on couch) act for director/cameraman Joe Sherlock on the set of *Lust of the Vampire Hookers*. Sound assistants are Dale Wilson and Rob Merickel (waving at camera).

my mailings and the website. I have sold tapes wholesale to some guys who are cult-movie distributors. In addition, I've got deals with Draculina Cine and Salt City Home Video. Draculina Cine basically markets my tape, and when they get an order they dub a copy from a master for that order and I get a couple of bucks. Salt City lists my movie on their Web site, and when they get an order they buy it from me at a wholesale discount. So far it has been cool to have the control of owning the rights to the movies and all, but it sure is a pain in the butt sometimes to have to pay for duplication, store the things, do all the promotion, mailing, et cetera. I'd like to get to the point where some of my movies are signed over to a distributor for several years and they can deal with the hassles of selling

and filling orders and just send me a check.

What's in store for the future? I've shot a lot of stuff. I have no less than four projects sitting around in some stage or another waiting to be finished. I've got a little bit of shooting left on them but mostly I just need to edit, edit, edit and get these things done. I still enjoy the science fiction and horror stuff, so I see myself sticking to it for some time. I'd like to start doing full-length features. Most of what I have done has been compiled onto anthology or double-feature tapes. I'd like to continue to make cool movies that are fun, maybe make some money, maybe work with some of the other video moviemakers I've met around the country and just see where it goes!

Anything you want to add? I've read my share of how-to books on making movies. They all basically boil down to the same thing: Just start making something. Robert Rodriguez said that you need to stop saying you want to be a filmmaker—you need to start saying you *are* a filmmaker, and then you will be one.

Ronnie Sortor

DIRECTOR/PRODUCER

Filmography: Sinyster (1995) Director, Editor, Co-producer, Co-Writer, Actor; *Living a Zombie Dream* (1996) Editor, Co-producer, Sound Effects Editor, Actor; *Ravage* (1996) Director, Writer, Editor, Co-Producer, Sound Effects Editor; *Vile 21* (1997) Actor; *Kitty Killers* (1998) Editor, Co-Producer, Sound Effects Editor, Actor

Influences/Aspirations: Once, I answered a question like this with, "Thirty years of watching bad movies made me say, 'Goddamn it, I can do better than that!'" But that's not really it at all. A lifetime of watching great movies made me want to contribute to the world of cinema. Being entertained and inspired. Being moved and inspired. Being moved and enlightened by what I consider the highest art form did it for me.

Influences include all the great filmmakers, of course, but also horror literature and to some extent, comic books. I love storytelling and I love the way movies lend themselves to the very act of experimental narrative. You see it, you hear it, and when a movie is successful—i.e., prop-erly made—you feel it. That's why you and I keep returning to our favorites again and again. We have an emotional investment there. It's like repeating a favorite song, only it takes a bit longer.

Aspirations? I'd like to make a living as a filmmaker. To actually profit from it. But that concept is just a dream and not what really motivates me. I'm compelled by that need for artistic catharsis. I have stories of my own to tell. Have images in my head screaming to be purged. Woe to the madman who chooses the movie screen to be his canvas. Personally, no other medium could adequately convey the experience I want to create. Art and aesthetics are a celebration of life. Movies are naturally the ultimate celebration of expression and imagination. Participating in this craft that I love so much is also a way for me to leave a personal legacy.

Film School: If you can afford film school you can afford to make your own film independently. If you don't care enough about film to learn it on your own as a personal obsession, as a dream, then

Killer and soon-to-be victim in Ronnie Sortor's *Ravage*.

fuck you. Go on to film school and make music videos.

Script: Sure, the script is important, but it's only a guidebook, a sketch. The essential element is the director's vision. The director already has the movie in his head, and there's only so much that the script can illustrate. The director should either write his own script or rewrite the shooting script if it's a collaboration. Every project I've worked on has made some script deviation and it's always been the right choice. I welcome criticism and suggestions from the cast and crew. Keep an open mind but know your material.

Format: [I use] S-VHS, for obvious reasons.

Budget: I'm not sure that I have any new advice here. Just heed the voices of experience. They'll tell you to get as much for free as you can, to keep locations to a minimum, et cetera, et cetera. People freak out when I tell them that *Ravage* cost less than $10,000. There was no budget when shooting started. We pooled our resources. My collaborators and best friends, Todd

Reynolds and Frank Alexander, were dedicated to the project enough to dig into their own deep pockets. Todd actually spent more on *Ravage* than I did. Frank bought all the special effects supplies and neither of them complained. They believed in the project and they had faith in me to pull it off. The best advice I can give is to ensure a good supportive team.

Actors: Once again, we pooled our resources. All of us act. (Some are indeed better than others, but what do you expect? Laurence Olivier?) Our city, Springfield, Missouri, isn't very big, so the talent pool is quite limited. But I've learned that it's really a blessing in disguise for many reasons. Actors with any ambition at all are inclined to do low-budget projects like ours because there's no other opportunity for exposure. The filmmaking industry is nonexistent here, you see. My actors are friends and acquaintances of friends, and people who have contacted us out of curiosity.

How long does it take to complete a film? Approximately one year from script to final cut. Three months writing and pre-production, four months of shooting (remember, this is micro-budget weekend and evening shooting), two months for post-production (editing and sound work for what amounted to a rough cut). And three more months of re-mixing, re-scoring and re-cutting multiple times due to technical limitations and errors.

Publicity: Again, I've no unique point to make here. Those that handle publicity with more control over their own product can educate you. You make a film to be

Director Ronnie Sortor fires away in *Kitty Killers*.

seen, and it won't' be seen if no one knows about it.

Distribution: I'm one of the few who does not distribute my own pictures. I don't have the experience, resources or money to do it. It seems like every

Lei Renniks in *Ravage*.

moviemaker gets screwed by a distributor at one time or another, myself included. But I have to wonder about the validity of [some filmmakers'] claims, because they're still around. Most of them are still churning out titles and claiming that they're not making money. However, their complaints seem to lack earnestness. Either they're lying or they're a hell of a lot more resilient than I am. I'm fucking broke and fucking burned out.

Music: If you've seen my movies, you've heard Clark Carter's music. He's the greatest! My advice, if you don't do your own scores, is to get demo music from all the musicians you can. Then see who will be willing to work closely with you. If you want to just use existing tracks from your local garage band, then go ahead. Just don't expect your movie not to suck

with it. Think of the score as the performance of your lead actor. You have to work with the musician to get the proper mood. The right emotion. You're not done directing after the cameras stop rolling.

Special Effects: Depends on the scope of your project. Getting an effects man is very much like casting an actor. It happens in pre-production. Special effects artists who know their craft, [who] read *Fangoria*, who are eager to work on low-budget projects. When you put the word out that a movie is being made, they might find you. Just be prepared to buy their supplies.

Todd Reynold (standing) and Dan Rowland in *Kitty Killers*, directed by Ronnie Sortor.

Mark Sparks

DIRECTOR

Filmography: Dark Reign 187 (1997); *Rage 187* (1999)

Mark has produced two feature length films, *Dark Reign 187* and *Rage 187*. (The 187 is police code for a homicide.) *Dark Reign 187* is a nonstop thrill ride when Marcus (M.A. Sparks) and best friend Dre (Andre Walker) decide to make a violent gang film in the hopes of making some quick money. But first they must convince others (Maurice Sparks and Darrick Pugh'O) to join in on their ploy. The tables turn when the wanna-be filmmakers are caught up in a series of real life murders during a packed house party. Each murder is more brutal than the last. Everyone is a suspect as each guest is systematically stalked and slain. The suspense builds to an explosive finale that pits predator against prey. Only time will reveal the true killer. Or will it?

Their next film, *Rage 187* is about a series of gruesome murders that plague a suburban African-American community. Each murder is increasingly violent and local authorities are at a loss to solve the crimes. Their only clues, and hope for stopping the murders, are the video tapes left with the bodies as the killer videotapes his vicious spree. Everyone is a suspect. A whodunit.

Biography: I was born in Denver, Colorado, and graduated from the University of Colorado in 1996. I started my filmmaking career in college. I had taken a number of screenwriting, film theory and film production classes when I decided to start making films. I had written a screenplay called *Dark Reign. Dark Reign* was a love story between an inner-city kid who was in love with the daughter of a Korean grocery store owner, with a twist of action. Needless to say, the *Dark Reign 187* that graces video store shelves is a far cry from the original screenplay. I basically rented a camera and hired a crew of two and shot the film. After that grueling learning experience we shot *Rage* about six months later, which was a little easier to maintain. Both movies were shot in under eight days for budgets I dare not mention.

Influences: I think my biggest influence in film comes from the narrative abilities

Director Mark Sparks on the set of *Rage 197*.

of earlier generations' directors, such as Oscar Micheaux, Alfred Hitchcock, John Ford, et cetera. However, there are a number of contemporary directors that are very influential for me as well: Spike Lee, Carl Franklin, Steven Spielberg, Kevin Smith and Robert Rodriguez.

While in college I went to an advanced screening of *Bad Boys*, featuring Martin Lawrence and Will Smith. I was blown away by the camera movement and the lighting. It was at that moment I was sure I wanted to direct films. Prior to that I had a real keen interest in making films but never pursued it. I had purchased *Making Movies, How to Make Your Own Feature for 10,000 or Less, Rebel Without a Crew* and *Feature Filmmaking at Used Car Prices*, but never went after it until I saw *Bad Boys*. That was the turning point for me. After that, I engulfed myself in the world of independent films. Those I was most influenced by were *She's Gotta Have It, Boomerang, El Mariachi, Do the Right Thing, Chasing Amy, Laws of Gravity, Boyz in the Hood* and just about anything by Hitchcock.

I would say Spike Lee was the biggest influence for me in terms of becoming a filmmaker. Spike conveyed the "if I can do it, you can do it" image that many aspiring African-American filmmakers needed. Spike was a role model when so few were present.

Film School: I think if you're going to attend a top school such as UCLA, USC or NYU, then the risks are probably worth it because of the experience of the staff and the industry contacts at your disposal. However, there are many that graduate from these very schools that never actually make it in the film industry. So my take is that film school is beneficial, but not crucial to a career in film. Talent and determination are far better determinants on who will succeed.

Script: You can have the best crew in the world, the most high-tech equipment and an eight-figure budget, but without a good script or story to tell you're not going to have a successful or entertaining film.

Format: Initially I used Betacam video because it's what I could afford to get the movie in the can. Thus, my choice was from a financial standpoint as opposed to an aesthetic reason. I am excited about the progress being made in digital video, but until it rivals 35mm film, my choice would be film for acquisition.

Budget/Funding: This is a funny area for me because when I was trying to raise funds for *Dark Reign 187*, only one investor could be found after months of looking (and that investment was only a small fraction of the budget). We tried everything but couldn't raise any funds. So what did we do? We shot video with the funds we had. Well, that gave us some credibility as far as being filmmakers was concerned, and we started receiving unsolicited investments for our follow up feature, *Rage*.

How did you cast your actors? We ran several advertisements in the local papers and had actors come in for cold readings. I also scouted local theaters and arts schools.

Music: For *Rage I* I wanted a definite street/hip-hop feel for the music score, so I solicited for material from local artists with already completed songs to put on a movie soundtrack. For the other half of the songs we created them so that they are in line with the film's theme.

How long did it take to shoot your first feature? It took about ten days with an on again, off again shooting schedule.

Special Effects: I think special effects are the most challenging part of the film because many of them are done in the post-production phase. However, despite the challenge of utilizing special effects I think they are crucial in heightening the value of your film. This is especially true for digital special effects.

Format/Equipment: Shoot video to learn your craft. Experiment visually to develop a style of shooting that is unique to yourself and story. Also have good storyboards and make sure every shot is planned prior to you calling action the first day of production. Lastly, just shoot your film with what you have: 16mm, Digital Video, 8mm, S-VHS—it doesn't really matter. Just shoot it and show you can tell a good story.

Publicity: We found out the hard way that publicity is crucial. You may have the next Oscar Award Winner but if nobody knows about it, then you're SOL (Shit Out of Luck). So be sure to work every angle of publicity you can. Try to find a unique perspective to highlight something about your production such as Robert Rodriguez and the $8000 *El Mariachi* story, Robert Townsend and the "I financed my film with credit cards" story. Just find something and exploit every possible angle.

Distribution: Distribution is a tricky area because as a low budget filmmaker with little media or festival exposure there is very little leverage for you to use when negotiating with a distributor. My advice is to make the best film you can, get some exposure via film festivals to create heat on your project, hold industry screenings with executives from various distributors present at the same screening, and finally, get a good attorney to analyze the deal.

Video box art for *Dark Reign 187*. Copyright SEG Productions.

Future Projects: For us, we are trying to move up to the next level of filmmaking. We need a bigger canvas to paint on. But you have to crawl before you can walk (and we're still crawling). We would like to tell bigger and more elaborate special-effects type stories, and to do so we're going to need the bigger budget to go along with it. So for us right now, we are chasing every possible funding source we can find to help us move to that next level.

Dave Sterling

PRODUCER

Biography: I'm originally from Chicago and have been in the entertainment business for 18 years, since 1980. I started out at mobile DJing at parties and I advanced to night clubs, doing stage lighting and videotaping bands. I also had a tele-shopping show on television in college. I'm a Columbia College (Chicago) graduate and moved to L.A in '88. I started making movies around 1990. I began to have in interest in films starting in '84, when I watched a lot of cable TV and read every issue of *Fangoria* Magazine that came out. One of the books I read at that time, which really got me interested in filmmaking, was a book called *Splatter Movies* by John McCarty. In it he talked about how people are making low-budget movies for $7,000. I thought, "I don't think I'm going to be making *Star Wars*, but I think I can get $7,000 together to do something." I still look at McCarty's book from time to time.

So I started making movies in '90, '91. That first movie was *Things*, which I hear people still rent (most recently re-released in 1997 through *Dead Alive*). It was first released through Vista Street, who do all the *Witchcraft* movies. I've since developed a real strong relationship with Jerry Pfeiffer at Vista Street. Pfeiffer believed in me, got me going (*Urban Combat*, *Human Prey*). He doesn't give me a lot of money to make movies, but with whatever amount he gave me I could nonetheless make a movie. And I'm also indebted to Dennis Devine and Steve Jarvis, who worked on *Things*.

I still don't think I'll be doing *Star Wars*, but my budgets are increasing.

What is your goal as an independent producer? I always wanted to be at the top in any field I was in. I look at Roger Corman, the king of B-movies, as my model. I'm not saying my movies are in his class, but he's one of the smartest and prolific people in the film business. He's done a thousand films that he was associated with. My goal is to be the top in the low-budget field, and I feel I'm in that class. I'd also like to make a good living at what I'm doing. Getting paid for your work is important because it shows that people are interested in what you are doing. Filmmaking is about people seeing your stuff.

179

Box art for *Things*, produced by David Sterling.

I couldn't even get a job in a mail room! I think schooling, in general, rounds you out and makes you think about things. I recommend that you should get a four-year degree in something, not necessarily filmmaking. Getting a degree helps you to learn how to complete something because filmmaking is all about completing hard tasks. Sometimes the less money you have, the less chance you have to complete it. I don't necessarily think going to film school is going to make you a filmmaker, but it might teach you how to think about things in general. Not everyone who wants to be a filmmaker can be. It's such a small business. People think it's large, but it is really tiny compared to any other business. And I'm not against someone learning another trade. Sometimes I wish I was better in management. You have to do filmmaking because you love it. You have to have talent, too, and have to go figure it out. A lot of people I know want to be Spielberg but simply have no talent to be Spielberg.

If nobody sees your movie, you make no money, and so what's the point? My goal is to be the top of my field and make a good amount of money doing it.

How important do you think film school is? I never went to film school. I wanted to be in the record business. But after I graduated from college I found out

What equipment and format do you use and why? I use all formats. I've shot stuff in 16mm, Super-VHS, Betacam and digital video. The format depends on the project, the amount of money, and what equipment is available. I still like to shoot on S-VHS, particularly if I do a really cheap low-budget movie—for $40 in tape stock you can go out and shoot something. [It's] easy to work with,

Publicity shot for *Camp Blood 2*, produced by David Sterling.

and you can always bump it up to a higher format, like Betacam. If you look at *Human Prey*, for example, all the outside shots look beautiful. *Public Enemy*, done for Wildcat Entertainment, was shot on digital video with the Panasonic EZ-1, and that looked okay. If you shoot digital, use a Sony, the best camera. Also, linear tape editing is not a bad way to edit. If you're editing on your computer and it crashes, all your work is gone.

How do you cast your movies? I put an add in *Dramalogue*. I then get the actor's pictures, close my eyes and start poking ... just kidding. In L.A. you put an add for actors, saying you can't pay, and you'll still get two hundred to four hundred professional actors, people with all kinds of credits, sending you headshots and resumes. So you start there and you set up a casting call. It's amazing what kind of people you can get out there. You get

different type of actors than you do in Pennsylvania.

Why do you produce instead of direct? I know I can direct, I've been on enough movies. But I don't think I'm a *good* director. I don't have the patience. I'm better putting people together, getting everyone lined up. An overseer. A lot of people want to do everything. You have to know what you're good at. I could probably direct better than most of the young video directors out there because I know what I need to sell a picture. If you're doing horror—I don't care how bad the story is—you have to put in tits and blood. Even if it's crappy you're still delivering the goods to the audience. After all, how great can it be on video? I've done some great stuff but they're not masterpieces. In producing I can have two, three, four projects going at the same time. I've produced two films in a week before—I don't think I'd do that

The killer is not clowning around in *Camp Blood 2*. **Produced by Dave Sterling.**

directing, and the second part in '92 with Jay Woelfel, who is probably the best director I've worked with so far. He did *Beyond Dream's Door*. That film still holds up. And because this was my first film, I didn't know too much about filmmaking then, didn't have all the resources that I have now. It's not unusual for your first film. I was working on other stuff during that time—in '93, *Human Prey*, and we did *Flesh Merchant* in '92. And I was working on another movie. Good thing about *Things* is that it got me going.

How important do you think special effects are at this level? I think when you do your first horror film special effects can really save your picture. What can you give your audience making a horror film? You're not making *Good Will Hunting*. A lot of new directors, they make these horror films and try to philosophize. Viewers want to see nude bodies and gore—eyeballs popping, fingers being ripped off, arms coming out of sockets, cool stuff like that. And monsters are really important. If you want to do good on your first film, then put a monster in it. *Things* was great because we had two monsters in it. People liked that. And by putting the monsters on the box art you have something with which to hook your audience. That's why I think the *Things* film still holds up, after all these years. I think people know me best for that particular film.

again, but I liked it. I look at it how I think Roger Corman would. And I think he's a good director when he wants to be. But he was a better producer than anything.

When you're in the film or movie business you have to make a lot of product. A lot of people can make one film and that's it. And I wonder what happens to them. For example, whatever happened to the people who did *Killer Nerds*? I mean, what are you going to do in Ohio making movies? Even Bookwalter (*Ozone*, *Sandman*) got out of Ohio, at least temporarily.

How long did it take you to produce the first film? It took a long time. It was an anthology and we did it in parts. We shot the first part in '91 with Dennis Devine

How important is the script? You have to give actors something to say. It's important, but keep it simple. Take a film that you like—such as *Friday the 13th*—and just copy it. Do a *Slumber Party Massacre* type of movie. And then on your next movie or the one after that, you can make it more original.

I like seeing a synopsis first, rather than reading the whole script. I did a movie for Vista Street called *Crystal's Diary*, sort of like an *Emmanuelle* film, but without nudity. But we had girls running around in underwear for five days, great music, and the script.

What is the best production tip you could give to the beginning filmmaker? You need other people to make a film. Surround yourself with people who have made films already. If you want to direct the movie, then work with a cameraman who can help you direct, find actors who have acted in real stuff—commercials, TV, et cetera. You don't have to pay them. Get a young special-effects guy who will do it for cost—he'll do a better job than a more established guy and will go the extra mile. Also, I never do this because I'm really cheap—but make sure you have food around. I'm so cheap people hate working with me, but after the film is done they love me—I'm their best friend. Because we got the movie done. If you have the will and some talent, you can get people to work on a movie.

Don't have a twenty-day shooting schedule. I can do stuff in five days because I've been doing this for a while. Give yourself eight days. Spread it out. Don't burn yourself out. Do it on weekends. Be serious but have fun with it, too.

What about publicity? It's very important to get your name out there. You need someone who likes to do that stuff for you, or count on your distributor to get you publicized.

It's cool when people say, "Hey, I rented your movie."

What about distribution? You have to find a distributor you trust, because they do a lot of the legwork in "getting the movie out there." But you have to decide what you want to do—be a producer, or a director or a distributor. It's hard to do all

Publicity photograph for *Iron Thunder*, starring Richard Hatch (middle).

Video box art for *Iron Thunder*, starring Richard Hatch, produced by David Sterling.

Unseen, in 16mm. And there's *Iron Thunder*, starring Richard Hatch of *Battlestar Galactica*. It's a tank movie.

How did you get access to a tank? We built a wooden tank and miniatures. We've been in post [production] for months. It's coming out good. *Unseen* is a *Predator* type movie. And then I have a few other, bigger things, plus a lot of small video features. *Executive Action* with James Tucker, a no-budget type thing, and I'm doing a four day vampire film, directed by Tim Sullivan, called *Vampire Femmes*. *Things 3* was completed in '98, directed by Ron Ford. I also did *Scream Queen* with Linnea Quigley, and we rented a house for $300 for three days. I worked with Brad Sikes, who did a film called *The Pack*. It's not too bad, and he's a young kid. On the strength of that movie I funded *Scream Queen*. Linnea is real nice to deal with and is trying to get her career back on track.

Hopefully I'll have some real big stuff coming up. I like everything I'm doing, though, for the time being. I have a few knock-off *Re-Animator* scripts being written, because I wanted to do my own version, called *Re-Animation*. With the two different scripts I might make two different movies. I still need my big break, though.

three things. Whatever you put into your movie, you have to put the same amount into distributing it if you distribute yourself. Vista Street is my main distributor. Many times I'm a producer for hire. Or I sell the movie outright, like I did with *Evil Sister*, *Urban Combat*, and *Crystal's Diary*.

What's in store for the future? I have a movie we're shooting on film, called the

Anything else? If you don't live in California, New York is the next best place to be for filmmaking.

Be smart about it. If you're going to

make a film, then complete it. If you start something you have to network. Don't think you're going to be Spielberg, because you aren't. But you have to meet other people doing what you're doing. Find people who will help you. If you met Spielberg, what are you going to say to him, "Hey, I'm this kid and I do these shot-on-video movies?" So what. But if you meet someone else on your level, you can pool your resources together and make a movie. Keeps things going. It's important to make a lot of this stuff because you're not going to get rich. You have to make a lot of product, a lot of sandwiches, so to speak.

Mike Strain, Jr.

DIRECTOR

Filmography: Vile 21 (1999)

Biography: Mike Strain, Jr., started doing special-makeup effects at the age of twelve, having been influenced by his father and his love of art. As he created basic appliances and rubber slip masks, he discovered effects artist Tom Savini, and Strain's work was greatly influenced by him. From the mid–1980s to the early 1990s Mike created effects for numerous commercials, plays, live shows, conventions and television shows such as *Rescue 911* and *America's Most Wanted*. In 1994 he was hired to create the special effects for his first motion picture (shot on video) *Sinyster*. Effects work for this movie was featured in issue number 164 of *Fangoria* Magazine. In 1995 he directed his first feature, *Vile 21*, a sci-fi action movie, which is currently available on home video. He is staying busy with his next feature, *Mystery Monsters and Magic*, a trilogy of short films to scare the soul, as well as on his book *Special Effects*, a how-to look at special effects of the first six movies he has worked on.

Influences: Special effects are where my heart will always be. My influences [include], of course, Tom Savini, [but also] Rick Baker, Stan Winston and many others. There are two very special make up artists who went above and beyond to help me. The first is F/X godfather Dick Smith. I found his phone number and address where he lived in New York and we corresponded regularly. I remember the first time I called him and asked his advice about doing mustaches on actors for an underwater scene. He told me, "Okay, get a pencil and paper," and he just let it fly. I loved every minute of it. The other big F/X artist was David Ayres, who was based out of Arizona (he did some of the aliens for *Close Encounters* and the giant ants in *Empire of the Ants*). I would call him every couple of weeks and talk or send letters. He'd write back with a Far Side comic copied to the top of it.

As far as directors who have influenced me, I'd say Lucas, Coppola, Michael Bay, and John Woo. There are so many greats. But my biggest influence is my father. He supported me in everything I did and just let me be. This is for him!

An explosive moment on Mike Strain's *Vile 21.*

Film School: I didn't go to film school. If you can afford it and you really want to go, then go for it. But remember, outside of film school there is a lot more to learn. What you learn in any kind of school is someone else's point of view. Go after what you feel is in your heart.

Script: A script is the most important part of the project. You can't take a bunch of effects shots and make a movie. They are simply one of many tools used to enhance the script.

Equipment/Format: Right now I shoot on Hi-8 video with a Canon L-2 camera. I've had good luck with it. But like most movie makers, I would prefer using film. The ultimate goal is 35mm. But for right now Hi-8 is the format I'm working in until I can hone in on a style and have a better sense of direction of where my career is going. Video is cheap and film is

not. I know there's people out there who say, "You're wasting your time with video," but I say, "What have you done?" Without investors or a budget, shooting on video is a smart alternative.

Music: Music is important to set the mood. Music can make or break a movie.

How long did it take you to make your first feature? It's taken almost eight years to finish my first feature. When we first started shooting *Vile 21* we were taping with an old three-quarter-inch video camera that had a separate deck. Two weeks into the project, half of the people involved quit, because it was too violent or because it was raining or because they had parties to go to or something else important. So *Vile* went on hiatus for five years, until the time was right. In the fall of 1995 shooting was wrapped, but I had no way to edit it because some of the people

Director/makeup-effects artist Mike Strain touches up actor on *Vile 21*.

involved didn't want to work on it any-more. One day I realized I had to give up one dream to have another, so I sold a classic car I owned, a 1950 Mercury Coupe (like the one Stallone drove in the movie *Cobra*), and bought the editing equipment I needed to finish the movie. No matter how long it takes, stick with it—and find a cheap edit suite!

Actors: For the first few movies I worked on or directed the actors were friends, family and people who wanted to act. For my latest project, *Mystery Monsters and Magic*, I have joined forces with a local talent agency, Ozarks Talent Resources, and together we are out to find good actors to fill each role. Doug Moody runs OTR, and being an actor himself, he knows the importance of finding real talent. All the actors work on a voluntary basis, except for those portraying the lead characters. We have a basic percentage

agreement that says that when the project makes money, they will be compensated for their time and effort. Remember, bad actors can sink a project. Take your time and check out the local guilds and talent agencies and advertise.

Publicity: Publicity is an important tool to generate interest but the best publicity is word-of-mouth. Send copies of the movie out to magazines to get reviewed and perhaps they will be interested in doing an article on your project.

Budget/Cost/Funding: All the money spent on my own features has come out of me and my wife's pockets, from working our measly little forty-hour-a-week jobs. Investors are probably a great help to achieve more or to get more done. Pitch your ideas to doctors, lawyers and dentists. They may not be interested, but you won't know if you don't try it.

Special Effects: A lot of people can create special effects, but not all special effects can be created by all people. If you're making a movie and you need specific effects and someone says, "I can do that," ask to see pictures of their work as well as a resume. A good effects artist will be humble, not cocky. If you want to make a movie and have limited funds, find a good effects artist who loves what he's doing, and hopefully he'll help keep your budget down by what he knows. Extremely low-budget movies don't have pipe-ramp car rolls, explosions or full body burns, but I was able to get these in my first movie. Stuntman Steve Kelly, who portrays Jon the Bum in *Vile 21*, is a good friend of mine and helped out with those effects. Being an effects artist helped me to decide how and where to spend money on the effects I needed.

Distribution: Most filmmakers will try to find someone to distribute their movie rather than try selling it themselves, like I did. Get lists of distributors from books and magazines and send copies of the movie out to them to see if they are interested.

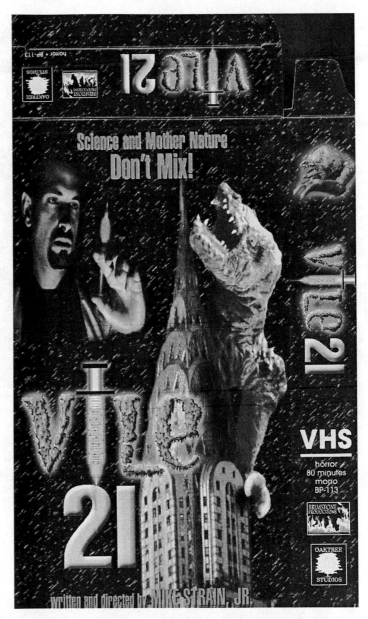

Video box art for *Vile 21*. Artwork designed by Lloyd Lathrop, copyright 1998 Brimstone Productions.

What's in store for the future? I'm working on a few more video projects such as *Until Sunrise*, a vampire story, and *Sarah's Secret*, which is written by my wife, Lacramioara.

If you really want to make a movie or work on a movie, then figure out a way to do it. Buy a camera. Donate your time on someone else's film project and learn. Don't let your talents go to waste. Make-up artist Dick Smith said that to be in this business you truly have to be a little crazy. If you do have the bug, then welcome to the world of the insane, the world of the moviemaker!

Director Mike Strain with a third hand on *Vile 21*.

Tips for the novice filmmaker: Make sure that you record good sound on the set. It's too hard to dub dialogue later on. Also, watch your back. If you get any suc- cess, someone will always try to take it away. And have fun with your first film. You can always be serious later.

Paul Talbot

DIRECTOR

Filmography: Campfire Tales (1991); *Freakshow* (1995); *Hellblock 13* (1998)

Biography: I was born on Friday the thirteenth in Salem, Massachusetts, so I was literally born to make horror movies. I moved to South Carolina when I was in junior high school, and I've lived down here ever since. I've produced and directed three horror anthologies which have been released on home videotape and cable television: *Campfire Tales*, *Freakshow* and *Hellblock 13*.

Influences/Aspirations: I've been interested in movies since I was born. It's the same story you hear from many filmmakers. I liked a lot of fantasy movies and shows when I was a little kid, like *Willy Wonka and the Chocolate Factory* and *H.R. Pufnstuf*. I was fortunate because the local TV stations showed a tremendous amount of movies. This was before VCRs. One station showed a double bill of A.I.P. horror movies every Saturday and another station showed a Universal classic every Sunday. Plus there was a local second-run theater that I could walk to, and I saw a double feature there every weekend. I could also walk to the library, and I checked out a vast amount of books on film history and filmmaking.

When I was in elementary school, my parents had a Super 8mm silent film camera. This was before the era of the video camcorder. I'd have kids come over after school and we'd shoot a little movie. Then I'd take it to the drug store for processing. It would be ready in a week, and we'd have a world premiere at school during the lunch break. It would cost $6 for a roll of film and $5 to process it, so a four-minute silent film would cost me $11. Now with camcorders, kids can buy a blank tape and shoot a sound feature for $2.99.

I kept making Super 8mm stuff throughout high school, eventually moving to sound. While in high school, I saw the movies that inspired me the most: *Night of the Living Dead*, *Carnival of Souls*, *Pink Flamingos*, *Last House on the Left*, and *Texas Chainsaw Massacre*. These movies were inspirations to me because they were very effective, but they were also obviously low-budget and crude on a technical level. I read articles on the making of those movies and I learned that these were all films made by people outside of the Hollywood system. And yet they were all distributed worldwide and became classics.

I studied media arts in college. In my senior year I took a 16mm film class. I made a short horror film with William Cooke, another student. When we graduated, we wrote a script for a horror anthology and included our existing short as one of the stories in our feature, *Campfire Tales*. We finished that movie in 1991 and made another feature, *Freakshow*. Then Cooke and I split up, and I recently made my third feature, *Hellblock 13*.

Film School: I have a bachelor's degree in media arts, but all of my production classes were worthless, and everything that I learned about filmmaking I learned on my own. I wasn't impressed by too many of my instructors. Most of them were idiots.

Having a degree does give me credibility in some circles, and I've received a number of grants that I never would have gotten if I didn't have a degree on my resume.

Being in college allowed me to get access to equipment, and I met other aspiring filmmakers who ended up helping on my shows. (Plus, I went to a lot of parties, met girls and had fun.)

I learned about filmmaking by watching a tremendous amount of movies and reading nonstop. It's amazing how much free knowledge is available to you at your local library. Most college courses are taught using books that you could have borrowed for free.

Script: The scripts for my three features were all designed to fit the budgets that we had. We wrote the scripts around specific locations that we knew we could get. Sometimes, we even wrote parts for specific actors that we knew.

When you're writing a script for a horror movie, you really need to dig into the dark corners of your mind and pull out your creepiest ideas. When you're watching a horror movie, you should get the sense that the creators are disturbed. Some of the sickest and most perverse horror movies were made in the 20s and 30s like *The Unknown*, *The Island of Lost Souls*, *The Black Cat* and *Kongo*.

Format: My three features have been shot on 16mm film. All post-production (i.e., editing, sound mixing) for *Campfire Tales* was also done on 16mm film, so we ended up with a film answer print.

On *Freakshow* we transferred the film negative and DAT tapes directly to Betacam SP and did all of the post-production on analog videotape.

For *Hellblock 13*, post-production was done on an Avid system.

I shoot my interiors with Kodak 7293 and exteriors with 7245. These stocks are my favorite and turn out the sharpest low-grain 16mm images. Kodak is introducing new stocks all the time. I didn't always use these particular stocks. Aesthetically, I prefer raw, semi-grainy images, but my movies have to look as sharp as possible if they are to have any chance of getting into the ever-shrinking TV and video markets.

All three of my features have been shot using an Aaton LTR 54 and an Arriflex BL. We used to record sound on a Nagra but now our recordist uses a DAT recorder.

Renting a non-linear (such as Avid) editing suite is expensive, but the editing process moves much quicker when you edit digitally. So ultimately you're getting a better product for less money.

Budget: Well, money is everything. Money is all that you need to make a movie. It's as simple as that. The biggest error I made in my youth was not major-

Shannon Michelle Parsons and monster in *Freakshow*, directed by Paul Talbot. Courtesy Crimson Productions.

ing in business in college. Once you have the money, everything else (actors, crew, locations, equipment) comes easily.

For my first movie, most of the budget came from my own pocket and co-director William Cooke. We also got some money from some local grant organizations. Grants are great because it's free money that you don't have to pay back. On the other hand, filling out a grant application is worse than writing a term paper and it takes months before you get a yes or no, and more months before you finally get your check. Plus, most grant organizations have had to fold, anyway.

For *Freakshow*, my second movie, the money came from proceeds from *Campfire Tales*, my own pocket, and private investors who invested in the film through a limited partnership.

For *Hellblock 13*, co-producer Jeff Miller and myself set up another limited partnership and raised the money through investors. An official limited partnership has to be set up through a lawyer in your state before you can start asking people for checks. We put together a prospectus that described the financial arrangements and explained the film. We handed these out to potential investors along with a demo tape that contained scenes that had already been shot.

Finding investors is one of the most frustrating aspects of filmmaking. You meet an astounding amount of bullshitters who claim that they want to invest.

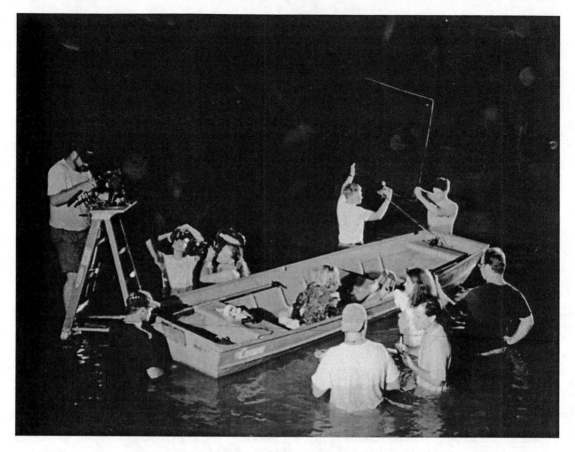

The crew of *Hellblock 13* spend a wet night on the set.

But after months of being strung along, and never getting a check, you realize that their true motive was to fuck actresses or get you to read a shitty script that they wrote. Of course, if you have a track record and have some successful projects behind you, it gets a little easier to find investors.

One important thing to remember is that most people with money tend to look fairly conservative, and they won't feel comfortable entrusting money to someone who doesn't look professional. You should always wear a coat and tie when you're meeting with an investor. Don't just tuck in your T-shirt.

When preparing a budget, you have to make sure to include everything, including the ice for the coolers. Make sure your production heads (costumers, effects,

sound recordists) understand that you need specific figures from them, not ball-park figures. Include a small contingency in the budget but realize that you cannot go over budget under any circumstances.

A low-budget movie set is no place to make decisions. When I'm shooting a movie, I have all of my shots meticulously planned out on paper. If you only have so many hours to shoot a scene, that's going to limit the amount of camera angles that you'll have time to light for.

I never have time or money to shoot any extra footage or alternate camera angles. All of the special effects should be storyboarded. The actors should be rehearsed beforehand so you're not wasting time on set discussing the characters. The gaffer and the sound person should visit each set prior to the shooting to see any problems with electricity or extraneous noise. You should try to think of everything that could possibly go wrong and plan a solution.

And never forget to include the costs of coffee and Gatorade when preparing a budget.

Actors: I usually try to use actors that I've worked with before. Most of the actors in my region usually don't have much camera acting experience. Their acting experience is limited to theater—acting for the stage isn't the same as acting for a camera.

To save time and money, I already have my movies edited on paper before I shoot, so I only shoot the camera angles that I know I'll use. I never shoot master shots or extensive coverage. This is confusing for the actors because the lines of dialogue and the blocking of the action is shot completely out of order. It's a very mechanical type of acting so I like to work with actors who already understand this weird method.

When you're making a low-budget movie, most of your actors won't have much experience, so it's important that you cast actors who physically fit the part. I usually don't have big casting calls. I just use my instincts and cast people that seem right to me.

Music: Well, you find your composers just like you find your actors and your crew, by networking. Nowadays, it's getting cheaper for serious musicians to have studios in their homes. The musicians that I've used have all had their own equipment in their homes. I've used several different composers on all three of my features. Whenever I'd meet a musician, I'd ask them to make me a sample tape of horror-themed music. I was very pleased with the score for *Hellblock 13*.

How long did it take to make the movies? *Campfire Tales* took four years to make, *Freakshow* took two years and *Hellblock* was done in a year. I should be able to make my next movie in a week. My movies have taken a long time to make because of the time it took to raise money and having to work around the schedules of the cast and crew.

Special Effects: The guy who does my special make-up and effects is Michael R. Smith. We started working together in high school. A large portion of my films' budgets go to the effects supplies. Most of the supplies have to be shipped from out of state.

The effects and the make-ups in the script are always based on what Smith knows that he can pull off and create within our budget.

In *Hellblock 13*, there's a scene where a spirit comes out of a dead girl's body. This effect was done with computer graphics in the post studio. Computer effects are getting cheaper and more accessible to low-budget moviemakers. But you have to be real careful because they can look cheesy.

Advice: Well, making a movie is a massive undertaking, and you just need to make sure that it's what you really want to do before you start to make one. It's important that you surround yourself with a group of people who will give support to you and your project.

Publicity: I grew up collecting movie posters and stills, so I've always understood how important promotional materials are. People aren't going to rent a movie unless they like the photos that are on the box.

Have somebody on the set take color slides and black-and-white prints. After you've shot an important set-up, get the

Left to right: Director of photography Paul Cornwell, actress Debbie Rochon and director Paul Talbot rehearse a shot from *Hellblock 13*.

movie camera out of the way and replace it with the still camera. Recreate all of the important scenes for the still camera. Make sure that you get plenty of different stills of your special effects, your "name" actors and the attractive female actresses.

Many low-budget moviemakers don't bother to shoot stills when they're in production. When it comes time to promote their movie, they have to track down the actors again to shoot some stills. Or they take stills directly off a video screen. I've

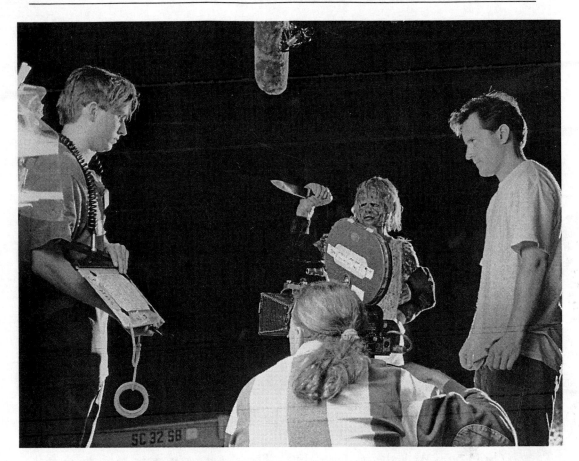

Left to right: Grip Wade Sellers, assistant cameraman Larry Lowe, actress Jessica Dunning, and director Paul Talbot rehearse a shot from *Hellblock 13*.

heard of some filmmakers who lost their distribution deal because they couldn't provide good promotional materials.

Choose your best black and white still, have it mass-produced as an 8 × 10 and include it with every press kit that you send out.

You should be careful about overhyping your movies and getting too much advance publicity. Many moviemakers get press releases published before they even shoot anything. Most of these movies never get shot or completed. You'll lose your credibility and people will know you as the Boy Who Cried Movie.

Distribution: I think aspiring moviemakers should spend time in prison before they make their first movie. That way they'll know what it's like to be raped and they won't be surprised the first time they deal with a distributor. Most distributors are so sleazy that I need to spray my phone with Lysol after I talk with them.

It's very important that you hire an experienced entertainment attorney to review your distribution contracts. Signing a contract without an attorney is like walking into a bad neighborhood without a gun.

One type of creep you must beware of are those that try to pass themselves off as "producers' representatives" or "sales agents." Most of these guys have a few addresses of distributors and claim to have connections but end up wasting the filmmaker's time and tie up [his] movie.

Left to right: Amy R. Swaim, Roxanne, Debbie Rochon and Jennifer Peluso star in the thriller *Hellblock 13* **from Crimson/Millman Productions.**

The Future: Well, the market right now for independents is pretty soft, to put it mildly. I'm going to carefully pay attention to what's going to happen to the marketplace.

But the independent film scene is always going to be the way it's always been. Those that really want to make movies, and not just talk about it, will do what it takes to get it done.

You just keep beating your head against the door and hope that the door cracks open before your head does.

Walking Between the Raindrops

After having made several direct-to-video horror features, I decided to try something different in 1998. I knew I was doing all I could do on the home video market, in terms of self-distributing my tapes and "getting them out there," and I would continue to participate in it. But I have never explored the film festival avenue and the prospect of getting a distributor to buy the film outright and take it off my hands.

I knew that horror and science-fiction films had a low likelihood of getting accepted (well, this was before *Pi* and *Blair Witch*), and I had been wanting to do a drama for some time. I was looking forward to the day when there would be no special effects, no knives and no blood. It would make a production so much easier, I thought. And, in part, I was right.

First, I had to decide on a script, which was simple because I had a specific script in mind. This was *Walking Between the Raindrops*, a relationship drama written by Evan Jacobs of Fountain Valley, California. He had shot a Hi-8mm video in '96 for about $200, which was crude, yet showed the power of the script. In fact,

it was one of the best-written films I'd seen in years, and it stuck in my mind as something that deserved a higher budget.

Synopsis

Stanley meets Sarah at a party. They begin casually spending time together as they juggle their responsibilities as college students in Southern California. Stanley is a film major and Sarah a psychology major. Their different career interests and values make for some very interesting and humorous conversations, which not only effectively highlight their unique personalities but also some of the major differences between men and women.

Told from Stanley's point of view, the movie steadily draws the viewer into Stanley's world and his developing feelings toward Sarah. As Stanley and Sarah spend more and more time together, Stanley discovers that he has fallen in love with her.

Through Stanley's internal dialogues and his comic, down-to-earth conversations with his friends Chris and John, the viewer becomes privy to Stanley's anxiety

Top: Actor-screenwriter Evan Jacobs as Stanley in *Walking Between the Raindrops*. *Bottom:* Evan Jacobs (left) and Rachel Stolte meet at a party in *Walking Between the Raindrops*.

about telling Sarah of his feelings and in turn finding out whether she feels the same toward him. Stanley's situation is further complicated, and his emotions sent into a tailspin, when he unexpectedly meets Sarah's boyfriend, Pete, at a party.

Although devastated at first, Stanley maintains his relationship with Sarah and continues to hope that his feelings are reciprocated. Stanley grows even closer to Sarah after she reluctantly shares with him the problems in her relationship with Pete. Shortly thereafter, when Sarah informs Stanley that she has broken up with Pete, he makes the decision to confess his love to her.

The two make plans to meet at a party. Stanley decides that this is finally the evening to tell Sarah of his true feelings. So, with a bouquet of flowers in hand, Stanley arrives at the party and goes looking for Sarah. However, to his great surprise, he finds Sarah flirting, laughing and thoroughly engrossed in a conversation with his best friend, John.

Dejected and crushed, Stanley quickly leaves the party and throws his flowers onto the pavement before driving away. In a voice over, Stanley explains his actions. He states that although some people may believe him hasty, he sensed something in their interaction that led him to realize that Sarah would never feel toward him

the way he wanted her to. They were just good friends and nothing more.

My wife Audrey's interest in production had been rekindled (she was a film/video major at University of Michigan), and after seeing Evan's first version of the movie, thought it would be a great project to do together, with a slightly higher budget. And the more we thought about it the more we were eager to do it.

First, I contacted Evan via the fax machine and proposed what I was willing to do, which was basically re-do the entire movie with as much of the same cast as we could get. He would get paid a flat fee for the script and then a set percentage if the movie ever made any money. Of course, he'd also be starring in it, as the part of Stanley could be played by no one but Evan. He would also get his credit as writer and production manager, as he'd have to get some logistical things organized before we went out there. Both my wife and I would produce and edit the project, and I would direct and shoot the movie. Audrey would take care of the sound, as well.

Evan was not only agreeable to what we proposed but extremely eager. During the next month or so he sent me a copy of the script, we figured out the shooting schedule, which would be several months

Left: **Stanley talks to his friend Sarah in** *Walking Between the Raindrops.* *Right:* **Rachel Stolte as Sarah in** *Walking Between the Raindrops.*

away, in June '98, and he figured out the logistics of location and getting the actors. All the actors except one returned to re-perform their roles.

As I could not be in California, it was extremely helpful that Evan was so familiar with the project. We faxed shooting schedules back and forth, and within another month or so had it pretty well figured out with what scenes we were shooting and when and where. Audrey and I booked our flight to LAX, made reservations at our hotel, located several miles from Evan's house, and prepared as much as we were able. A week and a half before the flight, I shipped the majority of the production equipment—lights, grip equipment, tape stock, boom pole, cables, et cetera—to Evan and made sure that he received all this before we arrived. I carried the digital camera on the plane.

Several hours after arriving at the hotel, we shot all the "talking to the camera" scenes with Evan, in our hotel room, shooting him against a plain white wall. These were the character's confessional scenes. This was the first time I met Evan in person, and we hit it off. Evan came with his friend, Mike Hartsfield, who proved invaluable as our production assistant and "everything assistant" during the week.

Compared to shooting a horror or science fiction film working on *Walking Between the Raindrops* was relatively easy. There was a great deal of work involved, but so much was done in pre-production that Audrey, Evan and I were able to minimize any potential problems. The cast, mostly Evan's friends, were perfect for the roles because he had them in mind when he first wrote the script—and he had worked with them on some of his other micro-budget projects. They were Mike Vogelsang (nicknamed "Popeye"), Chris

Lohman, and Rachel Stolte as Sarah. Erin Lander, Mike's girlfriend, portrayed Erin, Sarah's friend. Although the only people who had previously acted were Rachel and Erin, they were probably the most professional group of actors I've worked with. They knew all their lines, were on time and had good suggestions for the characters. Absolutely no attitude.

There were some surprises, though. Chris Lohman, who had been in the previous, black-and-white version of *Walking Between the Raindrops*, had lost 150 pounds, so he was no longer "the fat guy" in the movie, which changed the dynamic of the friends a bit, and when Rachel appeared on set I was surprised that she was a redhead. Then, there was Evan disappearing. Sometimes after shooting one of the scenes, when I'd have to readjust the lights or change tapes for the next shot, Evan would be gone. I'd be saying, "Evan—Evan?" and when there was no reply I'd have to send one of the other actors to go and find him. At the time I was thinking he thought I needed more time to set up the next scene but found out later that he was a bit nervous about the shoot and wanted to concentrate on the acting, not worry about the other stuff. So he was disappearing to mellow out for a few minutes. But it still drove me a little crazy that you'd call for him and he wouldn't answer. It was at the end of the shoot that he revealed he was deaf in one of his ears—and that was probably the reason for the lack of response!

We adhered 95 percent to the shooting schedule. The only day we lagged behind was during a night scene when it was very windy and we couldn't get rid of the wind sound from the microphone, even with an extra windscreen. So we had to shoot that scene the following night. There was also one night when we were shooting

Opposite: **Poster artwork for** *Walking Between the Raindrops.* **Courtesy Anhedenia Films.**

Walking Between the Raindrops

a scene in a large parking lot and someone's car horn or car alarm got stuck—and we kept on hearing this loud siren noise every few minutes, which drove me nuts. We had to wait for the noise to go away, shoot as much as we could in order to get good sound, and then wait while the noise went off again. That particular scene took a little longer than I planned on and was extremely irritating to get through. But we got all the coverage, and I knew it would edit together well.

Locations were shot in the actor's houses, and the scenes where Stanley is talking to Sarah in the car were shot in Evan's driveway, simply for the reason of being able to run extension cords from his house out to the production lights. These car scenes were supposed to take place in a variety of locations but because only the actors were lit, the background so dark, it didn't matter where we shot this. An establishing shot in the edited movie makes it clear where they are supposed to be.

One night we shot in the parking lot of a movie theater (Evan knew the owner), which worked out well. We were able to run an extension cord inside and get some power for our two lights. After the shoot, the owner insisted we show our footage on one of the movie screens since he had a video projector. I wanted to keep on schedule because we had several more hours of work to do that night, but everyone was so excited about this and the owner so insistent that I reluctantly agreed. I wasn't very excited, because it was raw footage and I didn't need to see it again so soon. I wanted to move on.

There was also one day where we were shooting some B-roll footage for a flashback sequence, and the restaurant was very reluctant to let us videotape there, even though Evan had cleared the location months before. The scene involved Stanley and his friends buying falafels and Stanley having a bad reaction to the food. Not only did the restaurant open an hour

later than they told us—the soonest they could make falafels was in an hour or so. So, rather than wait, I had Evan go to a nearby grocery store and buy some food to make some pseudo-falafels for them to eat in the scene. This took about a half-hour. When I was shooting the scene, all the actors kept making faces and seemed very reluctant to put the falafels in their mouths. I found out that Evan didn't buy lettuce to put in the pita bread—but cabbage, and it was really bitter! No wonder they didn't want to eat them. I guess it added realism to the scene, though.

At the end of the eight days, we had shot 13 hours of footage, which was a decent shooting ratio for a movie that would be 85–90 minutes.

To add a different perspective on the low-budget, guerrilla filmmaking approach we took while shooting *Walking Between the Raindrops*, here is Evan Jacobs' perspective, taken from the diary he kept during the production. I did not read this until six months after we were done with the film.

Evan Jacobs' *Walking Between the Raindrops* Diary

In 1993 I wrote a script entitled *Walking Between the Raindrops*. In 1995 I made the film on 8mm video, and it was edited on a SVHS player. As you can guess, the quality wasn't the best, but the story of a guy who is in love with a girl seemed to strike a chord with some people. I was given the address of a New York filmmaker by the name of Kevin Lindenmuth, and I figured the best way to help myself (and the film) would be to contact as many people as I could who had also made films themselves. Kevin really liked the film, and we started a friendship as basically pen pals.

I continued to make films on my own and even tried doing some projects with

Kevin, but for one reason or another things just didn't pan out. We kept on talking over letters, and Kevin was very helpful in directing me to publications and distributors for my films.

In the midst of pre-production on my most ambitious endeavor, *Shustermann Levine: A Boxing Fable*, I received a fax from Kevin. In it he said that he wanted to re-do *Walking Between the Raindrops*. He would shoot it digitally and then blow it up to 16mm film. After that, he wanted to enter it into film festivals and sell it to a larger distributor. Oh, yeah—he wanted to pay for everything. I thought about it for about a half of a second and faxed him back with a resounding "Yes!"

Now, remember, Kevin and I have never met. We've talked on the phone once, and anything else has been through faxes and the mail. Now we were going to make a movie with a 3,000-mile gap between us (I'm from Orange County, California, and he's in New York City). Obviously, we talked more leading up to the shoot, but we'd never actually met. The following journal chronicles the eight-day shoot which began the day Kevin and his wife Audrey flew out from New York.

6-8-98

Well, today is the first day of the *Walking Between the Raindrops* re-do. I honestly think it is going to be awesome. I feel so prepared, but at the same time I don't. I guess that that is good, because it leaves room for the magic to happen. Kevin was due in at 1:30 this afternoon, which would mean that he's been here for an hour. No word from him, but I'm not too worried. I feel that this week will be filled with many ups and downs, but that it will be a great and a growing experience, nonetheless. I honestly feel that the cast and everyone else is as prepared as they can be, and I feel that I am also. I just need

to keep on my toes, as does everyone else. Well, I'm gonna watch *Badlands* or write. I don't want to do too much. As dumb as that may sound I am going to give this everything I have. I am also pleased that I did everything I could do, in terms of rehearsals, props and locations. Well, to quote my boy Steven Soderbergh, "I heard it was bad luck to start a shoot on Monday. Fug dat shit." Yup, my sentiments exactly.

Later that night...

Well, it's 11:38 P.M. and the film is underway. Finally met Kevin in person and his wife Audrey, and I must say that they're good people. Kevin has a really awesome low-budget set up, and Hartsfield (my partner) and I are learning all the time. We did all of the Stanley confessional scenes and voice-overs in a little under four hours, and I'm pretty drained emotionally. I am so excited about this. I feel like I shouldn't relax, because then something will go wrong—that's a dumb attitude to have. I need to remain positive and upbeat, and believe that all will go well. Kevin seems to know what he wants as a director, and I am trying to give the best performance that I possibly can. I look forward to making a great movie, and I really believe that if I give everything that I have to this, then so will everyone else. I'm too used to being in charge of the camera—and everything else. I think that I really need to continue to work hard and give this project everything I have. Everything.

6-10-98

Well, another day and everything went awesome. For some reason I've felt sick to my stomach everyday this week, and I just got things prepared for the party scene. I got my clothes prepared, the food for the scene, and I come to find out that Kevin is going to be reimbursing me for

Rachel Stolte and Evan Jacobs.

everything. We shoot some scenes of me just driving in the car. I'm supposed to be thinking about Sarah (the girl that my character, Stanley, is in love with). By doing this we made sure that we have nothing to shoot on the 16th. It felt good and we also did the mailbox scene, where Stanley sends Sarah the letter that his buddies tell him not to send. We hang out with Kevin and Audrey and try to troubleshoot some possible problems, but everything looks fine. I've decided not to worry about any problems I can't control. I'll just have to roll with the punches. I rehearse with Rachel before we go to the party scene, and I really feel that she and I are doing a good job. All of this rehearsal is paramount to really giving a good performance. It's not just saying lines, it's talking like a human being. How did I ever make a movie and not rehearse? Yet

again an example of how I learn things too late. I really feel that I'll make my perfect, flawless film—when I'm 150 years old and have 150 flawed films behind me.

For the party scene almost everyone that I called showed up as an extra, and I'm really happy that my friends can all be a part of the things I'm doing. I realize that Kevin shoots party scenes differently than I do, and I must say that at first I was thinking that there's no way that we're gonna get anything done. Then, I realize that that's Kevin's department. He knows that we are up against time constraints. A director looks for certain things in performances, and they put the movie together while they're shooting. I then just submit myself to the process, and I feel that must be my attitude throughout the entire production.

Later that night...

I pick up my car from Rachel's house, and we shoot the scenes of Stanley driving before he gets to the party, and the scenes after he leaves the party. I bring us to Beach Boulevard, which I have used many times when I need a lit car. It works. I have come home so I can rest up for the shoot tomorrow. We're gonna get this done—you bet your ass we will!

6-11-98

Well, we went to Los Feliz, and Rachel's phone scenes came off pretty cool. I guess that my Dad's cell phone is messed up, because Rachel couldn't hear me when I tried to call her on it. I just did the scenes without the phone, and Kevin will dub in the sounds of the phone ringing when he edits the movie. Other than that, we ate at Mexico City (Kevin paid), and then we hit it back to Orange County.

Later that night...

Rachel and I rehearsed between lighting setups and I really feel like I did well in all of the scenes. I honestly think that Rachel and I are giving the performances that we need to give. I really feel that if Kevin can edit this together with the same charm that the first one had and at the same time draw on how good the performances are this time, we may have something here. I really do.

We fell behind schedule, though. Rachel forgot her pajamas for the store scene and the wind was making the scene where Rachel throws me to the ground inaudible. We've decided to shoot that scene on Sunday. It looks like there's a lot of exterior scenes that Kevin wants, so I'm just going to resubmit myself to the process and we'll get all the exterior scenes he needs. I want to send him back and I want to end this knowing that I did everything

Stanley (Evan Jacobs, right) asks the advice of his friends (Chris Lohman, left, and Mike Vogelsang) about Sarah.

that I possibly could to make this movie come off.

I am going to clean my cat's litter box and then go to sleep.

6-11-98

I didn't mention how Kevin is shooting the car scenes. We're getting exterior shots of the food places, people's houses, stores. And we're actually shooting all the car scenes in the driveway of my parents' house. Kevin is lighting everything, using gels and whatnot to give it a certain kind of night-time look. And the sound is good. This is Kevin's equipment, and he is obviously capable enough to use it and get the best performance out of it. I feel bad about that because I don't want to give off the impression that "It's not my job; I'm just acting; this was his idea"—but at the same time I don't want to seem like I doubt what he's doing. I'm just going to continue doing the best that I possibly can.

6-12-99

Well, Kevin called me and we went out and shot some exterior shots. I'm not too sure what he's going to be using it all for, but I have a feeling that it's a good idea that he's doing this. We then discuss Sunday's shoot and it appears that it'll go until two or three in the morning. I hope that everyone involved can remain composed and cool, and that we get everything done. We will because we don't have a choice. Looks like we're also going to be filming some at Captain Blood's (a movie theater). I called Todd, the owner, to see if we could run an extension cord out of the theater and he said it was fine. His exact words were: "Anything you need." Cool.

Later that night...

Well, last time we did the scenes at Lohman's house we started at 9:30 P.M. and only did shots from one angle. We got done at two or three in the morning. This time we got started at 7:30 P.M. and got done at 11:00 P.M. It was awesome. Popeye, Lohman, and I are doing a rad job. We seem to all have a really good sense of the material, and everything just seems to be going just as it should. Kevin then shot the opening monologue scenes and that was about it. I wasn't there for that and I think that's good. I've distanced myself from Kevin in a lot of these director's areas because I'm not the director. That's his deal. I'm going to do my deal for this movie and maybe that'll show on the film. Hopefully I'll look comfortable and good on camera. I didn't watch Popeye and Lohman do their monologues, and haven't watched Kevin film every shot, because I don't need to. This is his. Some say I'm dumb for giving this up, but I feel that in the long run it will benefit me and Anhedenia to let him have *Walking Between the Raindrops*. I have so much inside of me. So much I want to say. This is just the tip of the iceberg.

6-12-99

Well, it's about 4:35 P.M. and I'm feeling weird. Every day this week, except for Wednesday, I've woken up and felt sick. I need to start sleeping in my bed again. I've been staying on the couch and watching TV. I've done almost nothing today. Oh, have I mentioned that today is our day off? I've got a long weekend prepared.

6-13-99

Well, I get up and shower and get to work. I buy some props (juice and strawberry milk), and I prepare my clothes for the scenes. I get a call from Kevin because I'm four minutes late, and I'm wondering if today his moodiness is going to boil over. Not that he's been that moody, but I think that I have a way of bringing out the anger in people. Why this is I'm not sure, but I think it may stem from the fact that I'll ask someone any question on my mind. It's not a way to win friends but what is, nowadays?

We get over to Popeye's and scenes just flow. I've left everything in Kevin's hands. I am really trying to make people sympathize and root for Stanley. I don't want to seem pathetic or brooding but like a guy in love. That's it. I'm trying to have energy in every scene and on top of that I'm trying to be open and receptive to everyone's comments and questions about why I'm doing what I'm doing with the character. I give everything I have in the shower scene. We then film Stanley getting into bed after he finds out that Sarah has a boyfriend. Shooting during the day, we made the room look like night by using a blue gel. Kevin also made it look darker with the camera.

Later that night...

Kevin, Audrey, Popeye and Erin come over, and we shoot the scene in the car where Stanley first tells John about Sarah. We use a large flashlight to get some light in the cab of Popeye's truck, strapping it to the seat with a seatbelt. We shoot the scene with Kevin and Audrey in the back of the truck. Then we shoot some exterior scenes of Stanley and John driving, and we also get a shot of Stanley and John walking to John's truck. I'm not sure if it's supposed to begin the movie or if it's supposed to be used after the party scene where Stanley first meets Sarah. I trust that Kevin knows what he wants to get, and that he'll be able to really put this together well when he edits it. We record the sound for the driving scene in Popeye's truck and on the stairs in my house so that Kevin will have good, audible dialogue when he cuts this scene together.

I am realizing that coverage is everything and that you can make a movie with anything as long as you have the key points to say what you want to say. I look forward to working on my scripts and putting together my next film. I feel that I have learned how to make a better film with minimal lights, a boom microphone and a great script. If you have dedicated people then you can make a great movie. Fuck this "If it's not on film, it's not real" attitude. You use what you have and that's that. To not make a movie because it's not on film is crap because then what is the movie, anyway? The fallacy is thinking that film legitimizes your movie. Your belief in the project legitimizes your movie. If you don't believe in it, then you don't have anything.

6-14-98

Well, we had a long day and night, but I honestly don't feel that tired. We met at about 10:30 A.M. and went right into Jack's Tobacco shop and shot all of the liquor store scenes. Even though it was a tobacco shop, I think that we can pass it for a liquor store. We shot the scenes and just took our time. Jack, the owner, even appears briefly in the film when I walk up with the avocado that reminds Stanley of Sarah. I feel really good about it. We then shot the mailman and retrieving-the-letter scenes out in front of Rachel's house. It went really well, and her parents were very cooperative. We're basically sticking to what's in the script, and I'm very happy about that.

We went back to my house, had a lunch break and proceeded to film the scenes that are supposed to be in front of Sarah's house in front of my house. We needed some light in the back of the car to shine on Popeye. Kevin built a reflector out of the tops of two cardboard boxes and we taped aluminum foil on top of it. It

Stanley and Sarah take a stroll.

worked out great. We did the scenes a bunch of times from a couple of different angles and then we were done. It started to get hot, but we needed to film the scenes that take place in the car on the way over to Sarah's and after we get the letter. We also film some scenes of us just driving, and I'm sweating like a pig because it is so damn hot. Kevin gets an exterior shot of the freeway so that he can have more coverage, and I'm just trying not to die because of the heat. We get done around 3:00 P.M. and decide to meet up at 7:30 P.M. At this point I go back to Jack's to thank him for letting us use his place. He isn't there, but I thank the person who has been in the store all the times I've gone there.

I go home, clean up, hang out in my boxer shorts with the guys and basically just relax. I watch *Party Girl*, starring Parker Posey. Rachel calls and she's stressing out and tells me we need to start at 8:00 P.M.

Later that night…

Kevin comes over and we go over to Rachel's house and bust out scenes in the kitchen and of us playing Scrabble and watching television. These are all voiceover scenes, so it all goes quickly. Rachel and I both get into our pajamas and we head over to the Seven-Eleven. It goes well, and Kevin even gets to film inside. We change clothes at Rachel's, hit it over to Captain Blood's Theater, and Todd treats us like kings. We shoot the scene where Rachel and Stanley begin to talk about her boyfriend Pete and it goes well. Todd then lets us inside and we watch the scene we just shot on the big screen. On the same screen that million-dollar movies play, *Walking Between the Raindrops* was shown. The script that I wrote two pages a night on when I was twenty was tonight in a theater, being played by someone who wants to help us. We go back to my house and film three di-

alogue scenes, and I feel really great about how we're doing this. Rachel and I are sort of boxing each other and then we argue and she pushes me to the ground and gets on top of me. It's a really good scene, and we give our all for the rest of the shots. We then shoot some exterior shots of Rachel and me in the car in the empty parking lot, and then we move over to the park area and shoot some more. Rachel is done with all her scenes.

6-15-98

The guys come over and we go over to Frostee Freeze. Now, I'm not one to talk shit, especially when someone is doing me a favor, but they (the people at Frostee Freeze) told me that we could shoot there at around 10:30 A.M. So we show up at 10:00 A.M. and we knock, and they don't answer. Then the lady comes to the door and tells me that they don't open until 11:00 A.M. I remind her that we're filming a movie here (like we'd discussed months earlier), and she seems to remember that. We decide rather than paying her the money and wasting time for her to get falafels ready (which would take at least another hour) I go to the nearby store and buy some pitas, cabbage and tin foil. This should pass for falafels. I get back there, and this place is very unclean. There are ketchup and food stains on the trays and table! I'm getting the falafels ready and the owner tells me we have to get this done as soon as possible. I'm a little bothered by this. So we shoot the scenes that are pertinent to the story that I already told Rachel in the voiceovers. I feel that I did a good job of appearing grossed out by the falafel. Then I kicked it. The first few kicks were pretty pathetic, but on the third one I kicked the falafel all over the bushes. We decide that's a wrap.

6-16-98

I am very tired, so this will probably be short and sweet. This is the last day. We actually got done on the 15th, which has got to be a record of some sort if you consider the fact that we had Friday off as well.

Kevin, surprisingly, showed up late with Audrey, but we got to the Family Fun Center and cruised through the scene where Stanley and John talk to Chris about the video game. We just walked in and filmed the scene and it flew. Nobody said anything, and that was fine.

Then, we filmed the scene where Stanley runs into Amy and they talk, and he finds out that Sarah likes him "a lot." There's so much ambiguity in this script that it amazes me. We have a lot of sound problems because this woman had lost the keys to her van and she can't turn the damn alarm in her car off. What are you gonna do? We shoot the scene as many times as we can, sometimes with the alarm and sometimes without, then decide to go to another lot. I almost lose everyone because I drive too fast. But the light in this lot is different, and we decide we have to use the old one (for continuity's sake). We record just the sound of our scenes, just in case Kevin needs to use it (again, one of the many times that I am grateful not to have to edit this thing), and we go back and we film the scenes quickly. It feels weird because I have to act without an actor for a lot of this scene. Amy is with her boyfriend, but that's where the camera now is. So I'm just talking to Amy and the camera. The first take of it I think I did all right, but the second one I think I nailed it. That's it—we're done.

Later that night...

I go back to Kevin's hotel, and we talk about what each of us needs to do, in terms of getting music to him, release forms for the extras, and so forth. No worries. We talk a little bit about the festivals and the screenings, and Kevin seems to think that it will be ready by December. Is that the print or is that just the edited video version? Hey, that's his deal. I have *Schusterman Levine* and the 108 Documentary to finish and some scripts to rewrite. I have been working on this film stuff heavily for the past three years. I will not stop now. I'm just taking a break from actually making a film for a year. I am excited and I look forward to recharging my batteries, replenishing my mind, and making a living doing the thing I love. This is it, make no mistake where you are.

Finishing the Movie

Once Audrey and I flew back to New York City, we transferred all the digital tapes to Betacam and made three-fourth-inch window dubs for the rough cut edit. All the tapes were then logged according to the time code before we even started editing, deciding on paper what takes were good or not. This saved a bit of time. The entire rough-edit took a little over one month and then another two weeks to do the on-line Betacam edit.

Once the Betacam master was finished, we then sent it out to be transferred to 16mm film. Audrey and I had investigated this before we embarked on the project and decided the most economical way to do this was through a company here in New York City. They would transfer the video to film via a Kinescope, and we would have a 16mm negative with optical track, along with a print of the film (3 reels). We had several minutes of the film transferred first, to see the quality, and were extremely happy with how it looked. So, we then did the American thing and charged this to our credit cards, which was somewhere around $15,000, when all was said and done.

Although we were ultimately happy with the film transfer, getting the video transferred was a nightmare. It took a month after we submitted it before they even did the job—and when we saw the first film print there were some scratches on the film, not to mention audio problems. They said they would re-do the reel of the print; we wouldn't be charged for it. So, we took notes, deciding what scenes needed to be brightened or darkened, and they were then to make another print. Two weeks later we sat down to watch the "corrected print" in their screening room and were shocked to see that this print looked far worse than the first one we saw. We said so and they were insistent that they simply followed our notes in changing the exposure, et cetera. There was no arguing with them. Well, the first print was too dark in spots and the corrected print was too bright, so we decided to get a third print struck. Again, we sat down with one of their film guys and took notes on the exposures. Three weeks later we went to the screening room again to watch the third print, which looked better but still wasn't perfect. It was then that the projectionist admitted to us that he had the projector bulb turned on too high with the last showing, which meant all the over-brightness was caused by the projector, not the film itself. We had just spent another $1,500 on a third print and did not need to. We still had to pay for the print. Anyway, this last print had some scratches and problems on one of the reels (again), and they said they'd replace this for no charge, as that particular problem was their fault. This took another two weeks to get all the reels. So, the entire process of getting the movie transferred to film took from the end of August to the middle of October '98.

Then, to be able to show the film to festivals and submit it to distributors, we had to transfer this film print back to Betacam, which was another $1,200. In the midst of their transferring the film to video, one of the reels snapped, and they had to print up another film reel. This delayed the transfer for another two weeks.

Once everything was transferred and all the film and video paid for, I went to pick up all the material—and they did not want to give it to me. They said all the film was kept in their vault and that I'd have to go and fill out paperwork to get my film negative, which basically made this a day-long project. It should have taken an hour, at most. I have absolutely no idea why they made things so difficult. It wasn't like this was brain surgery.

Shooting and editing the movie was very smooth and enjoyable, and it really amazed me that this entire transferring process was such an unpleasant experience. I think I'm so used to doing the majority of work on a project and being in control of it that when I have to deal with an aspect of it that depends on other people—specifically people I feel I can't rely on—it drives me a little nuts. I was so happy when all the material was in my hands.

Walking Between the Raindrops turned out well. It was a small drama with interesting characters and some ultimate truths, perhaps one of my favorite movies I've worked on. We thought it was perfect for the film festival market.

We were wrong. The first festival that rejected it was Sundance—and this was followed by something like twenty others. It was really puzzling, because we had various showings of the movie here in the city (mostly in our apartment) and 99 percent of the people who saw it enjoyed it. It was a likeable movie.

The festival submissions went on for a year, about the same time we simultaneously sent out VHS screening cassettes to possible home video distributors. Around 150 screening cassettes went off to indi-

The New York City premiere of *Walking Between the Raindrops* **at the New York International Independent Film and Video Festival, 2000. Photograph by Audrey Geyer.**

Evan Jacobs (left) and co-actor Chris Lohman at the West Coast premiere of *Walking Between the Raindrops* at the Angelciti Film Festival in Las Vegas, 1999.

viduals and companies who expressed interest in seeing the movie. We only heard back from around 30 of these, some who said they liked it but it wasn't for them.

Finally, in October of '99, about a year after the movie was completed, a company called The Asylum said they really liked the movie and were interested in distributing it through Hollywood Video. They had recently worked out a deal with Hollywood to present them with new dramas, pictures by first-time directors. I told the guys at the Asylum that I had directed some other movies, but they said it was all right—those were horror movies and this is a drama. There won't be a problem, they said. They wanted the movie in Hollywood Video in January of 2000, so in December they faxed me the distribution contract, which stated that the movie was my first movie. There were some minor

things I wanted to have changed in the contract. Anyway, I email them back saying again that I had previously directed some movies and wanted to make sure this wasn't a problem. They then asked, "You're not listed on the Internet Movie Database, are you?" and I said, "Yeah, all my movies are." There response was, "This is a problem." Even though I had the contract in my hands they said they were now unable to take it.

On the one hand it was reassuring to know that a company had been so enthusiastic about the movie and had wanted it, yet it was frustrating because the film still wasn't out there on the home video market. The movie was shown at two festivals in the summer of 2000, Angelciti in Las Vegas and The New York Independent International Film & Video Festival, where I finally got to see it projected in a real theatre. The movie will eventually find its audience.

In the meantime, I had worked on finishing *Addicted to Murder 3: Blood Lust*, re-edited the movie *Vile 21*, which I dis-tributed, and directed and edited *Rage of the Werewolf*—all of this since *Walking Between the Raindrops* was completed in October of '98.

Theatrical Exhibition for Video Movies

By Tim Ritter

It's common knowledge that the independent exploitation video market killed the drive-in movie experience. And when shooting a feature on video (like S-VHS or Hi-8), moviemakers tend to think it's impossible to get their creation any kind of legitimate theatrical release. This is not so. If you have tenacity and a little bit of good luck on your side, you can get a shot-on-video movie some theatrical bookings in your area, and even at other select areas around the country if you really pursue it.

As the new millennium is upon us, digital video is offering even more possibilities than first anticipated for independent video makers. It's being embraced, for instance, by film giant George Lucas, who plans to shoot the last two *Star Wars* prequels on digital video! Then he plans to add his computer-generated special effects and transfer the whole thing to film. His plan also includes adding digital video

projectors to upscale theaters, who will play a digital video master of his creation! Once these are installed into theatrical auditoriums, independents can shoot directly on digital video and may even be able to get a limited upscale release like the big boys. This would be a huge step forward for the video moviemaker with a limited budget, who could then bypass the expensive video-to-film transfer and put all that money where it belongs: on the screen.

You might ask why you would want a smaller movie to play on the silver screen. The biggest thing a legitimate theatrical run (termed limited, regional or platform releases) will get you is more interest from video distributors when you release your flick on tape. When you mail them articles that include the theatrical booking info of your movie photocopied from real newspapers, it tends to make them take a closer look at your product. Also, with the new aforementioned digital

Tim Ritter is the director of such movies as Truth or Dare, Creep, Screaming for Sanity, Killing Spree, Dirty Cop *and* No Donut. *He was a contributor to my* Alien Agenda *series.*

Director/producer/writer Tim Ritter of Twisted Illusions, Inc., on the set of *Killing Spree.*

First of all, you have to have your movie finished, including your final sound mix. You've mastered it on digital video, Betacam SP, S-VHS or three-quarter-inch. Your poster art is ready, even if it's just the artwork for the front of your video boxes to come. Now you make a couple of half-inch VHS copies of your movie directly from your master tape. You are now ready for phase one.

Phase I

Get your local newspaper and check your area and the surrounding areas within at least a 90-mile radius. What you're looking for are second-run movie houses that charge only $2 a person and offer midnight movies on the weekend. You can also check out local theater chains that rent out their auditoriums, like some AMCs. Just call (or go in person) and chat with the manager. This is the more expensive way to go, having to pay a few hundred bucks to rent a place for a night and having to make the rental cost back as well as other costs. But some people have done this successfully.

The biggest thing you're looking for in your search is video projection capability. Video projectors are the monster machines that are very expensive but can project video images of any format (with the right deck connected) onto the silver screen. If you want to stay local, and nearby theaters don't have video projection, you can go to the hassle of renting a projection system from upscale rental outlets. Just check your Yellow Pages under **Video: Equipment Rental** and you'll usually find what you're looking for. Again, this route can get expensive.

For the no-budget moviemaker, it's better to find a theater that already has a

video cinemas it will become possible to have your work seen and reviewed by some of the more mainstream critics like Roger Ebert and Rex Reed. Your movie will be much more accessible.

With our company, Twisted Illusions Inc., Joel D. Wynkoop and I have released all our feature-length 16mm and shot-on-video (Betacam SP, three-quarter-inch, Hi-8mm and S-VHS) movies to the cinema. This includes *Truth or Dare?* (1986), *Killing Spree* (1990), *Lost Faith* (1992), *Wicked Games* (1993), *Creep* (1995) and *Screaming for Sanity* (1997).

Let me take you through the process step-by-step so you can see how to do this with your project in a successful, yet cost-efficient manner.

Opposite: **Theater billboard for the premiere of Tim Ritter's** *Screaming for Sanity.*

video projection system in place. As the technology expands and the prices of these systems become more affordable, I've found that many independent dollar theaters do indeed have such systems in place! Generally, they play *Rocky Horror Picture Show* and local business stuff on their equipment, and they're usually set up to play half-inch VHS video. So you simply isolate the theaters nearest you that have video projection and make that appointment to see the owner or manager.

Tell them you'd like to have your shot-on-video feature play theatrically and that you'll do all the promoting if they simply run your movie for a week or even just a weekend. Their part will include local paper listings (which they do anyway for all movies playing) and also putting your movie title up there on the big marquee. Beyond that, the rest is up to you.

With most of our movies, Joel Wynkoop would go in and make the deal with the theater owner. Then I'd discuss how much money we get out of the deal. Usually it's the standard distributor/exhibitor cut, which yields anywhere between 30 and 35 percent of the net profits. The house gets the rest. Plus the theater gets 100 percent of their snack bar sales. If you have videos, T-shirts or posters ready to sell, it's always wise to get them behind that snack bar for sales during your theatrical run. Selling those items, you call the shots on percentage cuts, giving the theater a smaller cut from your merchandise.

Phase II

This would be local publicity. Promote yourself and your project to any and all newspapers in the surrounding areas. Hit radio stations, colleges, public access television, local news stations and any-

Joel D. Wynkoop stands in front of the poster of *Screaming for Sanity.*

thing else you can think of, too. Go after it all—leave no stone unturned. You will inevitably get some negative reactions and doors slammed in your face, but generally the local press will love what you're doing and give you ample time for news coverage. Make sure you book your movie well in advance at the theater, giving ample time for news coverage. This is the hype stage, where you pull out all stops. Make your publicity stand out. You have to make people want to see your movie in this stage. Highlight controversial subject matter, problems you had shooting your movie, problems you had raising the funds, and any shooting anecdotes. Get cast members interviews with the press.

Sell yourself and the project. The key is promotion, and namely getting that hyped-up word-of-mouth out there. Create the buzz, that sensation, about your movie.

With one of our movies we made the mistake of booking the flick with only a week's notice to press, and it wasn't enough time to get the wheels of publicity going. Generally, give yourself at least four to six weeks to organize all the pre-publicity and to start that buzz on the local news. Be sure always to give the dates, times, and location of your movie's premiere night in all publicity.

Phase III

Another selling tool is movie posters for the theater. Hey, I know it can be expensive for big color posters, but some kind of poster is imperative for theatrical play. The color 18 × 24-inch posters for *Killing Spree* cost thousands of dollars. But it's not the same if your movie isn't represented by a one-sheet right next to the big-budgeted competition, right? Also, walk-up customers need to have an idea what to expect from your offering, and you need something for them to stare at as they wait in line to choose a flick. It's the spirit of showmanship that pushes you forward in this phase. Ad campaigns, taglines and artwork are all your responsibility.

The inexpensive answer goes back to having either your front video box art ready or even some sort of mini-poster drawn up professionally. If you're good with your home computer and desktop publishing, this problem is already solved.

Your original artwork will more than likely be small, either video-box size or standard typing-paper size. Head for the Yellow Pages again to find either a building contractor or blueprint printing shop's phone numbers. The best places are ones that make copies of blueprints for town developing, apartments or houses. If you don't see what you're looking for, call your local city hall and simply ask where they have large blueprints copied. They'll give you the info. Then just head over to the blueprint place with your artwork in hand.

When you get there, show them your artwork and tell them what you want—the provided artwork blown up to a decent size on inexpensive paper. They'll be able to tell you how big they can make it and whether they have to send it off to be copied or have the facilities to blow it up in-house. They'll also be able to show you how big they can blow it up. With today's technologies, they can print easily in color or black and white. Generally these blown-up posters of your artwork (done on blueprint paper) run anywhere from $10 to $20 each. We usually make up five, so you shouldn't have to spend more than $100 on the whole process! And they look great in the poster windows at theaters, behind that locked glass—just like the real one-sheets! If you want to sell posters, hang one up behind the concession stand and have people place orders for them. You can charge them a little extra on top of your expenses, that way you won't go broke printing up a hundred posters that don't sell. In the past, we've spent about $12 a poster and sold them for $18, making a nice little profit but not ripping anyone off at the same time. We always give cast and crew free videos and posters at printing cost so they can have a nice memoir of the project.

Phase IV

Now you've got the exhibitor locked in and psyched. Locally shot productions have a nice way of selling themselves to theaters that are in the same town. Your print, TV and radio press is chugging along nicely and scheduled to culminate on your movie's official release (or premiere) day. You've got your posters ready to plaster up, and the excitement and hype are building to a fury. What's the next phase? Word-of-mouth. Tell everyone involved with the movie about the premiere, and tell them to tell family and friends. This is the beginning of a grassroots publicity wheel. That's how most small independently distributed movies without millions of promotional dollars behind them make it into the limelight. Simple word-of-mouth. Start the ball rolling with the cast and crew. As more and more people see the movie, they'll tell their friends about it. The time your movie makes money and stays in the theater is referred to as its "legs." It will stay in distribution as long as it generates money for everyone involved.

Usually, an independent theater will book your movie for a week or even just a weekend and that's it. But if it makes them money, they'll hold it over. When you open up the newspaper and look at the movie section and see "Held Over" on an ad, that means the theater owner didn't think they were going to make much money on the movie and planned to keep it only for a short time—but it ended up making them more greenbacks than they had expected so they kept it longer to milk it for the money. Often you can make $500 a week if your movie performs well. Then it's up to your movie to keep generating funds. If the word-of-mouth is good, who knows where it will lead!

One way you can help promote your flick at this time (if you want to roll the dice) is to take out some late-night ads on cable television channels. Just cut a quick thirty-second to one-minute advertisement of your movie (being careful not to show any explicit content that may be in the flick) and include the theater infor-

mation with showtimes. It's rather economical to get on UPN channels, the USA Network and other local channels after midnight. Call your local cable carrier and they can give you an ad-buy rundown. Usually you can spend under $200 for three or four promotional spots that will give your project more consumer awareness. The best nights to buy on are Friday and Saturday nights, when lots of younger people do late-night television viewing. But take it slowly: You don't want to blow all of your box-office revenue on something that doesn't keep packing people in. Sometimes you can split these advertisement costs with the theater. All this work pays off in the long run, either way. Some big-time producer or actor may take note of your work. Or maybe some investment groups will take an interest in your business. On the other hand, you might just make a little bit of money and your movie might go away quick—but you'll still have the press clippings and theatrical-play info to hype during the video distribution phase. Either way, it translates into additional dollars in your pocket.

Another tip is to take video and stills of the marquee and theater front, showing customers buying tickets and waiting in line. Even get comments from audiences as they exit the auditorium, if they'll give them. You can create a neat video trailer intercutting their reactions and comments with quick clips from your movie, similar to the way Miramax advertises movies like *Scream*. Positive audience reactions can only help you in the video distribution phase.

Beyond your local area, if you have friends or other filmmakers you know in different parts of the country, you can have them assist you in getting video theatrical runs in their hometowns, as well. All you need to mail them is a few posters and a VHS copy of the movie. We've had movies play in Chicago, New York, Los Angeles

Actor Joe Zaso introduces the movies *Addicted to Murder* **and** *Rage of the Werewolf* **at the DE-TOUR Film Festival in Rome, Italy, February 1999.**

and Virginia. All these areas were in addition to our South Florida–based connections, where the movies were lensed. You'll want to trust in the individual handling your movie (and money) in a place where you won't be present to help supervise the release, of course. Or maybe you will go there to help promote the movie, if your funds and schedule are flexible.

Phase V

Part of the fun of releasing your movie in theaters is to watch people who have never heard of you or your movie plunk down the $2 to go in and view the flick. I like to sit in the back of the theater and watch audience reactions. I've seen audiences hoot and holler and scream at the right places while watching one of my horror films, and it was exciting to see and hear people enjoying all the work we put into the project. It's also a great learning experience—when you see your movie blown up to theatrical screen size and the sound is louder than a heavy metal concert, you (and the audience) tend to notice all of your mistakes. These reactions are all part of the learning process and will help you improve on future projects. I learned a lot about pacing a movie while watching one of my videos with a theatrical audience. I could see where to improve scenes that got bogged down with long dialogue when everything could have been explained quicker (and in a more entertaining way) with visuals and action. Also, you get to see how your story comes across, whether or not an audience can follow it. So this whole experience is a good way to learn while doing.

During *Wicked Game*'s theatrical run, I loved it when people walked out of the movie when it got too gory! That was a real compliment to me. I remember seeing audiences of movies like *Scanners* and *Friday the 13th* leave abruptly, visibly shaken. I knew my movies succeeded in the gore department. On the flip side of the coin, one night there was an intoxicated dude in the back of the theater that kept muttering, "Give me my money back; anyone could make this crap." So the process can also be very sobering for a moviemaker's ego, as well. Keep in mind that most general audience expectations are very high these days. People are used to seeing *Star Wars: The Phantom Menace* and other *Titanic*-sized productions in cinemas. Some people may simply not understand what you're trying to do on a miniscule budget, even if they're only paying a $2 admission!

The last thing I'd like to reflect on is the video projection format as a whole. Most of the older non-digital systems don't come close to giving you the clarity of a 35mm or 16mm film, so don't expect your movie to look like *Clerks* on the big screen. At times, darker scenes can be pitch black, and you can run into many other picture problems as well, depending on the video format connected to the projector and how clean the heads are.

My recommendation would be that before you and the theater manager completely commit to a video projection exhibition of your movie, you should both sit down and watch the movie in its entirety on the cinema's system. This can be done in the early afternoon before the theater opens or after the theater closes at night. This way no one gets any surprises come opening night. Keep in mind that this is still video, so it's never going to be perfect. You'll have to live with some imperfections, but make sure the sound is clear and the majority of the video can be seen so the audience can follow the story and not demand money back. We have had a couple of showings where equipment didn't do our movies justice, but generally I've been pleased with the results, considering our budgets and equipment. People have to keep in mind the difference between a $12 million budget and a $12,000 budget.

If you really believe in your project and want a new way for your fully completed independent video to be seen, get to the phone and get started!

Public-Access Television

BY KEVIN J. LINDENMUTH

Public-access television, though somewhat restrictive, is the perfect place for a beginning independent filmmaker to improve his skills and get his work seen by a potentially huge audience. "But isn't public-access that boring as hell community channel with the bad video, bad sound, and those godawful government meetings?" Yeah, it is. But it can also be something more.

The basic premise of public access, at least in the two places where I worked as a staff person in the mid–80s (at Ann Arbor Community-Access Television and WBRK, in Berkely, Michigan) was a non-profit television station that was to meet the needs of the community in terms of local events, news, and information. Where else could you shoot something on your consumer VHS camcorder and get it shown that evening, broadcast on your television? The down side of this was that there was very little quality control—as long as you were a member of the community and your video met standards (i.e., didn't have any glitches and wasn't obscene), you could get it on. Even though I always thought of public access as anti-

television, I learned far more in this venue than I did taking filmmaking classes in college. I was finally able to get my paws on some equipment and utilize those film-making theories I was learning in lectures.

Although I did my share of City Hall meetings and local news shows, I was always more into the entertainment aspect. I wanted to make my own twisted little films and get them shown. And I did. One of the more notable endeavors was a project called *Beyond Sanity*, which was an hour long series of skits, written by me and a friend. The show, which featured such segments as *Shopping Spree of the Blood-Crazed Sorority Girls, Don't Fuck with the Unknown, Cooties: A Nation's Problem, a Nation's Shame* and *Roadkill*, probably incurred more viewer complaints at that station than anything they had aired in the past decade. Hey, I was thrilled. I knew people were watching the show.

Another program I compiled as a fledgling producer (I was twenty years old) was *Videospace*. This was a half-hour anthology showcasing independent films and videos. Its sole purpose was to give film-makers exposure they normally wouldn't get. As a filmmaker, I wanted people to see my work and figured others felt the same with their own films. After all, what's the point in making a movie if you aren't going to show it to someone? It's the driving force to do what we do, right? The first dozen episodes of this show were limited to fellow students' endeavors. I'd usually videotape an interview with the filmmaker and include this on the show before I showed the film. Later, when I moved away from public-access (to New York City), I continued the show, getting it broadcast over a dozen public-access stations across the country, from Cambridge to St. Louis. Although I discontinued the show in '91, with over 75 half-hour episodes (30 hours of some really weird programming), it continues in Boston under the name of *Videospace Boston*.

How can you get involved with public-access?

Very few public-access stations are set up exactly the same way. The ones I worked at, for example, were part of City Hall, so community functions were always given priority. Other stations I've heard are self-supporting, charging for use of the video facilities. Call up your cable company, get the number of your station and see what their procedures are for getting a program broadcast or about becoming a participating member.

Getting your show broadcast should be easy. You simply have to prove (via license or utility bill) that you are a member of the community. They should be able to fit you into their programming schedule. There are always gaps in programming, because most people don't take the time to do anything.

If you decide to become a volunteer at a local station, the best aspect is that you get access to the equipment (like studio cameras, editing equipment that's too expensive to rent), and the more you work on the local show, sporting events or whatever, the more you improve your skills. And you don't just work at one thing—one day you might do audio, the next day camera, and after a while actually direct a multi-camera show. Of course, you don't get paid for this—you're a volunteer—but think of everything you're learning and wouldn't normally have access to. The worst thing that can happen is that you come across kindred spirits that are as demented as you are.

Appendix:
Ordering Information

Joe Bagnardi
JB Productions
P.O. Box 164
Rensselaer NY 12144

Pat Bishow
Amusement Films
P.O. Box 26
NYC NY 10028
www.amusementfilms.com
email: amusefilms@aol.com
(212) 388-2319

Michael Bockner
Michael Bockner Productions, Inc.
605 Finch Avenue West, Suite 910
North York Ontario M2R IPI
Canada

Mark Borchardt
Northwest Productions
P.O. Box 635
Menomee Falls WI 53053
www.americanmovie.com

John Bowker
Pipedreams Entertainment
P.O. Box 856
Corvallis OR 97339
http://members.xoom.com/oregonvideo

Mike Burchett
B+ Productions
P.O. Box 621
Amelia OH 45102

Elisar Cabrera
Vista Street Entertainment
1720 20th Street, #202
Santa Monica CA 90404

Dennis Devine
Cinematrix Releasing
22647 Ventura Blvd. Suite 352
Woodland Hills CA 91364
www.unknownproductions.com

Tommy Faircloth
www.horsecreekproductions.com
(803) 791-1928

Michael Fox
B+ Productions
P.O. Box 621
Amelia OH 45102

Bruce G. Hallenbeck
E.I. Independent Cinema
68 Forest Street
Montclair NJ 07042

Andrew Harrison
www.leatherface.com
www.sloanmusic.freeserve.co.uk/

Evan Jacobs
Anhedenia Films
PMB 171 17860 Newhope Street
Fountain Valley, CA 92708
email: anhedenia@hotmail.com

Marcus Koch
Undead Entertaiment
3440 Enterprise Road
E Safety Harbor, FL 34695
email: subgenre@aol.com

Jeff Leroy
Thorton Productions
3509 E. Broadway
Suite 8
Long Beach, CA 90803
(562) 439-8106

Kevin J. Lindenmuth
Brimstone Productions
www.lindenmuth.com
email: transtill@aol.com

Santo Marotta
Marotta Productions
234 E. 88th St Suite D
New York NY 10128

Ted V. Mikels
TVM Studios
3230 W. Hacienda Ave #307
Las Vegas NV 89118
(702) 261-0051
http://www.tedmikels.com
email: TVMSTUDIOS@aol.com

Brian O'Hara
www.rrfrankenstein.com

Andrew Parkinson
15B Arlington Gardens
London, W4 4EZ
U.K.

Brett Piper
Kinetic Image Co. Ltd.
14900 Deer Park Road
Bainbridge OH 45612
(603) 437-5348

Mark Pirro
www.loop.com/~pirro

Mike Prosser
Playground Films
2952 Buxton Court
Forest Grove OR 97116

Tim Ritter
Subrosa Studios
P.O. Box 5515
Syracuse NY 13220

Joe Sherlock
P.O. Box 856
Corvallis OR 97339
http://www.proaxis.com/~sherlockfam/drsquid.
　html

Ronnie Sortor
Salt City Home Video
P.O. Box 5515
Syracuse NY 13220

Mark Sparks
SEG Productions
P.O. Box 461164
Aurora CO 80013
www.segfilms.com

Dave Sterling
(949) 757-9580
Vista Street Entertainment
1720 20th Street #202
Santa Monica CA 90404
email: vistastr@pacbell.net

Mike Strain, Jr.
Oaktree Studios
9405 N. State Hwy. 13-E
Willard MO 65781
email: stillfx@msn.com

Paul Talbot
Crimson Productions
PO Box 50021
Columbia SC 29250

Index

Numbers in italics refer to photographs.